ATF Series: 9

Faith and Freedom

Christian Ethics in a Pluralist Culture

edited by David Neville & Philip Matthews

The ATF Series is a publication of the Australian Theological Forum. Each volume is a collection of essays focusing on a theological investigation of the interaction between the Christian faith and issues of a cultural, social or scientific nature.

ATF Press
Adelaide

Series Editors
Veronica Brady IBVM
Hilary Regan

ATF Series 1
Faith In The Public Forum,
Neil Brown and Robert Gascoigne, editors, 1999.

ATF Series 2
Civilising Community for Us All,
Libby Davies and Francis Sullivan, editors, May 2000.

ATF Series 3
More Than A Single Issue: Theological Considerations Concerning the Ordination of Practising Homosexuals,
Murray Rae and Graham Redding, editors, 2000.

ATF Series 4
Spirit of Australia: Religion in Citizenship and National Life,
Brian Howe and Alan Nichols, editors, 2001.

ATF Series 5
Prophecy and Passion: Essays in Honour of Athol Gill,
David Neville, editor, 2002.

ATF Series 6
Rethinking Religion: Exploratory Investigations,
Douglas Pratt, 2003.

ATF Series 7
Spirit of Australia II: Religion in Citizenship and National Life,
Brian Howe and Philip Hughes, editors, 2003.

ATF Series 8
Church and Civil Society: A Theology of Engagement,
Sue Leppert and Francis Sullivan, editors, 2003.

ATF Series: 9

Faith and Freedom

Christian Ethics in a Pluralist Culture

Edited by

David Neville & Philip Matthews

ATF Press
Adelaide

First published 2003

National Library of Australia
Cataloguing-in-Publication data

Faith and freedom: Christian ethics in a pluralist culture
Includes indices
ISBN 1 920691 16 2

1. Christian ethics - Australian. 2. Christianity and culture - Australia. I. Neville, David, 1958- . II. Matthews, Philip, 1959- . III. Australian Theological Forum (Series: ATF Series ; 9).

241.

Published by
ATF Press
An imprint of the Australian Theological Forum
P O Box 504
Hindmarsh SA 5007
Australia
ABN 68 314 074 034
www.atfpress.com

Printed by Openbook Print, Adelaide, Australia

Contents

Abbreviations

General Abbreviations

BCE	Before the Common Era (= BC)
CE	Common Era (= AD)
cf	*confer* (compare)
chap(s)	chapter(s)
ed(s)	edition; editor(s)
eg	*exempli gratia* (for example)
esp	especially
ET	English Translation
n	note
nd	no date
NT	New Testament
OT	Old Testament
p or pp	page or pages
rev	revised
trans.	translator or translated by
vol(s)	volume(s)
vs	versus
WCC	World Council of Churches

Books of the Bible

Gen	Genesis
Ex	Exodus
Lev	Leviticus
Num	Numbers
Deut	Deuteronomy
1-2 Sam	1-2 Samuel
1-2 Chron	1-2 Chronicles
Qoh	Qoheleth (Ecclesiastes)
Isa	Isaiah
Jer	Jeremiah
Ezek	Ezekiel
Dan	Daniel
Hos	Hosea
Mic	Micah

Hab	Habakkuk
Zech	Zechariah
Mal	Malachi
Mt	Matthew
Mk	Mark
Lk	Luke
Jn	John
Rom	Romans
1-2 Cor	1-2 Corinthians
Gal	Galatians
Eph	Ephesians
Phil	Philippians
Col	Colossians
1-2 Thess	1-2 Thessalonians
1-2 Tim	1-2 Timothy
Heb	Hebrews
Jas	James
1-2 Pet	1-2 Peter
1 Jn	1 John
Rev	Revelation

Periodicals, Reference Works and Series

AB	Anchor Bible
ABD	David Noel Freedman (ed), *Anchor Bible Dictionary,* 6 vols (New York: Doubleday, 1992).
ABRL	Anchor Bible Reference Library
BAGD	Walter Bauer, William F Arndt, F Wilbur Gingrich and Frederick W Danker, *A Greek-English Lexicon of the New Testament and Other Early Christian Literature,* 2nd ed, revised and augmented (Chicago and London: University of Chicago Press, 1979).
CD	Karl Barth, *Church Dogmatics* (1956–1975).
DBWE	*Dietrich Bonhoeffer Works*, English edition (Augsburg Fortress)
MQR	*Mennonite Quarterly Review*
TDNT	G Kittel and G Friedrich (eds), *Theological Dictionary of the New Testament*, trans. Geoffrey W Bromiley, 10 vols (Grand Rapids, MI: Eerdmans, 1964–76).

Foreword

St Mark's and ATF: Speaking Up and Speaking Out on Theology in Public

St Mark's National Theological Centre is delighted to co-sponsor with the Australian Theological Forum (ATF) this important series of essays in what tends to be called these days 'public theology'. To many observers, both inside the church and out, 'public theology' is a contradiction in terms. The public realm, so the argument runs, is concerned with the political and economic life of our nation. These aspects of life operate wholly within the dynamic of human power and human decision-making. The object of theological interest—God—is to all intents and purposes irrelevant to the operation of and discussion about this human world. The public realm is a secular realm through and through. If God and thinking about God have any contribution to make to contemporary Australian life, it can only be in the 'spiritual' realm, which means the personal, private, inner worlds of individual people who are interested in such matters.

Recent public debate in Australia has shown this simple separation of human life into two spheres, public/political and private/spiritual, to be much too simple. From the secular side, widespread criticism has been directed at the church for its failures, particularly abuse of vulnerable people placed in its care. The criticism reached to the highest levels of society, and it has been sharp, unapologetic and certainly public. Rightly so. No one can say these issues are not a matter of public concern and accountability. The church must respond to this critique with all seriousness; it cannot claim special separateness or immunity that somehow absolves it from public scrutiny and judgment.

On the other hand, in recent times the churches have spoken out in Australia with a clear and unified voice. A strong critique of public policy on reconciliation with indigenous people, treatment of asylum-seekers and making war in Iraq has hit the headlines again and again. This time it has been hard for the politicians and policy-makers to duck for cover. Predictably, however, the 'two-sphere' argument that theology has no place in public life and should stick to 'saving souls' has been the first line of defence for some of our leaders. But these public matters have an irreducible theological dimension to them. The church cannot simply be quiet in public.

The debate that takes place in the headlines and television 'grabs' is merely the media take on a much deeper, careful and sustained conversation that has been part of the life of our nation and our churches across many decades. St Mark's, founded in the 1950s by that socially 'meddlesome priest', Bishop Ernest Burgmann,[1] has consistently fostered critical dialogue between church, theology and Australian social and cultural life. Our journal, *St Mark's Review*, provides a window on to some of this dialogue during the last forty-five years.

The work of the ATF through its conferences, journal and books has greatly enriched theology in the public realm in Australia since its founding in 1993. The publication of *Faith and Freedom* as a joint enterprise of the ATF and St Mark's represents an exciting development of this work. David Neville, Lecturer in NT at St Mark's and the School of Theology of Charles Sturt University, Philip Matthews, who lectures in the School of Philosophy and Ethics at the University of Notre Dame in Fremantle, and Hilary Regan, Secretary of the ATF, are to be congratulated for their work in preparing this volume for publication.

The essays in this book are written mainly (but not exclusively) by Australians, and they speak mainly (but again, not exclusively) to issues in Australian public life, from war and peace to ecology and reconciliation. They draw upon a long tradition of Christian theological reflection upon and action within public life and reveal impressively that this tradition has a great deal to contribute to the search for a just, open and compassionate society 'down under'.

Rev'd Dr Stephen Pickard, Director
St Mark's National Theological Centre
Canberra, Australia

1. See Peter Hempenstall, *The Meddlesome Priest: A Life of Ernest Burgmann* (St Leonards, NSW: Allen & Unwin, 1993).

Introduction

David Neville

With one exception, each article or essay in this book was first published in *Faith and Freedom: A Journal of Christian Ethics* between 1992 and 1998.[1] During this period, *Faith and Freedom* also explored the following social and ethical issues: Aboriginal land rights following the High Court's recognition of native title on 3 June 1992; 'Aboriginal reconciliation'; the role of women within the leadership structures of the various churches; Christian feminism; child sexual abuse; the AIDS crisis; ministry among sex workers; euthanasia; gene therapy; environmental, health and business ethics; the power of money; conflict resolution; Arab Christian perspectives on the Israeli-Palestinian conflict; religious liberty; ministry within the church and discipleship; and Australian spirituality. Most of the articles addressing these issues were written for their day and are now dated, even if the issues themselves continue to be important.

As might be expected in the Australian context, the editors gave special attention to legal, social and political dynamics associated with 'Aboriginal reconciliation', which we understood to mean a process of reconciliation between indigenous and nonindigenous Australians based on the understanding that 'the High Court's [native title] decision exposed that fallacy hitherto lying at Australia's heart, the lie of *terra nullius* and the cruelty, humiliation and injustices that accompanied it'.[2] Shortly after the High Court's native title decision on 3 June 1992, Frank Brennan summarised the social and legal ramifica-

1. The essay by Rowena Curtis, 'Christ and Power', was scheduled for publication in the December 1998 issue of *Faith and Freedom* (Vol 6, No 3), but for a number of reasons (not least because of the increasingly prohibitive cost of printing on recycled paper) the journal was forced to cease publication.
2. This is how Sir Ronald Wilson expressed the significance of the High Court's native title decision in his guest editorial, 'Is there Reconciliation after Mabo?', *Faith and Freedom* 3/1 (March 1994): 2-3.

tions of this historic decision.[3] In 1993, *Faith and Freedom* issued 'A Call for Reconciliation':

> Since the establishment in 1788 of the first British penal colony in Australia, the original inhabitants of this land have been mistreated, dispossessed of their land and discriminated against by social and governmental institutions. Unfortunately, many Australians do not recognise the extent of this systematic abuse or the social effects of this maltreatment on present-day Aboriginals and [Torres Strait] Islanders. Within the Christian church, which must acknowledge its complicity in the alienation of indigenous Australians, there are now many at the forefront of the process towards reconciliation. In this International Year of Indigenous People, we call on the Christian community in Australia to respect Aboriginal culture and spirituality. We also express our solidarity with Aboriginals and Islanders in their quest for justice, self-determination and land rights, which should not be understood as land 'granted' gratuitously but as land restored belatedly.

In 1994, Sir Ronald Wilson's editorial, 'Is there Reconciliation after Mabo?', documented both the background to the federal government's Council for Aboriginal Reconciliation Act 1991 and the affirmations written into the preamble to this Act. The preamble acknowledged that for thousands of years before British settlement in 1788, Australia had been occupied by Aborigines and Torres Strait Islanders, many of whom suffered dispossession and dispersal from their traditional lands. As part of the process of reconciliation, which was hoped would be concluded by the centenary of Federation (2001), the Commonwealth committed itself to seek 'an ongoing national commitment from governments at all levels to co-operate and coordinate with the Aboriginal and Torres Strait Islander Commission as appropriate to address progressively Aboriginal disadvantage and aspirations in relation to land, housing, law and justice, cultural

---

3. Frank Brennan, 'The *Mabo* Case: Aboriginal Land Rights in Australia', *Faith and Freedom* 2/1 (March 1993): 30-32.

heritage, education, employment, health and economic development'.[4] Despite the establishment of a Council for Aboriginal Reconciliation, whose task was to search out ways for indigenous and nonindigenous Australians to share this country as equals, 2001 has come and gone without much cause for celebration among those concerned for justice in Australia.

In 1996, Stephen Hall wrote a disconcerting account of 'The Church and Child Removal'.[5] In addition to outlining the history of child removal, the 'philosophy of assimilation' underlying the policy and practice of child removal and its long-standing effects, Hall also pointed out that without the co-operation of the churches and Christian organisations, government bodies could not have implemented the policy of child removal as effectively as they did. In other words, in this respect those in the churches were no better than anyone else. Hall pointed out that it would be disastrous for churches in Australia to fail to accept responsibility for their part in supporting the policy of child removal from their families and thus causing long-term psychological and social disruption. Indeed, according to Hall, '. . . now that the stolen children inquiry is complete, how churches in Australia approach the question of this injustice will be a clear test of their resolve and commitment to the concepts of justice and reconciliation'.

In a 1998 editorial on 'Native Title and the Political Process: *Kairos* and the Freedom of the Church', David Hunter observed that 'the political process has so far failed to deliver an answer on native title and reconciliation'. On the other hand, he noted that many in the Australian church had come to see the issues of native title and reconciliation as crucial for the spiritual health of the nation. 'While there is much work to be done', he wrote, 'deep reflection on the church's role in Australia is now issuing in a public theology with depth and strength.'[6]

None of these editorials and articles was appropriate for this collection because each was written specifically for its time. Nevertheless, in the Australian context few issues are more pressing than

---

4. Wilson, 'Is there Reconciliation after Mabo?', 2-3.
5. Stephen Hall, 'The Church and Child Removal: No Better than Anyone Else', *Faith and Freedom* 5/4 (December 1996): 3–8.
6. David Hunter, 'Native Title and the Political Process: *Kairos* and the Freedom of the Church', *Faith and Freedom* 6/1 (April 1998): 2-4.

that of justice for indigenous people, as evidenced formally in recent years by the 1991 Report of the Royal Commission into Aboriginal Deaths in Custody, the 1992 *Mabo* decision, the 1993 Amnesty International report, 'Australia: A criminal justice system weighted against Aboriginal people', the 1996 High Court Wik decision, the 1997 'Bringing them home' report of the National Inquiry into the separation of Aboriginal and Torres Strait Islander children from their families conducted by the Human Rights and Equal Opportunity Commission,[7] and the proposals to sustain the process of reconciliation set out in the documents released by the Council for Aboriginal Reconciliation in 2000.[8] These milestones were accompanied by a growing popular movement for reconciliation expressed in the dynamic public art of the 'Sea of Hands', the nation-wide marches for reconciliation in May-June 2000, the ongoing commemorations of 'Sorry Day' and the concurrent 'Journey of Healing'. The formal landmarks and the popular movement both challenged and drew strength from the churches. In 1996 Thorwald Lorenzen wrote:

> The greatest challenge to Australian society in general and to the Christian church in particular is our attitude to the indigenous people of Australia. In 2000 and 2001, the eyes of the world will be on Australia. But God's eyes are on Australia now. Lazarus is lying at our doorstep. Our attitude to him is our attitude to God.[9]

Although no essay in this book directly addresses the issue of justice for indigenous Australians, many are nevertheless relevant for Christian reflection on this crucial matter.

The essays in Part I, The Bible and Christian Ethics, examine either the Bible's relevance to Christian moral deliberation or aspects of bib-

7. See also the Bringing Them Home Oral History Project funded by the Commonwealth Government and edited by Doreen Mellor and Anna Haebich, *Many Voices: Reflections on Experiences of Indigenous Child Separation* (Canberra: National Library of Australia, 2002). For an assessment of this historically significant publication, see David Hunter's review in *St Mark's Review*, Number 193 (2003): 33-34.
8. See especially 'Roadmap for Reconciliation' at www.reconciliation.org.au/
9. Thorwald Lorenzen, 'Baptist Heritage and Relevance in a Changing Society', *Faith and Freedom* 5/3 (September 1996): 5.

lical moral teaching, especially in the NT. The first essay, 'Is the Bible a Handbook for Ethics?' by John Dunnill, explores the role of the Bible in dealing with moral problems. After demonstrating the inadequacy of some simplistic responses to the question of the Bible's moral relevance, Dunnill recommends a perspective that understands the Bible as presenting a vision of the good life, which Christians are challenged to live out in response to God's grace. Informed by the recent re-emphasis on virtue and character as central to the practice of ethics, he articulates a point of departure for thinking more profoundly and more practically about the Bible and ethics.

Chris Marshall's essay on 'The Moral Vision of the Beatitudes' argues that the beatitudes, so often dismissed (even by Christians) as idealistic or utopian, are holistic, kingdom-oriented, community-dependent and christologically defined. For Marshall, 'the beatitudes are best understood as descriptions of a *whole way of life* that we as a Christian *community* are called to live, a life *modelled on Jesus* and bearing witness to the transforming reality of the *kingdom of God*'. To demonstrate this fourfold characterisation of the beatitudes, he discusses each beatitude in turn. In so doing, he shows how they are applicable to people's daily lives, provided they are understood as presenting an alternative perspective on the way things really are.

Rowena Curtis begins her reflections on 'Christ and Power' with the following christological declaration: 'Our understanding and use of power needs to be anchored in Jesus Christ. If Jesus Christ is the one we follow, then how he used or did not use power is basic to how we use or do not use power today.' She recognises the ambivalence of power and highlights various abuses of power within the Christian community, but nevertheless affirms the use of power for the legitimate ends of love, life and justice. After exploring the theme of 'Christ and Power' in the Gospel of Matthew, in which the story of Jesus subverts the idea of power as domination, Curtis provides examples of 'ways to name and unmask abuse of power' within the church and wider society. She also endorses the legitimate use of power for justice, peacemaking and compassion.

Bill Loader's study of 'Christian Communities in Earliest Christianity' reminds us that 'small Christian community began with Jesus', especially his vision of God's kingdom characterised by justice and peace. Among those who gathered around Jesus and shared his lifestyle, 'community in the here and now became a sign of God's kingdom'. The Jesus movement was countercultural because commitment to God's kingly rule led Jesus' followers to see all other values in a different light. Loader shows that after Easter, Christian communities within and outside Palestine struggled with internal disputes and tended to dilute the radical egalitarianism of the Jesus movement. Yet in the face of such challenges, Christian communities continued to flourish, provided their identity and reason for being were shaped by Jesus' kingdom vision. Much the same applies today. 'It seems to me', Loader opines, 'that we need to take our bearings afresh from the radical nature of the kingdom community of Jesus.' He shows that to take such a challenge seriously involves redefining ministry within the church, including traditional leadership roles. The following claim by Loader also implies the need for a reappraisal of the church's ministry to those outside the church: 'We are called more to community than to congregation, more to intimacy than to formality, *more to modelling justice and equality than to patterns of authority and monopoly*. We are still called to be the community of the kingdom.'

'The Boundaries of Freedom' by Rick Strelan explores the NT understanding of Christian freedom and indicates some implications of such an understanding for the Christian community, not only for interrelationships within itself but also for its relation to the wider world. Strelan connects biblical concepts of liberty and liberation with God's creativity. He also shows that freedom in the biblical sense creates new relationships, not only between people and God but also among people and between people and nature. However, Christian freedom is self-limiting, 'defined and confined by boundaries', as Strelan puts it. By focusing on various episodes in the gospels and on the teaching of the 'apostle of freedom', Paul, he examines ways in which the 'law of love' limits personal freedom yet also leads (or should lead) disciples of Jesus to transgress social and interpersonal boundaries that marginalise people. For Strelan, 'Being in Christ is not to be released from prison into the vacuum of free choice', but equally, 'Christian freedom calls Christians to love in the world, to push against and even to dismantle boundaries within society'. Love is the measure that not only sets boundaries for Christian freedom but also challenges Christians to transgress dehumanising boundaries in the world. By being an agent of reconciliation, the church is (or should be) a witness to the world of its intended destiny. Until then, Christians live out their freedom in hope.

The essays in Part II, Theological Perspectives and Resources, either explicate key theological topics or explore the contributions of important writers for thinking theologically about ethics. Graeme Garrett begins his essay, 'Open Heaven/Closed Hearts: Theological Reflections on Ecumenical Relations', by proposing that Christians desist from excluding one another from the Lord's table. In view of the pluralist context in which the church currently finds itself, he advises: 'Given our increasingly marginal status as Christians in Australia, if we are going to achieve anything beyond the cultivation of individual piety in the next century, it will have to be in co-operation, not competition, with each other.' Garrett traverses such themes as 'sacramental sensitivity' and the 'dissenting tradition', each of which is found in some church traditions more than in others and therefore needs to be shared more widely, and he also explores the ecumenical meaning and relevance of the mystery of God, courtesy and conversation. He ponders whether ecumenical fellowship is a *status confessionis* issue, that is, a crisis that threatens the very being of the church. 'There is a sense in which a divided church is a contradiction in terms', he writes. 'It is a theological nonsense and a discipleship scandal.'

If Garrett's essay focuses on 'exterior' relations between Christians from different church traditions, Thorwald Lorenzen's essay, 'Jesus Christ and Spirituality', might seem to focus on the Christian's 'interior' relationship with God, Jesus or the Spirit. Yet for Lorenzen, ecumenical relations are no less a part of authentic Christian spirituality than prayer and Bible-reading. He argues that Christian spirituality must be grounded in Jesus Christ, whom God raised from death to give meaning and structure to people's lives. As a result, Christian spirituality cannot be solely concerned with the interior life; rather, it must be a spirituality of changing things in accordance with God's purpose for the world revealed in Jesus Christ. True Christian spirituality repudiates dichotomies such as sacred and profane, reclaims a holistic anthropology, anticipates God's ultimate transformation initiated in the resurrection of Jesus, agitates for justice and sustains people on their faith journey.

The essays in Part II by John Howard Yoder and me were first published in 1993 to evaluate the legacies of Martin Luther King, Jr, Thomas Merton and Karl Barth a quarter-century after their deaths in 1968. Yoder begins his essay by remarking that 'the coincidence that three quite different men died in the same year is an odd reason for seeking to juxtapose their ministries or their thought'. Yet he shows that although these influential figures were products of different environments, they came to see that they could not but swim against the stream of their respective traditions. Having reached that point, they travelled similar journeys and moved towards similar destinations. In short, as Yoder concludes, 'they were on the same pilgrimage'.

While many regard King, Merton and Barth as representatives of a bygone era, there are aspects of what they learned and stood for that are too valuable to be forgotten. In a pluralist context, it is worth remembering that while all three were Christians, their faith motivated them to live socially engaged, responsible lives, albeit in different ways. This is obvious in King's case, but Merton was not simply a reclusive contemplative and Barth was not simply a 'theologian of the Word of God'. My essay seeks to show that central features of their respective legacies remain indispensable for Christians concerned to live responsibly in the world. While Yoder's essay covers similar ground, it is enriched by his personal contact with both Merton and Barth. Of particular interest is his critique of Merton based on his involvement in a retreat on the 'Spiritual Roots of Protest' convened by Merton in November 1964 for people involved in the peace movement.

In 'An Unmistakable Accent: Remembering Dietrich Bonhoeffer', Frank Nichol singles out Bonhoeffer from among other influential European theologians of the twentieth century (including Barth,[10] Emil Brunner, Rudolf Bultmann and Paul Tillich) as one who provided a meaningful theological interpretation of his contemporaries' profound sense of God's absence. According to Nichol, 'It may be that in this bold stroke and what flows from it is to be found his most positive and creative contribution to our theological and ethical thinking.' Nichol also indicates three central themes in Bonhoeffer's writing that merit closer attention today. First, Bonhoeffer's christology (epitomised in the phrase, 'Jesus, the Man for others') reshaped his understanding of both God and the church in creative, world-affirming ways. Second, Bonhoeffer's theology entails an ethic of witness (rather than prescription), which respects the integrity of cultural values and norms. And third, Bonhoeffer chose to accentuate

10. Cf Frank Nichol, 'Learning from Karl Barth', *Faith and Freedom* 2/4 (December 1993): 38-40.

the suffering of God, a theme with radical implications for the church's self-understanding and the shape of the Christian life.

Charles Birch is a widely respected population ecologist and process theologian who has written extensively on the environmental crisis and the relation between science and religion. In 'God of Compassion', he identifies compassionate love as a focal point for thinking about God's relation to the world. For Birch, God acts only as compassionate and persuasive love, never coercively; it is therefore more meaningful to speak of divine purpose than divine design because to speak of design implies predetermination. Lest such a view of God seem to limit God's power, Birch affirms that the only power that ultimately matters is that of persuasive love. God acts in the world through our response to God's compassionate love. 'God acts in human life by being felt by us as persuasive love that is transforming', he writes. 'This is incarnation.' Birch shows how this understanding of God has profound implications for the natural environment. Finally, he affirms God's passion as well as compassion; God experiences both the joy and suffering of the world. Birch maintains that the view of God he outlines is more helpful than traditional theological perspectives for confronting the social and ecological challenges facing us today.

The Australian author and Nobel Prize winner, Patrick White, was no theologian, but in '"A Grandeur Too Overwhelming to Express": Patrick White's Vision of God', Veronica Brady reveals that White had a deep interest both in God and in issues of faith. By investigating the faith-stance of several characters in White's novels, Brady discovers viewpoints that resonate with the thinking of Barth, Bonhoeffer and Simone Weil. She also shows that White was attuned to God's intangible presence in the world: 'God is never far from Patrick White's world, to be found not only in suffering but, as White wrote, "less in what is said than in the silences. In patterns on water. A gust of wind. A flower opening."' Something similar can be said of Tim Winton, among others. Alongside its intrinsic value, literature is a potent stimulus for theological and ethical reflection.[11]

11. For a discussion of fiction as a resource for theological reflection, see Alex Wright, *Why Bother with Theology?* (London: Darton, Longman and Todd, 2002), 73-93.

Part III, The Politics of Jesus and Christian Pacifism, directs the spotlight to an issue that featured prominently in the pages of *Faith and Freedom*. Before the journal's association with the Baptist Peace Fellowship of Australia and, later, Baptist Inner City Ministries in Sydney, the journal was published by the Perth Christian Peace Community, whose vision statement indicated its indebtedness to the peace-church tradition:

> In the tradition of the 'historic peace churches', the Perth Christian Peace Community affirms that the active pursuit of peace is central to the Christian life and not simply an optional extra. Peace is not at the periphery of Christian faith but at its heart. We refuse to accept the implication that the pacifist stance is a deviation from authentic Christianity; indeed, we like to remind people that Jesus and the early church were pacifist. However, pacifism should not be confused with 'passivism'; it involves us in the active struggle against all forms of injustice. Furthermore, pacifism is not only a philosophical stance on war and physical violence; it also involves a firm commitment to all that is required for peaceful relations between people. This includes confronting 'economic violence', which is responsible for more deaths worldwide than all the wars of the twentieth century. We are committed to a 'style of life' that reflects this broad understanding of what it means to be Christian.

In 1992, the Mennonite theologian and Anabaptist historian, John Howard Yoder, accepted an invitation to write an article to commemorate the twentieth anniversary of his book, *The Politics of Jesus*.[12] Yoder understood Jesus as one who responded in a politically distinctive and creative way to first-century Jewish aspirations for justice and liberation. As such, Jesus was someone whose political stance is relevant for Christians today. In the opening chapter of *The Politics of Jesus*, Yoder wrote that the purpose of his book was 'to let the Jesus

12. John Howard Yoder, *The Politics of Jesus: Vicit Agnus Noster* (Grand Rapids, MI: Eerdmans, 1972; 2nd ed, 1994).

story so speak that the person concerned with social ethics, accustomed as he [or she] is to a set of standard ways to assume Jesus not to be relevant to social issues, or at least not relevant *immediately,* can hear'. He also claimed that 'Jesus is, according to the biblical witness, a model of radical political action'.[13] In 'Jesus—A Model of Radical Political Action', Yoder restated the central thesis of *The Politics of Jesus* that the life and teaching of Jesus are not only relevant but normative for Christian social ethics.

So began an association with Yoder that saw him publish three further articles in *Faith and Freedom*.[14] In addition, the June 1996 issue contained ten essays written as a tribute to Yoder for what he had taught the church about faithful Christian discipleship. The essays by Stanley Hauerwas and Ian Barns, which first appeared in 'A Tribute to John Howard Yoder', explore the relevance of Yoder's thought for the church in the Australian context.[15] Hauerwas notes differences between how Yoder is understood in Australia and in the USA, and he comments on how Yoder's theology might help Australian churches respond to the challenge 'to become disciplined communities that are able to resist the secularism surrounding them that is legitimated in the name of freedom'. Barns draws upon Yoder's writings to sketch a 'post-Constantinian' public theology relevant to Australia's recent public policy debates. In doing so, he contests the judgment of those who dismiss Yoder as 'sectarian'. During the second half of the twentieth century, the label 'sectarian' was used pejoratively to marginalise or dismiss theological voices that allegedly safeguard the integrity and distinctiveness of Christian faith at the expense of responsible par-

---

13. Yoder, *The Politics of Jesus*, 2nd ed, 2.

14. In addition to 'Three Unfinished Pilgrimages' (reprinted in this volume), see his 'Christianity and Protest' (Vol 3, No 2), which enumerated various preconditions for authentic Christian protest both in society and within the church, and 'Gospel Renewal and the Roots of Nonviolence' (Vol 4, No 4), which examined biblical and historical bases for a nonviolent Christian ethic.

15. Two other essays first published in *Faith and Freedom* 5/1-2 (June 1996) were republished in Stanley Hauerwas, Chris K Huebner, Harry J Huebner and Mark Thiessen Nation (eds), *The Wisdom of the Cross: Essays in Honor of John Howard Yoder* (Grand Rapids, MI: Eerdmans, 1999): Glen H Stassen, 'The Politics of Jesus in the Sermon on the Plain' (150-67); Marva J Dawn, 'The Biblical Concept of "the Principalities and Powers": John Yoder Points to Jacques Ellul' (168-86).

ticipation in society. On various occasions Yoder answered the charge that his theological stance was not 'responsible', but never more forcefully than in the collection of essays published shortly before his death, *For the Nations*,[16] in which he addressed this accusation by expositing the ethical implications of his concept of the church. If, as Yoder maintained, the mission of the church is to be the vanguard of God's new world on the way (or, as Barns puts it, 'an image to the wider world of its true destiny'), then its very presence in the world is a social ethic, and its practices, when authentic or faithful, are exemplary or paradigmatic for the wider world. Yoder's own challenge to those who dismiss his position as sectarian was encapsulated in these words:

> Let those who fear sectarian self-sufficiency and seek 'public' relevance show us how they can articulate, in reasonable discourse describing the nature of things so that all our neighbors will come along, the relevance and the realism of servanthood, enemy love, and forgiveness. This, and not domination, ethnocentricity, and punishment, is the divinely given nature of things that we are called to show the world.[17]

In 'Pacifism—Not Passivism', Philip Matthews argues that while passivism and its dualist world-view have little to offer those who advocate and agitate for justice, pacifism (peacemaking) is consistent with radical (yet nonviolent) activism on behalf of the marginalised and oppressed.[18] 'Rather than passive bystanders', he writes, 'the ma-

---

16. John Howard Yoder, *For the Nations: Essays Evangelical and Public* (Grand Rapids, MI: Eerdmans, 1997). Each essay seeks to show that 'the very shape of the people of God in the world is a public witness, or is "good news," for the world, rather than first of all rejection or withdrawal' (6). Yoder had in mind at least three further collections of essays: (1) a scholarly set of essays on the just-war tradition; (2) a collection on nonviolence; and (3) a volume of missiological writings.

17. Yoder, *For the Nations*, 48. Another important book that explores biblical and theological bases for responsible yet nonviolent Christian involvement in a pluralist context is Duane K Friesen, *Artists, Citizens, Philosophers: Seeking the Peace of the City* (Scottdale, PA: Herald Press, 2000).

18. Similarly, in 'Anabaptist Pacifism', *Faith and Freedom* 6/2 (August 1998): 12–16, I document divergent views on pacifism among the early Anabaptists and

jority of Christian pacifists are now active participants in the struggle against injustice of all sorts.' Matthews also documents the varied types of pacifism within one trajectory of the peace-church tradition, showing how there was movement among Mennonites during the twentieth century from nonresistance to nonviolence.

Like the essays by Hauerwas and Barns, my critique of CS Lewis's argument against pacifism first appeared in the tribute to Yoder and is informed by Yoder's Christian pacifist perspective. An important strand of Yoder's corpus is his criticism of influential theological figures and movements. In particular, he engaged two of the most forceful theological voices of the twentieth century, Karl Barth and Reinhold Niebuhr, on the contentious issue of the legitimacy of violence and war for certain ends. Proceeding from the Anabaptist conviction that the life and teaching of Jesus are normative for Christian ethics, Yoder maintained that violence is inimical to Christian discipleship. No assumption about the way things are, whether Niebuhr's 'Christian realism' or Barth's *Grenzfall* (exceptional circumstance), takes precedence over the Christian responsibility to relate to others, whether neighbour or enemy, in such a way as to mediate God's self-giving, indiscriminate love displayed in the social stance, or politics, of Jesus. From that perspective, Lewis's defence of state-sanctioned violence is troubling, especially given his widespread popularity not only as a Christian apologist but also (and perhaps more importantly) as the author of the Narnia chronicles.

Australian Christians live in a pluralist context. This makes the issues of faith, freedom and their interrelationship all the more critical. Faith that is authentic and seen to be so may well be the church's most vital and persuasive apologetic. To that end, the church must retain its freedom to follow faithfully its pioneer and perfecter. Yet in a pluralist culture, the church's faith and freedom must be expressed and embodied in a coherent rather than discordant way. The ecumenical movement was one of the most important theological developments of

---

argue that two principal reasons why pacifist Anabaptists were pacifist remain valid, relevant and binding for Christians today. While I affirm the pacifism of pacifist Anabaptists, I do not defend their dualism or separatism. See also Ross Langmead, 'Anabaptist Perspectives for Mission', in D Neville (ed), *Prophecy and Passion: Essays in Honour of Athol Gill* (Adelaide: Australian Theological Forum, 2002), 328–45.

the twentieth century, but the church as a whole needs to travel further down this road and some churches have significant catching up to do. The contributors to this collection represent the Anabaptist, Anglican, Baptist, Lutheran, Methodist, Presbyterian, Roman Catholic and Uniting Church traditions, yet the dominant chords sounded are in harmony—for faith and freedom.

Part I

The Bible and Christian Ethics

Is the Bible a Handbook for Ethics?

John Dunnill

An informal survey of conversations in bus-queues and bars indicates that as a society we are well aware of moral dilemmas. A moment's reflection reveals, however, that this seldom helps us to arrive at agreed solutions. For example, people are aware of the prevalence of child abuse and the lasting damage it can do to young lives. Nevertheless, is it right to remove small children from their families on suspicion that they are being abused? In combating the spread of AIDS, does the promotion of condoms offer a solution that in the long run makes matters worse by creating a climate in which sex is 'OK' so long as it is 'safe'? Will the misery of a Bosnian debacle be helped or compounded by armed intervention of outside powers?

The Bible has a contribution to make to these and other moral questions. But does it have the answer? Is it, in other words, a handbook by which such knots can be unravelled? If not, how does it help us?

1. A book of rules?

We can think of the Bible as a handbook in at least two ways. The first is as a law code, a book of rules. The Bible certainly contains law codes, most notably in that section of the Pentateuch stretching from Exodus 20 through Leviticus to Numbers 6 and resuming in Deuteronomy 5–26, but also in the prophetic writings, in Jesus' teachings and in parts of the Pauline and post-Pauline letters. In different ways, these parts of the Bible are plentiful in commands about what shall be done and not done if one is to lead the good life. For example, 'You shall not commit adultery' (Ex 20:14) or 'You shall not see your neighbour's donkey or ox fallen on the road and ignore it; you shall help to lift it up' (Deut 22:4). There is also the following command in Deut 21:18-21:

> If someone has a stubborn and rebellious son who will not obey his father and mother, who does not heed them when they discipline him, then his father

> and his mother shall take hold of him and bring him out to the elders of his town at the gate of that place. They shall say to the elders of his town, 'This son of ours is stubborn and rebellious. He will not obey us. He is a glutton and a drunkard.' Then all the men of the town shall stone him to death. So you shall purge the evil from your midst; and all Israel will hear, and be afraid.

Some of these laws will be more to our taste than others; some we shall think it right to modify or ignore. That people have always exercised discernment in applying scriptural laws presents a problem for a fundamentally simplistic ethic that looks for a set of clear imperatives laid down by authority. There has to be a way of resolving contradictions. On divorce, for example, when Deut 24:1-4 (which allows it) conflicts with Mk 10:2–12 (which prohibits it), Jesus' authority may, for Christians, outweigh that of Moses. But then, how do we resolve variations in what Jesus is reported to have said (permitting divorce, according to Mt 5:31–32, even if only on the grounds of adultery)?

Terms must also be defined. At what point is a son irredeemably 'stubborn and rebellious'? What kinds of activity constitute 'adultery'? For example, should Jesus' strong definition of adultery in terms of the lustful glance (Mt 5:27-28) lead to the death penalty as prescribed in Lev 20:10? In trying to obey the command of Deut 22:4, how can we know whether *this particular* lame donkey should be helped unless we ask, like the scribe in Lk 10:29, 'Who is my "neighbour"?'

If laws are not to be completely arbitrary, they must be interpreted and applied. Inevitably a system of case law develops like that of the Jewish *Talmud* or the English common law; what begins with a desire for a clear, simple set of rules turns into something complex and subtle. Curiously, it is often those who call for a 'rule book' approach to the Bible who criticise Judaism for being legalistic.

What is at fault here is not the laws themselves—two of those quoted above are fundamental to our concepts of marriage and compassion—but how we treat them. We are not entitled to choose which federal laws to obey; nor can we do so with the laws of God. If we adopt a principle for selecting which laws apply and which do not, then we grant moral authority to that principle rather than to the laws themselves or to the Bible in which they are contained.

2. A guide book?

Perhaps we should think of the Bible not so much as a book of rules, but as a guide to holy living and to what constitutes godly approaches to moral problems. Doing so will enable us to widen the field of biblical data to include not only laws but also miscellaneous sayings and stories. Thus the tale of Susanna and the elders found in the Apocrypha's additions to the book of Daniel gives us a concrete image of integrity and wisdom in the face of pious corruption. In Acts 5 and 9 two men called Ananias model for us, respectively, deceit and obedience as alternative ways of relating to God.

However, this broader approach opens up a richer field of contradictions. Should Christians share all their property, like the earliest Christian community in Jerusalem described in Acts 2:44-45 and 4:32-37, or, like Job at the end of his life, rejoice in what they own as God's blessing? How does this approach enable us to choose between Ruth and Boaz or David and Bathsheba as model couples? Such an approach also confines us to the historical particularity of the world within which the Bible was framed, for example, the Bible's failure to question the role of slaves and women as forms of property or the absence from the NT in particular of an appeal to justice as the basis for transforming society.

Nor does the Bible reveal the principles we might be seeking in such an approach, since these are rarely articulated within the text. 'Sanctity of life' may be a compelling principle, but it is not found in the Bible. It is an ethical abstraction based on a theology of creation ('all life belongs to God') and buttressed by some commands, of which the most obvious example is, 'You shall not murder' (but permitting legal and military exceptions to the rule). Yet again, we must take our thinking to a higher level if we are to have any settled way of determining what a moral system based on the Bible might look like.

3. Atomism

The problem with both approaches discussed above is that they are atomistic, treating each issue as though it were separate and unrelated. This appears to be what 'morality' means in the popular media: Should I sleep with X? Is it okay to 'borrow' equipment from my workplace? Why shouldn't I bend the rules in financial dealings if no-one loses out in the process? In this perception, which separates every individual from every other ('my decision-making') and every moment from past and future, there is little room for moral principles or values. Inevitably decisions turn on consequences: What will cause pleasure or pain? What can I get away with? This 'airport bookstall' morality is only the romantic side of a fundamental amorality that permeates much of our society, even in high places and in positions of responsibility and public trust.

But the desire to be ruled by law is equally atomistic if it entails handing over our own responsibility to a set of rules for every situation—where the question 'What should I do?' really means 'What does the book say?' This is abdicating our duty to be responsible agents; it encourages the development of rigid and dependent personalities incapable of dealing with unclear and borderline cases or of knowing what to do when the application of a good principle may lead to evil consequences. Yet this is what is promoted by many who urge us to 'return to traditional morality'. It is also promoted by the recent papal encyclical *Veritatis Splendor*; beneath the structure of argument drawn from natural law lurks an authoritarianism that insists there is a rule for every occasion.

If there is one good that Christian witness can do, it is to relieve the world of this appalling reduction of life to a mass of disconnected selves making agonising decisions or blindly obeying rules in a moral void. There is an alternative. It is to see the primary business of ethics not as helping to make decisions or as framing rules for behaviour, but as forming persons of a particular kind and shaping societies within which human life can be properly lived. This approach is generally described as 'teleological' because it is concerned with the goal, purpose or end (Greek: *telos*) of human life. It seeks not to solve crises but to develop virtues that enable people to recognise and solve them or to contain them within a stable life-pattern. Such an approach is not exclusively Christian, indeed, most Christian thinking along these lines derives from Aristotle, but it is indispensable to any meaningful concept of Christian discipleship or to the idea of the church as a community of personal growth.[1] This approach may give us a better sense of what the Bible is and how it can help.

1. On this kind of ethical approach, see Stanley Hauerwas, *A Community of Character: Towards a Constructive Christian Social Ethic* (Notre Dame, IN: University of Notre Dame Press, 1981).

4. A vision of responsive relationships?

What is the overarching vision of life that the Bible depicts through its laws, myths, histories, prophecies and hymns? It offers us a vision of life lived in relation to God, a relationship arising from a response to an act of God. The Bible's world is therefore not human-centred, nor is the life-pattern it describes a human creation but a human response to divine initiative. Plainly, if the Bible is to provide us with an ethic it will be an ethic that includes God. Three forms of that vision of life and ethics in relation to God are 'covenant', 'kingdom' and 'life in Christ'.[2]

4.1 Covenant

The fundamental reality of the OT is Yahweh's choice of Israel, a choice expressed in the covenant of Sinai. A 'covenant' is a solemn contract freely entered into by two equals or granted by a superior to an inferior, who accepts its terms. The laws of the Pentateuch express those terms in an outward way, describing what would constitute, for individuals or the nation, a true and faithful response. From the divine side that choice is expressed in God's loving-kindness (*hesed*), faithfulness (*emunah*) and holiness (*sedakah*), and these are fundamental values also expected of Israel. The legal material is not to be understood as 613 separate laws (the atomistic view) but as Law (*Torah*), the enunciation of a life-pattern pleasing to God, characterised by obedience, service and praise. Looked at in this way, Law is not a burden but a life-giving joy; this viewpoint helps to make sense of Psalm 119, a delicate acrostic that finds 176 ways of praising the Law and therefore God, whose will and love the Law expresses.

Because the covenant relationship survived many phases of Israel's attempts (and frequent failures) to obey God, the ethical outworking is not uniform. For example, holiness may mean avoiding impurity (Leviticus), or acting with concern for the neighbour (Deuteronomy), or orientation on God (Wisdom). In ancient Israel and its scriptures, these variations lead to different solutions to particular problems, for example, different attitudes to strangers, war or the land. But the variations are not random. They are all expressions, within their historical context, of a basic relationship. For us, whether as

2. For an exploration of these three 'moments' in the biblical witness, in relation to different types of moral thinking, see Thomas Ogletree, *The Use of the Bible in Christian Ethics* (Oxford: Basil Blackwell, 1983), chapters 3-5.

church or society, this offers a paradigm of both the possibility and the problems of being 'God's people'.

4.2 Kingdom

Central to Jesus' teaching is the concept of the 'kingdom of God', a concept present in other Jewish teachings but seldom used in the NT outside the first three gospels. It forms Jesus' basic presupposition: the presence and power of God in the world striving to manifest itself in the life of individuals and nations. If God's kingdom is present, then all is possible: people can choose God and God's way (Lk 7:36-50), leave all to follow Jesus (Mk 2:14), give up their wealth and the dependence it generates (Lk 19:2-10), love those who hurt us and turn the other cheek (Mt 5:38–48).

Jesus' parables depict a world of possibility in which employers give work to those who need it (Mt 20:1-15), ancient racial antagonisms are overcome by human concern (Lk 10:30-37) and fathers forgive rebellious sons (Lk 15:11-32). Jesus refused the role of judge, so although there are detachable pieces of advice in the gospels, it is not helpful, as has often been done, to squeeze Jesus' teachings into the framework of a 'new law'. Rather, they present a vision to which we are called to assent, repenting and responding in trust, a way demonstrated by Jesus in his own life and death. The kingdom of God is for us, as individuals and as a church, a paradigm of the possibility and cost of radical discipleship.

4.3 Life in Christ

The fundamental claim made by Paul in his letters is that the idea of God's kingdom has been made absolutely specific and concrete in Jesus Christ, crucified and risen, and that in relation with Christ a 'new covenant' has opened up, a new mode of human living characterised by love, joy, peace, patience, kindness, generosity, faithfulness, gentleness and self-control (Gal 5:22-23). Paul's letters also contain much practical advice to the churches he was addressing and to groups and individuals within those churches. Usually these come at the end, as concrete applications of the vision expounded in the early part of his letters. Wrenching Paul's practical advice from its theological context contradicts one of Paul's central thrusts by preferring law to faith.

However, Paul is not always his own best interpreter. The 'risen life', as he sees it, can be worked out in various ways. Thus, for some the ideal state may be marriage while for others it may be celibacy (1

Corinthians 7); Jewish cultural norms of religiosity and behaviour have no superiority over pagan norms 'in Christ' (Gal 3:28; Rom 14:13-19). But this openness to God's working through means that appear less than ideal or even ungodly requires a suspension of certainty, which occasionally deserts Paul, as it deserts us all, and makes him reach for more definite frameworks of right and wrong: either his inherited Jewish law or the conventions of Greek society (1 Cor 11:2-16 displays both). The result is that in much of Paul's writing, and in that of his disciples, the connection between vision and discipleship is largely severed, at cost to both. Nonetheless, Paul's vision of 'life in Christ' is for us Christians, in both our inward and outward life, a paradigm of the possibility and risk of 'risen living'.

5. Which way?

The word 'ethical' has so far been used to mean much the same as 'moral'. I have argued that the Bible is not a 'handbook for morals' because it does not, in itself and without interpretation, tell us how we should behave. However, it may be claimed that the word 'ethics' should be reserved for discussion at a higher level, namely, discussion about the *principles* of morality by which we decide how to behave. An immediate answer to the question posed by my title would then be 'No', because the Bible contains little of that kind of discussion and certainly not couched in a philosophical mode. On the other hand, I have tried to show that the Bible is deeply concerned not only about morality (because it matters how we behave) but also about ethics (because it matters how we decide to behave).

Even if not philosophically, but through the use of theological symbols such as 'covenant', 'kingdom of God' and 'life in Christ', the Bible exercises a profound critique of the ways we make moral decisions. As it does so, it becomes its own critic too, passing judgment not only on those who fail to observe God's way, such as King David, but also on some of the ways otherwise faithful disciples have chosen to keep it (1 Corinthians 1–4). The example of Paul's failure to work consistently from his own theological symbols highlights the tension between vision and sight, between life in Christ and life in the world—a tension that led to Israel's exile in Babylon, to Jesus' death and to the collapse of Jesus' and Paul's eschatological teaching into 'law'. Far from abolishing this tension, the Bible—and the life seeking to live out the vision articulated in the Bible—witnesses to its uncomfortable, creative presence in the world.

Is it asking too much that we should overcome this tension? Perhaps. But the Bible has spiritual value only if it offers us power as well as vision. If we need *vision* to lift us from desire to duty, from 'I want' to 'I should', we also need *power* to transport us from duty ('I should') to freedom ('I shall'). Understanding the vision is the task of theology (theory); the business of discipleship (praxis) is laying hold of the vision's power by allowing our lives, both individually and collectively, to be formed by it and transformed by it until 'problems' present themselves within a world-view oriented on God and derive their character, as well as their solution, from that source.

Any of the examples outlined above could be worked through to illustrate what this might mean in practice: what it means to be in a covenant relationship characterised by loving-kindness, faithfulness and holiness; what it means to be obedient to a sovereign God; what it means to be human when life has been 'raised with Christ'. However, I conclude with another example, based on the biblical doctrine that the world is created in love and that humanity is made in God's image, an image tarnished in the tension between vision and praxis but presented perfectly in Jesus, the creating Word-made-flesh.

At least three consequences follow from this vision of the world's createdness. First, I am no accident but a vessel of love, and so is everyone else. Therefore, I shall not be at ease with myself or the world unless I can *love* myself and others and respond with *love* to the needy and the stranger. Second, created life is more than 'flesh', and I shall understand nothing unless I view the world in *faith* and search for the source of life in the power of God's Spirit. Third, if the world is alive with the life of God, who is infinite possibility, it is never true that we are governed by necessity and that there is no other way; the reality of 'problems' is found in their ability to call out from us new depths of *hope*.

To call us, and empower us, to rise to the vision of living together in faith, hope, love: that is the measure of the Bible's contribution to our ethical confusion. It is a vision whose truth can only be tested in practice.

The Moral Vision of the Beatitudes: The Blessings of Revolution

Christopher D Marshall

Christian attitudes to the Sermon on the Mount in Matthew 5–7 are deeply ambivalent. On one hand, we extol Jesus as the greatest moral teacher of all time and treasure the Sermon on the Mount as 'the most searching and powerful utterance we possess of what concerns the moral life'.[1] Even non-Christians share this estimate. Mahatma Gandhi described the Sermon on the Mount as 'the world's finest collection of ethical teaching',[2] while the contemporary Jewish scholar Pinchas Lapide terms it 'the quintessence of Judaism . . . the original creation of one of the great luminaries of human history'.[3]

Yet, on the other hand, despite Jesus' reputation as an ethical teacher, the Christian church has all but ignored his ethical teaching. At a practical level, the church has often failed lamentably to live up to Jesus' demands; it has evaded or domesticated his words, or postponed them to some future age. At a theoretical level, the teaching of the Sermon plays a very limited role in standard textbooks on Christian ethics. Historically, Christian ethics has been shaped far more by moral philosophy and natural law than by the distinctive ethic of Jesus.[4] Our professed admiration for the noble sentiments of the Sermon on the Mount has been matched only by our determination to minimise its impact on Christian thought and practice.

There are several reasons for this paradoxical state of affairs, but the main one has to do with how rigorous and uncompromising so many of the Sermon's demands are. Jesus allows no half measures. There must be *no* anger, *no* desire to retaliate, *no* hatred, *no* anxiety, *no*

1. AN Wilder, 'The Sermon on the Mount', *Interpreter's Bible*, vol 7, 156.
2. Quoted in RH Mounce, 'Sermon on the Mount', *International Standard Bible Encyclopedia*, vol 4, 411.
3. Pinchas Lapide, *The Sermon on the Mount: Utopia or Program for Action?* (Maryknoll, NY: Orbis Books, 1986), 7, 9.
4. See AE Harvey, *Strenuous Commands: The Ethic of Jesus* (London: SCM Press, 1990), esp chaps 1, 2, 9.

divorce, *total* purity of heart, *total* forgiveness of others and *uncalculating* generosity. Worse still, Jesus sets up God as a feasible model for human behaviour: 'You therefore must be perfect as your heavenly father is perfect' (Mt 5:48); 'love your enemies . . . so that you may be children of your Father in heaven' (Mt 5:45); 'forgive . . . as your heavenly Father has forgiven you' (Mt 6:14). God's own character and conduct are prescribed as the norm for human behaviour. Jesus demands a perfection of inner attitude and intention, which may be possible for God but is surely unattainable for ordinary people. A great gap seems to exist between what Jesus expects of his hearers and what people, even at their best, can accomplish. No wonder then, as one commentator puts it:

> Christians spend a lot of their time and energy explaining why Jesus couldn't possibly have meant what he said. This is understandable: Jesus is an extremist and we are all moderates. What is worse, he was an extremist in his whole life—not just some narrowly 'spiritual areas' . . . but in everything. So we have to find ways to dilute his teaching.[5]

To take the Sermon on the Mount seriously is clearly a difficult and disturbing business. Jesus has an uncanny knack of making us feel uncomfortable. The same lofty ideals and moral absolutism that win our respect leave us reeling in disbelief or despair. 'Such wonderful words . . . but surely he can't be serious! Life is not that black and white. A dose of starry-eyed idealism may be good for the soul, but it is unrealistic for the workaday world!'

---

5. John Alexander, 'Why We Must Ignore Jesus', *The Other Side* (Oct 1977): 8.

1. Even the Beatitudes?

But what about those delightful, sonorous words that introduce the Sermon on the Mount in Mt 5:1-12, the so-called 'Beatitudes'?

> Blessed are the poor in spirit, for theirs is the kingdom of heaven.
> Blessed are those who mourn, for they will be comforted.
> Blessed are the meek, for they will inherit the earth.
> Blessed are those who hunger and thirst for righteousness, for they will be satisfied.
> Blessed are the merciful, for they will receive mercy.
> Blessed are the pure in heart, for they will see God.
> Blessed are the peacemakers, for they will be called children of God.
> Blessed are those who are persecuted for righteousness' sake, for theirs is the kingdom of heaven.
> Blessed are you when people revile you and persecute you and utter all kinds of evil against you falsely on my account. Rejoice and be glad, for your reward is great in heaven; in the same way they persecuted the prophets who were before you.

Are these heartwarming assurances of God's blessing really so discomforting, so extreme, so hard to take seriously? Indeed they are, although most readers often fail to recognise it. They are so familiar to us that we have become deaf to the scandalous radicalism and costly challenge embedded in them. As John P Meier observes:

> The most dangerous passages in the Bible are the familiar ones, because we do not really listen to them. The sharp stone of God's Word, smoothed down by the river of time, no longer cuts. Instead of being challenged by hard thought or hard choices, we lean back and savor pretty words. No pericope in the Gospels is more exposed to this familiarity, that contentment, than the beatitudes in Matthew's Gospel. Nine beatitudes, nine spiritual bonbons. No sooner is

> 'Blessed are the poor . . .' intoned than eyes become glassy or moist, the heart is strangely warmed, and no one notices that Jesus the revolutionary is heaving a verbal grenade into our homiletic garden.[6]

In what follows I explore the revolutionary message of the beatitudes. Before examining each 'verbal grenade' individually, I make some generalisations about the focus and significance of the beatitudes as a unit. First, however, a comment on the term 'beatitude' itself.

The name comes from the Latin *beatus,* which means 'happy'. The Latin term translates the Greek word *makarios,* which begins each of the statements in Mt 5:1-12. This Greek term is usually rendered into English as 'blessed', since 'happy' sounds altogether too anaemic and secular. Yet most experts agree that 'happy' is the closest English equivalent to the normal meaning of *makarios.* 'Beatitudes', then, are pithy statements about happiness. They are wise insights ('wisdom sayings') into the universal human quest for happiness or bliss. They depict the conditions necessary for finding true contentment, joy and fulfilment.

This means that the Sermon on the Mount commences with Jesus 'teaching his disciples the way to be genuinely happy'.[7] But what a strange kind of happiness this is. The truly happy are the poor and persecuted, the hungry and thirsty, the meek and the mournful. As Lüthi and Brunner wryly observe, 'This is evidently a very *quiet* kind of happiness'.[8] The happiness in question is obviously not simply a feeling of emotional elation. By no stretch of the imagination can the blessedness of those who mourn (5:4) be an emotional exhilaration. By 'happiness' Jesus apparently has in mind that sense of security or well-being that comes from experiencing God's companionship in situations of need, together with a deep certainty that God intends, eventually, to bring that need to an end. It is the blessedness that comes from knowing you are not alone and your plight has not gone unnoticed by God, that God is *with* you and *for* you.

---

6. John P Meier, 'Matthew 5:3-12', *Interpretation* 44/3 (1990): 281.
7. Meier, 'Matthew 5:3-12', 282.
8. W Lüthi and R Brunner, *The Sermon on the Mount* (Edinburgh/London: Oliver & Boyd, 1963), 12.

2. The focus of the Beatitudes

The beatitudes in Mt 5:1-12 are more than a random collection of isolated moral maxims. They form a coherent unit that introduces the entire Sermon on the Mount and sets the tone for all that follows, including the most austere of Jesus' demands. To understand how the beatitudes function in this way, and how profoundly challenging they are, I want to identify four realities upon which they focus. There are four co-ordinates we need to keep in mind to appreciate the stunning vision of reality the beatitudes exhibit.

2.1 A whole-of-life focus

The beatitudes are often regarded as individual spiritual virtues or 'be happy' attitudes, expressions of an inner posture or mental outlook that attracts God's blessing. But while the beatitudes undoubtedly do refer to interior attitudes and intentions, they go far beyond these. They demand qualities of conduct as well as designating qualities of the heart.

It is true that, grammatically, the beatitudes are in the indicative, not the imperative, mood. That is to say, they are formulated as descriptions of certain conditions, not as ethical demands calling for obedience.[9] Jesus says, 'Blessed are those who *are* poor in spirit', not 'You must *become* poor in spirit, then you will be blessed'. This is a crucial insight, to which I will return. But indicatives can function as implicit imperatives, and do so here. As indications of those qualities of life that God blesses, the beatitudes constitute an implied summons to perform corresponding deeds of obedience. Jesus is not simply wanting to reassure his followers of God's approval, but also to provoke certain ethical commitments. For example, the remarkable blessing promised to the 'pure in heart', namely, that 'they shall see God', carries with it the implicit imperative, 'Therefore you must be pure in heart in order to see God'.[10] Furthermore, several of the beatitudes are matched by explicit imperatives later in the Sermon on the Mount. Jesus pronounces blessing on 'those who hunger and thirst

---

9. The only imperatives in the list of nine beatitudes are 'rejoice and be glad' in Mt 5:12.
10. Cf Georg Strecker, *The Sermon on the Mount* (Nashville: Abingdon Press, 1988), 33. See also WD Davies and Dale C Allison, *The Gospel According to Saint Matthew*, vol 1 (Edinburgh: T&T Clark, 1988), 439-40.

for righteousness' (Mt 5:9); later he warns his disciples that their righteousness must 'exceed that of the scribes and Pharisees to enter the kingdom of heaven' (Mt 5:20). He blesses the merciful and the peacemakers (Mt 5:7, 9); later he commands his followers, 'Love your enemies and pray for those who persecute you' (Mt 5:43-48).

The beatitudes, then, are both blessings and requirements, gifts of grace and demands of conduct. They commend not only inward sentiments but a concrete style of living and acting in the world. To be 'meek' is not simply to have an inner attitude of humility, but to live a lifestyle of powerless dependence on God. To be a 'peace*maker*' is not merely to *enjoy* peace, but to *work* for peace by acting positively to resolve conflict.

One further comment on this point: It is often said that Luke's version of the beatitudes concentrates on external conditions whereas Matthew's focuses solely on inner attitudes. In Luke, Jesus blesses 'the poor' and 'those who hunger and thirst' (Lk 6:20-21). In Matthew, he blesses 'the poor *in spirit*' and those who 'hunger and thirst *after righteousness*'. Matthew, it is alleged, 'spiritualises' the beatitudes by shifting the emphasis from socioeconomic need to subjective attitudes of spiritual hunger and poverty.[11]

Certainly there are differences between the two versions. But Matthew's concern is less to 'spiritualise' the statements than to clarify the link between Jesus' actions and the messianic promises of Isaiah 61, to which the beatitudes allude. Matthew shows how in blessing the poor Jesus fulfils the eschatological role of the Isaianic servant.[12] In technical language, Matthew's redactional activity is christological in design; it is concerned to highlight the identity of the speaker of the beatitudes rather than to change the identity of those about whom he speaks.

In any event, even if Matthew intentionally accents the attitudinal and spiritual dimension more than Luke, he still assumes that these attitudes, values and commitments will work themselves out in corresponding ethical practice, for a tree is known by its fruit (Mt 7:15-20). Matthew would consider it extremely difficult to be both 'spiritually poor' and materially rich; indeed, 'it is easier for a camel to go through the eye of a needle than for a rich person to enter the kingdom of

---

11. See, for example, Strecker, *The Sermon on the Mount*, 24-47.
12. So RA Guelich, *The Sermon on the Mount* (Waco, TX: Word, 1982), 109-111. Cf Davies and Allison, *The Gospel According to Saint Matthew*, 1:436-39.

heaven' (Mt 19:23-24). Later in the Sermon, Matthew includes Jesus' instructions about not storing up treasures on earth or attempting to serve two masters, God and wealth (Mt 6:16-34). Spiritual poverty, in other words, is demonstrable in how one handles material wealth. The same connection applies in Luke. When the wealthy Zacchaeus becomes spiritually poor, he redistributes his wealth (Lk 19:1-10). For all their differences, both versions of the beatitudes presuppose an inseparable link between inner posture and outer conduct.

2.2 *A kingdom focus*

The beatitudes describe the quality of life appropriate for those who have entered the kingdom of God and who live in conscious submission to God's rule. Just as the Decalogue begins with a declaration of fact, God's liberation of Israel from bondage in proof of his love (Ex 20:2), so the Sermon on the Mount begins in the beatitudes with a declaration of fact: God's compassionate turning towards the disadvantaged, bringing them into his liberating reign of peace and justice.[13]

Jesus began his ministry by announcing that God's long-awaited kingdom was drawing near in his own person and deeds (Mt 4:17). A new saving reality was breaking into the world of suffering and oppression. Through Jesus a new order, a new age, a new reality was being inaugurated. God's kingdom was dawning, though it was not yet here in all its fullness. Ancient hope was being fulfilled, though the final consummation was still to come.[14] Not surprisingly, Jesus found the warmest reception for his message of liberation and hope amongst the most needy, amongst the sick and possessed, amongst the victims of human unkindness (Mt 11:2-6). For them in particular, the coming of God's kingdom was truly good news.

The beatitudes presuppose Jesus' announcement of what God has done to change the history of the world. They describe how reality now looks in light of God's irruption into human affairs in Jesus. In the beatitudes, true happiness is defined not by present circumstances and prosperity, but by the sure knowledge of God's ultimate triumph over evil. The poor and the persecuted, the meek and the mournful are

13. Cf Lapide, *The Sermon on the Mount*, 36-37.

14. See Chris Marshall, *Kingdom Come: The Kingdom of God in the Teaching of Jesus* (Auckland: Impetus, 1993).

declared to be happy not because they are poor and wretched but because they participate in God's kingdom. They are blessed because they know for certain that when God's kingdom comes in its fullness, they will find consolation, mercy and justice. The absolute certainty of this future transformation brings blessedness to those who suffer now because they can be sure that present pain will be swallowed up in future victory.

But this hope is more than 'pie-in-the-sky-when-you-die'. Jesus is not telling the oppressed simply to accept their present plight and wait passively for the happiness of heaven. For the good news of the kingdom is that God's eschatological reign has *already* begun to operate in the present age. God is already acting, in Jesus, to begin to put right what is wrong on earth. A new day has dawned; change has begun; the blessings of the future kingdom are even now the possession of the poor.

This is perhaps why the first and last beatitudes are in the present tense. 'Blessed are the poor in spirit for theirs *is* the kingdom of heaven.' 'Blessed are those who are persecuted for righteousness' sake, for theirs *is* the kingdom of heaven.' The intervening beatitudes are in the future tense, but the reward of the future kingdom is framed by references to the blessings of the present kingdom. The promise of future blessing for the meek and mistreated on earth is matched by the present blessing of belonging to God's kingdom, which is already active to bring an end to their suffering. The liberating reality of God's heavenly rule is even now at work in their present experience.

But where is this to be seen? How does it work? In what ways does participation in God's kingdom concretely affect the situation of the poor and persecuted? It does so because the kingdom of God becomes a *social reality* in the community of Jesus' disciples, a community committed to God's new order, a people called to live out the vision and values of the beatitudes here and now. For as Lapide observes, the splendour of God's future triumph 'ought to inspire radical alteration of the present'.[15] Our vision of the coming kingdom should kindle in us 'a fire of happiness that cannot sit still',[16] that seeks to further God's lordship in this world through co-operative acts of obedience. This is why Klaus Wengst describes the beatitudes as 'declarations of war

15. Lapide, *The Sermon on the Mount*, 32.

16. Lapide, *The Sermon on the Mount*, 31.

against poverty, hunger and tears: they are concerned for radical change'.[17]

This is where the beatitudes acquire their disturbing radicalism. We must not see them solely as a source of consolation and hope for future change (though they are that too); we must also accept them as a *charter for Christian action in the present*. The primary way the poor and oppressed will find the blessedness of participation in God's kingdom now is in and through the community of God's kingdom, amongst other recipients of God's saving grace who are committed to embodying the values of the beatitudes in their common life and to working for the agenda of the kingdom in the world around them. This leads to the third focus of the beatitudes.

2.3 *A communal focus*

Traditionally the beatitudes have been understood as descriptions of personal virtues or private character traits that every true believer ought to display. Consequently, sermons on the beatitudes usually leave a legacy of guilt or inadequacy. Living up to any one of these virtues seems impossible, let alone displaying all of them all the time!

But before despairing, it is worth observing that the beatitudes are addressed to the disciples as a group (Mt 5:1), that they are all in the plural and that they take the form of descriptions rather than demands (even though, as argued earlier, demands are implied). These observations suggest that Jesus is talking not primarily about private moral qualities but about what the messianic community ought to look like. The beatitudes are Jesus' attempt to define the ethos of the messianic community as a colony or showcase of God's kingdom. They set forth the values and priorities that the Christian community will incarnate in the world when it is faithful to its vocation. The sayings about purity, love, generosity and mercy are not simply individual virtues but 'representative portraits of the new community's daily life of discipleship'.[18]

---

17. Klaus Wengst, *Pax Romana and the Peace of Christ* (London: SCM Press, 1987), 65.

18. R Lischer, 'The Sermon on the Mount as Radical Pastoral Care', *Interpretation* 41 (1987): 159. See also Stanley Hauerwas, 'The Sermon on the Mount, Just War and the Quest for Peace', *Concilium* 215 (1988): 36-43.

The entire Sermon on the Mount presupposes participation in the community life of a people prepared to be radically different from the world around it, a community that honours the poor, demonstrates integrity, craves for all that is right, prefers mercy to punishment, makes peace not war and suffers for its commitment to Jesus. This of course requires that each individual member strives to live in conformity with Jesus' demands. But it is impossible to do so without the support and trust of others. It is precisely as isolated individuals that we are most likely to fail as disciples. We will be inspired and empowered to live 'beatitudinally' only in so far as we are surrounded by fellow believers who share our commitment and whose collective direction will sustain us when we fail individually. And *we will fail*, repeatedly. But the community is more than the sum of its individual parts. The corporate faithfulness of a nurturing community pursuing the same vision will uphold us when we falter and challenge us to try again. As Stanley Hauerwas and William Willimon insist:

> The Sermon, like the rest of Scripture, is addressed neither to isolated individuals nor to the wider world. Rather, here are words for the colony, a prefiguration of the kinds of community in which the reign of God will shine in all its glory. So there is nothing private in the demands of the Sermon. It is very public, very political, very social in that it depicts the public form by which the colony shall witness to the world that God really is busy redeeming humanity, reconciling the world to himself in Christ. All Christian ethical issues are therefore social, political, communal issues. Can we so order our life in the colony that the world might look at us and know that God is busy?[19]

In the first instance, therefore, the beatitudes are neither individual character traits nor a strategy for changing secular society; they are 'imaginative examples of life in the kingdom of God', as realised in the community of faith.[20] But where do these values come from? How do

---

19. Stanley Hauerwas and William H Willimon, *Resident Aliens* (Nashville: Abingdon Press, 1989), 92.
20. Hauerwas and Willimon, *Resident Aliens*, 84.

we know what 'poverty in spirit', 'meekness', 'righteousness' or 'peacemaking' actually means? Where do we look for guidance on how these qualities should work out in practice?

2.4 A Christological focus

The beatitudes do not commend a set of abstract moral principles that any reasonable person can understand and follow. They are not the ethics of common sense, even sanctified common sense. They are the ethics of the eschatological kingdom. They are disciplines of discipleship. More specifically, they are descriptions of the kind of person Jesus, the bearer of God's kingdom, is. They are 'the autobiography of Jesus, a perfect self-portrait by the Master . . . the only fully happy man who ever lived'.[21]

Jesus embodied his own teaching. His life gave content to his words; his actions and relationships illustrated his demands. We therefore learn what the humility, mercy and peacemaking of the beatitudes mean by looking at how Jesus lived. Jesus pronounces God's blessing upon the meek (Mt 5:5). The word 'meek' occurs only twice elsewhere in Matthew's Gospel, both of which refer to Jesus himself (Mt 11:29; 21:5). We learn to be meek by emulating Jesus' own meekness. Jesus blesses peacemakers (Mt 5:9). Jesus himself is God's ultimate instrument for bringing the peace of heaven to earth (Lk 1:79; 2:14; 19:38, 42; Acts 10:36). We learn what peacemaking entails by looking at how Jesus operated. Jesus blesses the mournful (Mt 5:4); he also mourned (Mt 26:38; Lk 19:41). He blesses those who hunger for righteousness; he himself 'fulfilled all righteousness' (Mt 3:15; 5:17-18; 27:4, 19). He extols the merciful (Mt 5:7); he himself showed mercy (Mt 9:27; 15:22; 17:15; 20:30-31). He comforts the persecuted (Mt 5:11-12); Jesus was also persecuted and reproached (Matthew 26–27).

So, the content and implications of the beatitudes are defined by considering the practices of Jesus. He actualises his own words and thereby becomes the standard or model to be imitated by his followers. And for Matthew, imitating Jesus means imitating God (see Mt 5:44-48; 3:17), which brings us full circle: These heart-warming, ennobling beatitudes truly are 'verbal grenades' that give expression to that revolutionary rigorism in Jesus' ethical teaching with which the Christian church has so long struggled.

---

21. Meier, 'Matthew 5:3-12', 285.

3. The vision of the Beatitudes

The beatitudes are best understood, then, as descriptions of a *whole way of life* that we as a Christian *community* are called to live, a life *modelled on Jesus* and bearing witness to the transforming reality of the *kingdom of God*. They offer us a vision of reality that stands in stark contradiction to the way reality looks to the world around us. The radicalism of the beatitudes only makes sense, and will only seem practical, if we accept Jesus' assertion that the world as we know it is passing away and God's new creation is being born. The question we face is whether we accept the truth of God's perspective or the common sense perspective of the existing world order. 'Let God be true, and everyone else a liar' (Rom 3:4). As Hauerwas and Willimon so insightfully put it:

> We can only act within that world which we see. So the primary ethical question is not, What ought I now do? but rather, How does the world really look? The most interesting question about the Sermon is not, Is this really a practical way to live in the world? but rather, Is this really the way the world is? What is 'practical' is related to what is real. If the world is a society in which only the strong, the independent, the detached, the liberated, and the successful are blessed, then we act accordingly. However, if the world is really a place where God blesses the poor, the hungry, and the persecuted for righteousness' sake, then we must act in accordance with reality or else appear bafflingly out of step with the way things are.[22]

Only when we take the beatitudes seriously as our corporate charter of life can we hope to be effective agents of God's kingdom in the world. That is why the list of beatitudes is followed by the famous sayings on salt and light: 'You are the salt of the earth; but if salt has lost its taste, how can its saltiness be restored? It is no longer good for anything, but is thrown out and trampled under foot. You are the light of the world. A city built on a hill cannot be hid' (Mt 5:13-16). Salt adds flavour and creates thirst; light exposes things shrouded in darkness and encourages growth. When we, as Christ's community, believe in

22. Hauerwas and Willimon, *Resident Aliens*, 88.

and embody the values of the beatitudes, we will be a truth-affirming, life-enhancing, thirst-creating, growth-inducing manifestation of God's kingdom in unbelieving society.

In sum, the beatitudes have a twofold significance for Christians. On one hand, they are a source of comfort and reassurance that God's kingdom will eventually triumph, evil will be vanquished, sorrow and suffering will come to an end. On the other hand, and more discomfortingly, they are a summons to Christian action; they are declarations of war by the Christian community on poverty, hunger, misery and injustice, in the name of God's impinging kingdom.

4. The revolutionary challenge of the Beatitudes

With this in mind, it is easy to see why each of Matthew's eight or nine beatitudes can be thought of as 'verbal grenades' heaved by 'Jesus the revolutionary'. Each has an explosive message.

4.1 Blessed are the poor in spirit, for theirs is the kingdom of heaven.

This initial beatitude functions as a rubric or summary heading for the entire list that follows. The remaining beatitudes spell out in different terms the meaning of both parts (pronouncement and promise) of this introductory beatitude.[23] Each of the ensuing pronouncements defines and describes what is entailed in being 'poor in spirit'. To be spiritually poor is to be meek, merciful, mournful, persecuted, pure in heart and so on. Similarly, each of the ensuing promises demonstrates what is meant by the assurance, 'theirs is the kingdom of heaven'. To receive the kingdom means to be comforted, to inherit the earth, to be satisfied, to receive mercy and to see God. The first beatitude, then, is 'related to all the other beatitudes as the thumb is to the fingers, and belongs to them all. None of the beatitudes that follow can be rightly understood if they are not approached through this one'.[24]

In Luke's version, Jesus blesses 'you poor' (Lk 6:20), whereas in Matthew he blesses 'the poor in spirit'. At first glance, Matthew appears to 'spiritualise' and 'interiorise' Luke's socioeconomic designation. But appearances can be misleading. When each designation is viewed in the context of the total symbolic world of their respective gospels, it is clear that Matthew and Luke have the same group of

23. So Davies and Allison, *The Gospel According to Saint Matthew*, 1:446, 449, 460.

24. Lüthi and Brunner, *The Sermon on the Mount*, 14.

addressees in view,[25] whom we might term 'the godly poor'. Both designations imply a *combination* of external and internal circumstances. The poor or poor in spirit are those who, facing an external situation of need and vulnerability, adopt an internal posture of trusting dependence on God. Unable to guarantee their own physical and material security because of poverty, oppression or prejudice, they rest their confidence in the power and grace of God.

The *New English Bible* glosses 'the poor in spirit' as 'those who know their need of God'. This is a wonderful rendering that captures the idea of the poor's response to God. But it misses the note of desperation implied in the original. Poverty of spirit is more than the settled piety of the spiritually sincere; it is the determined response of trusting reliance upon God in face of the most extreme need.

But why does Jesus declare the desperately needy who respond in this way to be 'blessed'? It is because God *never* ignores such pleas for help; he gives them 'the kingdom of heaven'; he intervenes to help. Two points need emphasising here. The first is that it is not the extreme need itself, be it poverty, oppression, sickness or bereavement, that is the blessing. Deprivation and suffering are not good in themselves. They express the tragedy and brokenness of the world. But loss and pain may yet become an *occasion* for blessing, in so far as they drive the needy in desperation to God, for God is never deaf to the cries of the poor.

The second point is that it is the *fact* of God's response to the poor, more than its immediate tangible results, that is the source of blessing. God's action on behalf of the poor is not intended to make them materially rich. It aims more profoundly to confer upon the poor a consciousness of their dignity in God's eyes, reflected in their privileged citizenship in God's kingdom. This awareness of their value to God enables the poor, in partnership with others in the new community, to rise up from the dust, repudiate the value system that calls them trash and find ways to participate in their own transformation. As Jürgen Moltmann observes:

> An inner acceptance of the meritocracy's system of values is always the greatest hindrance to the self-liberation of the poor, because this acceptance en-

25. For a full analysis, see Guelich, *The Sermon on the Mount*, 59-72; cf pp 81-83, 101-102.

> genders self-contempt. Faith overcomes this self-hate and raises up those who are bowed down. 'The kingdom of heaven is yours' is not cheap consolation, a sop designed to keep the poor quiet. It is the authority to get up and bring peace to the world of violence, as children of God's kingdom. Jesus doesn't set the poor on the road to social advancement so they can be as rich as the rest. He sets them on the road of fellowship, whose culture is a culture of sharing, as the feeding of the five thousand shows.[26]

The next beatitude further defines the poor in spirit as those who grieve and identifies reception of the kingdom with the experience of divine consolation.

4.2 Blessed are those who mourn, for they will be comforted.

Ever since the patristic period, this saying has been taken to refer to the penitential mourning of sinners over personal acts of wrong-doing. But this is not the primary thought here. The beatitude alludes to Isa 61:2, where God's people mourn over their oppression by their enemies. They grieve because judgment has befallen the nation, because the righteous suffer at the hands of the wicked.[27] Against this backdrop, the mourning of Jesus' beatitude fundamentally denotes a sense of anguish over the sorry state of God's world—where evil triumphs, where cruelty and greed despoil God's good creation, where sickness and death stalk and where wicked people do unspeakable things to the weak and helpless. It is the lament of those who recognise that God's will is *not* done on earth as it is in heaven (see Mt 6:10).

One profound expression of spiritual poverty, then, is a deep distress at the distortions of God's world, a holy discontent with the unjust status quo, a longing for the triumph of divine justice. God promises comfort to those who so mourn. Comfort comes from the sure knowledge that the present evil age is not final, that God's saving intervention is assured to 'wipe away every tear from every eye' (Rev 21:4; Isa 25:8). Such assurance is based on the fact that God is even now at work in Jesus, bringing his promises to fruition. Comfort also comes

---

26. J Moltmann, *Jesus Christ for Today's World* (London: SCM Press, 1994), 18.
27. Guelich, *The Sermon on the Mount*, 80-81.

from belonging to the community of Jesus, which is already beginning to experience the liberation of the future.

4.3 Blessed are the meek, for they will inherit the earth.

In the third beatitude, the poor in spirit are further depicted as the meek or humble. Meekness here probably denotes an external condition more than a mental attitude. It is a condition of vulnerability or insecurity in the world. It is the state of the dispossessed, disenfranchised or disempowered, those with no economic or political leverage, no capacity to protect themselves from the strong and the greedy.

Meekness was despised in the ancient world; humble circumstances were a sign of weakness. Things haven't changed much. Our society rewards ambitious, aggressive 'go-getters'. I once heard a prominent business leader quip, 'The meek may well inherit the earth, but they're damn well not going to get the title deeds to it!' But Jesus says the exact opposite. Not only does he commend meekness as a condition and disposition God prizes; he asserts that the meek *shall* get the title deeds to the earth. What a remarkable assertion! The meek shall *inherit the earth*. Possession of territory is generally achieved through brute force or power politics; the strongest or the most devious get the biggest slice. But here it is allotted to those who have no power, whose deeds are determined not by anger, brutality or enmity but by trusting reliance on the power of God.

When will the meek inherit the earth? When God's kingdom comes in fullness, when God's will is done on earth as it is in heaven (Mt 6:10). Then creation will be healed, the social order will be transformed and those who have been denied rights of possession in the present unjust order shall 'belong' in a way they have not experienced hitherto. The dispossessed shall possess the renewed earth.

It is worth pausing to consider some implications of this remarkable beatitude for contemporary Christian ethics. One is that Christians must *care for the earth*. It is significant that receiving the kingdom of heaven in the first beatitude is here identified with inheriting the earth. God's kingdom will be consummated on earth; the meek shall inherit the earth, not heaven. Getting people into heaven is not the ultimate goal of redemption. God's ultimate goal is to bring the reality of heaven to earth (see Rom 8:18-24; Rev 21:2ff). This planet has a glorious future. If redeemed humanity is to inherit this earth, then we must cherish our inheritance now.

Another implication is that followers of Jesus must *care for the weak and oppressed on the earth*. If God is on the side of the meek, those persistently denied power, dignity and their rightful share of the earth's resources, then God's people must also be concerned for them. The kingdom of God is especially good news for such people; it is the task of the Christian community to show *how* it is good news.

A third implication of this beatitude is that all Christians, including those who are powerful and well-off, must strive to *practise meekness in all that they do*. Our methods must match our message. We cannot rely on violence, wealth and worldly power to extend God's kingdom. We serve a meek king (Mt 11:29; 21:5) and must do so in meekness. This leads naturally to the fourth beatitude.

4.4 Blessed are those who hunger and thirst for righteousness, for they will be filled.

The imagery of this beatitude is striking. Jesus uses the two strongest biological drives, two basic human needs, as metaphors to describe a human craving for righteousness. Hunger haunted the ancient world, and drinkable water was always scarce in the hot, arid Middle East, so the metaphor would have been even more powerful for Jesus' first hearers. Clearly Jesus has in mind more than a nodding assent or mental agreement with the demands of righteousness. The metaphor expresses a passionate, energetic commitment to see righteousness done, a longing of such intensity that, by its very nature, drives us to action. As hunger compels the action of eating and thirst that of drinking, so hungering and thirsting for righteousness will, if present, compel us to *work* for righteousness.

But what is this 'righteousness' we are to be so desperate for? Some commentators suggest that it refers to a righteous status before God, a longing to be 'justified' or to have right-standing in the sight of God.[28] But this is to read Paul's theology into Matthew. 'Righteousness' in Matthew usually refers to ethical conduct in keeping with God's will rather than to 'justification' before God (Mt 5:10, 20; 6:1, 33; cf 3:15; 21:32). In any case, the Sermon on the Mount is addressed to those who have already embraced God's kingdom, who are already in right relationship with God (Mt 5:1).

---

28. Cf Guelich, *The Sermon on the Mount*, 86-87, 102-103.

To hunger and thirst for righteousness is better understood to refer to a *striving after what is right,* a longing to see God's moral will done on earth as it is in heaven and to see human life lived as God intends it to be lived.[29] Moreover, the righteousness in question is a social or relational reality more than an individual moral quality. It describes social relationships functioning in the 'right' way, the entire social order being as it ought to be. In this connection, 'righteousness' in this beatitude could well be translated as 'justice', since justice is our term for social righteousness.

Jesus, then, is pronouncing God's blessing on those who toil to see God's justice done in an unjust world, not those who only think it's a good idea but those who seek after it with the primitive force of hunger and thirst. Such passionate longing for justice comes most readily to those who at present are the victims of injustice, for they are the ones who need it most. For the rest of us, it is only when we identify with such victims that we will share their craving for God's new order.

Experience teaches, however, that suffering injustice can often lead to vengeful hatred and violence. The oppressed can themselves easily become oppressors. The next beatitude summons a very different response.

4.5 Blessed are the merciful, for they will receive mercy.

In biblical tradition 'mercy' is preeminently a characteristic of God. Most biblical references to mercy are descriptions of what God is like. When human beings are summoned to show mercy, it is in emulation of God's mercy. As Jesus puts it, 'Be merciful as your Father is merciful' (Lk 6:36).

Jesus has a great deal to say about mercy, especially in Matthew's Gospel. Twice he quotes Hos 6:6, 'I desire mercy, not sacrifice' (Mt 9:13; 12:7), and he attacks the religious leaders for neglecting 'weightier matters of the law: justice and mercy and faith' (Mt 23:23). The merciful, then, are those who demonstrate the Godlike conduct of offering pardon to those in the wrong and kindness to those in need. It is *because* God is merciful that those who live under God's rule must show mercy. To show mercy is an act of loyalty to God. And the mercy shown must correspond to the fullness of God's mercy. It must not be a resentful, grudging refusal to press charges but a free, boundless

29. Cf Davies and Allison, *The Gospel According to Saint Matthew*, 1:452-53.

pardon. This is the only beatitude in which the promise corresponds precisely to the pronouncement; those who show mercy shall receive mercy. Yet the ability to show mercy in the first place is enabled by God's prior mercy. Divine mercy is both the beginning and end of human mercy. This thought leads directly to the following beatitude.

4.6 Blessed are the pure in heart, for they will see God.

The phrase 'pure in heart' is often assumed to refer to moral or, even more specifically, sexual purity, to cleanness of thought and speech. But this is not the meaning here. Purity of heart is an OT idiom (eg Psalm 24:4-6) for something even more basic than thoughts or words.

In biblical thought, the 'heart' denotes the centre of one's being, the source of thinking, willing, feeling and doing. Purity of heart denotes consistency between one's intentions, thoughts and actions. It is what today we call 'integrity', 'sincerity' or 'genuineness', where there is true integration between outward action and inward motivation. It is the opposite of pretence, duplicity or hypocrisy. JB Phillips's translation is apt: 'How happy are the utterly sincere.' To be pure in heart is to be transparent and straightforward, to do what you say and say what you do. It also means singleness of devotion, a wholehearted desire to do what is true above all else.

Such people are comfortable in the presence of God. Why? Because they are not trying to hide anything or to appear as anything other than they are. The reward Jesus promises them is therefore appropriate: 'they shall see God'. They shall know God fully. As they have allowed themselves to be fully known by others because of their honesty, openness and integrity, so God shall allow God's self to be fully known by them.

There are two biblical traditions about seeing God. One denies that it is possible for mere mortals to see God because of God's transcendent holiness and human unworthiness (see Ex 3:6; 19:21; 33:20, 23; Jn 1:18; 1 Tim 6:15-16). The other makes seeing God the goal and destiny of human existence, something that is only possible because God graciously makes it possible (Psalm 11:7; 17:15; Job 19:26; Rev 22:4.) Jesus' beatitude reflects this second tradition. The goal of the beatific vision will only be reached by those who seek after God's will with integrity of heart. This notion of seeing or knowing God leads naturally to the next beatitude, which focuses on one of God's most astonishing attributes.

4.7 Blessed are the peacemakers, for they will be called the children of God.
At the time of Jesus, one of the most frequently used titles for God in the synagogue liturgy was 'Peacemaker' or 'Pacifier', the One who brings peace.[30] Peace or *shalom* was highly valued in Jewish piety. According to the rabbis, 'All commandments are to be fulfilled when the right opportunity arrives. But not peace! Peace you must seek out and pursue.'[31]

In Jewish tradition, *shalom* is not simply the absence of war, as suggested by the Greek term *eirene*, nor is it an enforced pacification of hostile forces by a preponderance of might, as in the Roman *Pax*. Biblical *shalom* is a state of total well-being, integrated wholeness and harmony, a condition of 'all-rightness', of 'having it together' in the way God intended. It is the world at rest under God. The original *shalom* of creation was shattered by the entry of sin. Ever since, the 'God of peace' (Rom 16:20) has been actively and redemptively involved to restore peace to rebellious, sinful creation.

Jesus is God's ultimate instrument for bringing the peace of heaven to earth, a theme accented in particular by Luke. At Jesus' birth, the angels sang, 'Glory to God in the highest heaven, and on earth peace among those whom he favours' (Lk 2:14; 19:38). Zechariah blessed the infant Jesus as 'one sent to guide our feet into the way of peace' (Lk 1:79). Through his life, death and resurrection, Jesus taught and demonstrated 'the things that make for peace' (Lk 19:42; Acts 10:36), the things that bring about the restoration of harmony between God and humanity (Rom 5:1-2) and between hostile peoples (Eph 2:13-18; Gal 3:28). Jesus' entire ministry was one of divine and human peacemaking.

Accordingly, in acclaiming peacemakers Jesus is blessing those who participate in his own great work of peacemaking. 'To make peace', explains Robert Guelich, 'is to engage actively in bringing God's redemptive purposes to bear in all of our broken society.'[32] Note again the action-emphasis of the beatitude. Jesus does not bless peace-*lovers,* those who avoid conflict at all costs, but peace*makers,* those who confront conflict and seek to bring about reconciliation and wholeness, those who demonstrate love even for their enemies (Mt 5:43-48; Rom 5:10).

---

30. Lapide, *The Sermon on the Mount*, 35.
31. Lapide, *The Sermon on the Mount*, 35.
32. Guelich, *The Sermon on the Mount*, 107.

Of course, the peace that is sought, God's universal *shalom*, is the goal of the entire plan of salvation, something that ultimately can be achieved by God alone. But Jesus invites human collaboration with God's peacemaking efforts. Lapide speaks of the 'theo-politics of small steps', of doing small things for the sake of peace, such as curtailing conflicts, blunting confrontations, being flexible, waiving rights and so on, as a constituent part of the reconciling work of the great Peacemaker.[33] Those who make peace, Jesus says, will be called (by God) 'the children of God'. To be a 'child of God' implies two things. It implies being like God in character by being someone who does what God does, that is, makes peace. It also implies enjoying intimacy with God, knowing God as openly and personally as a child knows its parents.

But peacemaking is costly; it is every bit as costly as war-making. It proved costly for Jesus and it will prove to be so for those who follow Jesus. No wonder, then, that Matthew's list of beatitudes concludes with a double blessing on those who pay the price.

4.8 Blessed are those who are persecuted for righteousness' sake, for theirs is the kingdom of heaven.

Matthew's list of beatitudes concludes with a twofold blessing upon the persecuted. (Strictly speaking, there are two beatitudes here, but they make the same essential point.) It is an inherent part of the kingdom's progress in the world to encounter opposition, both verbal abuse ('when they revile you and say all manner of evil against you falsely') and physical violence ('persecution'). It happened to Jesus, and it continues to happen to those who identify with Jesus and with his agenda.

Two causes of persecution are mentioned in this twin beatitude.[34] The first is 'because of righteousness'. Whenever people are committed to seeing God's justice realised in situations of oppression and injustice, they will suffer. The second is 'because of me'. Whenever people are stubbornly faithful to Jesus in situations where Jesus is rejected, they will suffer.

Neither should occasion surprise, 'for in the same way they persecuted the prophets who were before you'. God's redemptive work

33. Lapide, *The Sermon on the Mount*, 35.

34. Cf Strecker, *The Sermon on the Mount*, 42, 45.

always provokes resistance. This should not be a cause for despair; on the contrary, 'rejoice and be glad, for great is your reward in heaven'. Present suffering becomes meaningful and therefore bearable when it is seen against a larger canvas, in this case, as part of the whole course of God's saving action reaching back in history ('so they persecuted the prophets before you'), into the present ('theirs *is* the kingdom of heaven') and forward to future triumph ('great is your reward in heaven').

5. Conclusion

Too often in Christian usage the beatitudes have been domesticated into comforting platitudes directed to solitary individuals. They are far from that. The beatitudes are not a list of private virtues for isolated believers but wisdom sayings addressed to a discipleship community. They describe what the church, the social embodiment of God's kingdom, ought to look like when it is true to its vocation. The beatitudes are the characteristics of a messianic community prepared to be radically different from the world around it. They express a perspective on reality that the world does not accept as normal, but which the eyes of faith may perceive as the way things really are when seen from God's perspective. When the Christian community today takes the beatitudes as its charter for life, it will once again look different from the prevailing social order. It will look different because it will look like Jesus.

When Jesus blesses the poor in spirit, the pure in heart, the meek and the merciful, he underscores the importance of moral character and commitment, the supreme value of integrity, humility, compassion and sincerity. The beatitudes do summon individual moral transformation, not merely as a private, subjective experience, but as the result of belonging to a transformed 'beatitudinal' community that nurtures the ongoing conversion of its members in service of its redemptive mission in the world.

When Jesus blesses those who grieve over the world's pain, those who hunger and thirst for God's justice and those who strive to be like God in making peace, he blows apart any narrow restriction of the gospel to merely spiritual matters. Each beatitude implies an engagement in the affairs of this world in the name of God's encroaching kingdom.

When Jesus blesses those who are persecuted for the sake of justice and because of loyalty to himself, he reminds us that serving the cause of the kingdom is no picnic. The gospel of the kingdom confronts the whole of life with an agenda of radical change, and it calls us to invest all that we have and all that we are in God's work of renewing and transforming the world.

Christ and Power[1]

Rowena Curtis

Christ—the word brings images to mind. Some of these images hit us with great intensity, even those of incidents long past that still produce fear. Some images come more gently: 'gentle Jesus, meek and mild'. Some evoke anger, the anger of a son whose father's house has been desecrated. Christ Almighty, another image—not blasphemy, but a victorious image leading crusaders off to war in the holy land or in Vietnam. Or the crucified Christ, an image of suffering, pain and death. Jesus Christ, the Christ of God, God's self-revelation in truth and love, bringing life, grace and hope.

Power—the word brings images to mind. Some of these images hit us with great intensity, even those of incidents long past that still produce fear, of angry shouting and violent actions. Some images come more gently, reminding us of our own power and our own lack of power, times when we made a positive contribution and times when we felt powerless and confused.

There are current images flashed across the screens and pages of the media, images that lodge in our minds and often make us feel powerless: images of unresolved civil war, of natural disasters, of children dying of hunger. But from time to time there are also images that stir something deep within us: images of protesters at Woomera, of the Wik people dancing outside Parliament House, of a father cradling his child, of a woman being ordained.

We are confronted by these images over and over again. The media does not tire of showing us the misery and celebration of the world. Sometimes what we see makes us think a little; sometimes what we see makes us feel a little. But we rarely act. As Christians, our minds are constantly fed more and more information about our faith, more and more details about the scriptural text. Sometimes our hearts may be stirred, but rarely do we act. Someone has called this phenomenon 'constipated Christianity'. I suggest that not only as Christians are we

1. This paper was originally presented at a 'Baptists Today' conference in Can-berra (13 August 1998).

constipated with information overload, but also as world citizens. This saps our power because if we know more than we can process with our feelings and more than we can act upon, our thinking becomes confused, our feelings are repressed and we do nothing.

Christ. Is it a religious word? A name of faith? For many of us, it has become a faith word. *Power*. Is it a dirty word? Perhaps for many of us it has become a dirty word. So, when we put these two words together, we are confronted to do some thinking and feeling about how these two words relate to one another—and to act on that thinking and feeling. We are confronted to resolve how we think about power, how we feel about power and how we use our power as followers of Jesus Christ.

Our understanding and use of power needs to be anchored in Jesus Christ. If Jesus Christ is the one we follow, then how he used or did not use power is basic to how we use or do not use power today. We live in a vastly different world from that in which Jesus lived, so it is not always possible to make a direct transference. Nevertheless, in our complex world we must find ways to use our power legitimately, and we can gain direction in this from Jesus Christ.

Many Christians do not use their legitimate power. I believe that many Christians are afraid of power and perhaps do not think they have any power. There are also many Christians who abuse their power, so we need guidance to discern between the use and abuse of power.

We all have power because we Christians have been promised power by the risen Christ: 'You shall receive power when the Holy Spirit has come upon you . . .' (Acts 1:8a). But what is this power for, and how can we be responsible stewards of it?

For the purposes of this paper, I define power as the ability to influence, bring about or resist change. This definition is neutral, but the use of power is not neutral because it can be used for good or evil. Power can be abused to dominate, manipulate and control. Yet power can also be used for love, life and justice.[2] So, in answer to our question, What is power for, and how can we be responsible stewards of it? the following questions provide useful guidelines: Is our power

2. For a discussion of power as control and power as life, see Sally B Purvis, *The Power of the Cross: Foundations for a Christian Feminist Ethic of Community* (Nashville: Abingdon Press, 1993).

used out of compassion? Is it life-giving? Does it contribute to bringing about justice in our relationships and in the world? Or is our power abused by trying to control people around us, by trying to maintain our own position or even by trying to dominate those who are weaker than we are? In whose social, religious, economic and political interests do we exercise our power?

If we consult the biblical text, we see a variety of ways in which power is expressed and used. Hans-Ruedi Weber divides these different expressions of power into trajectories that run through the OT, the intertestamental period and into the NT. It is possible to trace these trajectories through church history up until the present day. In the ecumenical and global family of churches, the diverse understandings of power are clearly evident, as faith communities emphasise different parts of Scripture according to their context.[3]

But where is power located within the ecumenical and global family of churches? Who has the power to interpret the scriptural text, and who has the power to give priority to any trajectory within that text? Traditionally this power has been held by professional, white, western males. These 'gentlemen', whether academics or clergy, have had an interest in preserving their own power base, which means that their interpretations will generally preserve the status quo. This easily leads to disempowerment of others in the faith community because the interpretation of the text they hear often denies their life-experience and may even be used to justify a negative or abusive life-experience.

This need not be the case, however. There is an alternative way to share the power of the text, namely, to encourage the whole faith community to interpret the text out of their life-situation. This leads to the empowerment of the whole group. In this case, the clergy and academics put themselves at the service of the faith community, disempowering themselves as exclusive interpreters by sharing the power of interpretation with the entire faith community.

---

3. Hans-Ruedi Weber, *Power: Focus for a Biblical Theology* (Geneva: WCC, 1989). Weber's power trajectories within the Bible are: (1) God's liberating acts; (2) God's royal rule; (3) God's empowering wisdom; (4) God's holy presence; (5) God's vindication of the poor; and (6) God's renewing judgment. He argues that all of these trajectories converge in Jesus of Nazareth.

1. Christ and power in Matthew's Gospel

My research in the NT has focused on the role of women and children in the text of Matthew's Gospel, so I will concentrate on the theme of Christ and power as depicted in the Gospel of Matthew. It is important to note that all of Scripture, including the Gospel of Matthew, was written in an androcentric culture by androcentric authors. That is, the cultural assumption that surrounded and informed the author regarded male experience as normative. Feminist scholars have done a great deal of work in analysing the text from women's experience. This challenges the status quo but brings to light much that is fresh and pertinent for followers of Jesus today. This new-found freedom of interpretation is part of the phenomenon of deconstruction in the postmodern world, and it has had a liberating effect on exegesis for marginalised groups such as Christian women.

By asking new questions, new readings of the biblical text have been discovered, many of them life-giving to women in ministry and in the church. Women are using their God-given power to think and feel and act theologically. We cannot ignore this new work.

There is no question that Matthew portrays Jesus as one with power, indeed, as one who has *legitimate* power and authority. From the beginning of the Gospel, Jesus is introduced to the reader as 'the Christ', that is, the one anointed with the power of God. Matthew stresses titles and names for Jesus like Emmanuel ('God with us') and 'Son of David'. These titles indicate Jesus' legitimate power and authority, and they are reinforced as ordinary people respond to him throughout the Gospel. Disciples and needy crowds respond by following Jesus, and they gather around him for healing in their bodies, minds and souls. They call out that he teaches with authority. They call him 'Lord' and 'Son of David' as they cry out for healing. The crowds marvel that no one before in Israel has achieved such deeds of power. They elevate him above all the great leaders, kings, priests and prophets of their history.

Early in Matthew's Gospel Jesus' legitimate use of power is set in stark relief by contrast with King Herod's abuse of power (Mt 2:1-18). The reader is shocked by Herod's murder of innocent children in his attempt to kill the infant Jesus, a perceived rival to his position of power. Jesus' legitimate power is also emphasised in the temptation narrative (Mt 4:1-11) and repeatedly in his conflict with the religious and cultic leaders, whose power, whether secular or religious, Matthew portrays as the abusive power of domination and control. So, when the question of power arises amongst the disciples, Jesus tells them: 'You know that the rulers of the Gentiles lord it over them, and their great men exercise authority over them. It shall not be so among you; but whoever would be great among you must be your servant and whoever would be first among you must be your slave; even as the Son of Man came not to serve but to serve, and to give his life as a ransom for many' (Mt 20:25b-28).

Jesus' words and deeds demonstrate to his followers that the power that God bestows, the power of the kingdom of God, is different from secular or religious domination. When the disciples of John the Baptist ask if Jesus really is the one from God, Jesus points to what they can see and hear, what they have witnessed of his power and authority: 'the blind receive their sight and the lame walk, lepers are cleansed and the deaf hear, the dead are raised up, and the poor have good news preached to them' (Mt 11:4b-5).

Yet Matthew also presents Jesus as the powerless one. Jesus is 'God with us' in a powerless child (Mt 2:1-18). Jesus is 'God with us' in the hungry and thirsty one, the strange one, the naked one, the sick one and the imprisoned one (Mt 25:31-46). Jesus is 'God with us' in the reviled, forsaken, crucified one (Mt 27:38-50). This powerless Christ on the cross assaults the dominant idea of power. For in his ultimate identification with the powerless, Christ changes the course of history. In his powerlessness Christ opens the way for God to act in liberating, loving power in the resurrection of Jesus. The power that creates life is the power that resurrects life, the power of life in the face of death.

In his ministry Jesus gives special attention to the powerless. The Matthean Jesus clearly identifies those included in the kingdom of heaven and those who will lead the righteous into the kingdom. The beatitudes (or blessings) in Mt 5:3-10 form an *inclusio*, that is, the first and last blessings are framed with the words, 'for theirs is the kingdom of heaven'. The *inclusio* indicates that not only the people mentioned in the first blessing (the poor) and the last blessing (those persecuted for justice) are given the kingdom, but also those in between, those who mourn and work for peace. Matthew's Jesus also welcomes other groups into God's kingdom: children (Mt 18:1-6; 19:13-15); tax collectors and prostitutes (Mt 21:31); and those who do the will of God (Mt 7:21; cf 12:46-50).

This is significant for us. Many of us in the church may see ourselves as working for peace and justice, as ones who do God's will, although generally not persecuted for it. But the kingdom is not only for us. It is for poor, sad, downtrodden people, children, sex workers and those who are despised. This awareness provides us with a clear idea of whose company we should keep and whose feelings and interests we should attempt to understand and act upon.

In addition, if we look closely at the experience of women and children in the text of Matthew's Gospel, we see many reversals that Jesus inaugurates. These reversals are identified by Jesus' words, 'Many who are first will be last, and the last first' (Mt 19:30; cf 20:16). Those who had no power under patriarchy are given a place in the kingdom, an opportunity to use their power to think, feel and act. For example, we find women elevated by Jesus for their faith and service (Mt 8:14-15; 9:20-22; 15:22-28; 26:6-13; 27:55-56). We find that children have a place as followers of Jesus (Mt 14:21; 15:38). Towards the end of Matthew's Gospel we find Jesus in the temple. First he deals with corruption in the temple, then he does what should be done in the temple: he heals the sick. The blind and lame come to Jesus in the temple and are healed, and children praise God (Mt 21:12-17). The children see that Jesus' powerful deeds of healing are wonderful and marvellous. Perhaps they shout out praises because they have experienced his care at some point during his ministry. Perhaps one of them is the little rich girl brought back from death to life; perhaps one was the boy freed from the power of evil; perhaps some were in the crowds that Jesus fed.

This radically new understanding of power experienced by the earliest followers of Jesus, who for a time lived in his company, is recorded rather unevenly in the NT. This sharing of power forms one trajectory, one understanding of power, but there are other trajectories, other understandings of power in the NT. Christian feminists such as Elisabeth Schüssler Fiorenza have noted a movement from the 'discipleship of equals' to the 'repatriarchalisation' of Christian experience.[4] She argues that in the earliest churches women moved out of patriarchy into a more equal experience of shared power with men, but later, probably due to pressure from the surrounding culture, Christianity became institutionalised and hierarchical, and power was again

4. Elisabeth Schüssler Fiorenza, *In Memory of Her: A Feminist Theological Reconstruction of Christian Origins* (New York: Crossroad; London: SCM Press, 1983).

held by a few men. For example, in Mt 12:50 a 'discipleship of equals' is expressed in Jesus' claim that whoever does God's will is 'my brother, my sister, my mother'; yet Mt 10:1-4 indicates the prominence of the twelve male apostles. So it is possible to trace a trajectory of Jesus giving love and life and justice to a whole range of people, who then share power as a community of equal disciples. It is also possible to trace a trajectory of Jesus calling males only, giving them authority and power over the rest of the community. I suggest that the latter, traditional interpretation is no longer perceived as loving, life-giving or just by a growing number of people.

2. Christ and power today

We must find ways to name and unmask abuse of power. We need to recognise abuse of power in our society, in our church and within ourselves. We are to resist its seduction in all areas of life, and we are to protest against it.

In many situations, even people of good will misuse their power. This misuse of power is based on a lack of awareness of its consequences, rather than an intentional will to control, manipulate or dominate. Often this misuse of power stems from accepting the assumptions of society or a particular institution. Clearly in the institution named the church, good people can collectively abuse their power, especially when these same people are questioned about their decisions or their use of church procedures and processes. We all have power, but if we choose not to use it in a liberating way, if we choose not to protest its misuse, then we allow abuse of power to continue unchecked.

Abuse of power is an intentional will to control, dominate and manipulate. There is an element of choice for those who abuse their power. They resist change in order to maintain their power, even when they hear the protests of those who seek legitimate change. Indeed, many people work hard to increase their power, clearly at the expense of others in the church and in society.

In the same way that Herod abused power 2000 years ago, many do so today, although in many cases such abuse of power is far more subtle. Why is so little said about the abusive power of wealthy British investors who profit from the manufacture of land mines? They have destroyed the lives of thousands of children and their families in the poorest parts of the world. In the face of such facts, they cling to their power no less vigorously than Herod did.

And what of Ansett, HIH, Enron and WorldCom? Such companies represent corporate power exercised at the expense of thousands of jobs, thousands of families, indeed, of entire cities left struggling to survive. This imbalance of power is more and more acute in society: some pastoralists and mining companies continue to push the rights of indigenous peoples aside; some people have dozens of houses while others are homeless; some people have more money than they can spend in dozens of lifetimes while others live from day to day on meagre earnings or pensions.

But we cannot simply rant and rage against secular society. We must confront abuse of power at home, that is, within the church. Most of our experience of power in society and church is that of control. Many Christians seem to have a schizophrenic idea of power. We like to think that power in the church is shared. This is especially true of church denominations that affirm the priesthood of all believers and local church government. But most Christians accept and actually practise a controlling form of power. This has the disastrous effect of marginalising whole groups of people, and it greatly limits the ministry of the church.

In 1998 the Southern Baptists in the USA formally adopted a protocol that identified patriarchal power as biblical and 'official' in Southern Baptist homes and churches. This decision was justified on the basis of texts like Eph 5:22-33, which suggests that a marriage relationship should be organised so that the male partner is dominant and the female partner is submissive. This understanding institutionalises power as control,[5] and it creates a hierarchy within marriage. It allows women to be controlled and even abused.

Such control is not neutral; it leads to abuse of power. We know of abuse against children in church-run homes and of abuse against women in the church. There are Christian women who cannot go into a church because for them a church is a dangerous place.

> Several years ago we interviewed the father of two young daughters, who sat as a board chairperson of the congregation . . . He sought us out for counsel when he learned that a year previous an older member of the congregation had sexually molested the

5. See Purvis, *The Power of the Cross*, 35.

> pastor's young daughter. The pastor, however, had decided 'for the sake of the ministry' not to disclose the incident and had instructed his daughter to tell no one.
>
> After one year, the pastor's daughter told her friend, the board member's daughter, who then told her father. The board member talked to the pastor, but the pastor begged him to tell no one, stating that if the incident became public, it would ruin the church.
>
> The board member was distraught and went to the only psychologist in the area for help in deciding what to do. The psychologist, a long-time therapist in the community, told him that over the past 30 years she had heard of many such incidents in the same congregation. She had spoken to several pastors over the years who, upon learning of the incidents, had chosen to leave the congregation without making the situation public . . .[6]

This case of abuse of power had become part of that church's culture or system. The pattern of sexual abuse against young women had been passed from one generation to the next and was maintained as a secret. The unwillingness to name and to unmask this abuse of power ensured that the abuse continued, as did unwillingness to use power legitimately to confront evil and to protect the innocent.

There is another way to understand and to use our power, the way Jesus used power. The greatest difficulty is that this use of power is rare, even within the Christian community. How can we find ways to imagine power as life and love, to feel its potency in our lives and to use it for compassion and justice?

Beverly Harrison speaks of mutually shared power as loving one another into being: 'It is within the power of human love to build up dignity and self-respect in each other or to tear each other down.'[7] It is remarkable how people I have worked with in the inner-cities of Mel-

---

6. N Shawchuck and R Heusen, *Managing the Congregation* (Nashville: Abingdon Press, 1986), 273-74.
7. Beverly Wildung Harrison, *Making the Connections: Essays in Feminist Social Ethics*, edited by Carol S Robb (Boston: Beacon Press, 1985), 12.

bourne and Sydney have affirmed this sharing of power and become empowered in their own lives. In Woolloomooloo this was evident through the manner in which a diverse range of people identified themselves with the small worshipping community I was privileged to pastor. In a variety of ways, indigenous people, white people and other cultural groups, people who were unemployed, homeless or struggling with drugs and prostitution, and Christians from the suburbs wanting to be involved in ministry all found dignity and self-respect in the presence of that worshipping community. It was not only my job to empower others; it was the task of everyone in the 'church' to empower each other.

Many people would not understand that loving each other into being is really an expression of power. But it is this power, I would want to argue, that God intends for us to use, the power of living life toward right relationships, toward mutuality, toward justice. It may take a long time for powerless people to be empowered. It may take a long time for powerless people to take the risk, in Sally Purvis's words, of '. . . feeling the power of God, offered patiently, tenderly, over and over, that the hurt will be healed [so they] can grow again. The power of life is stronger, finally, than the power that harms or kills'.[8] I have seen this in a young offender getting his first job, in an elderly Torres Strait Islander staying off the drink for nine months, in a woman freed from the sex industry being baptised, and in a local Christian family fostering two abused girls who now laugh and have stopped wetting their beds. I could tell other stories of life, love, hope and liberation. And I know there are many other stories, many other lived experiences in which power is exercised to produce life, compassion, justice and hope, even in the smallest of worshipping communities and even in the most remote and unexpected places.

We cannot rely on governments, big business, the media, the legal system or even, it seems, the institutional church to show us how to approach power. These systems are unwilling to tell the truth about power and how they abuse power to serve their own interests. We should approach power in the way of Jesus Christ: grappling with current issues; grappling with the biblical text; grappling with Christ in prayer; and grappling with each other's stories.

---

8. Purvis, *The Power of the Cross*, 43-44.

We are to use power legitimately for justice, for peacemaking, for compassion. We are called to empower others. Some of us will need more encouragement to use our power than others. We need to look to and listen to indigenous leaders, our young people and women in our churches who have played second fiddle for 2000 years. We are called to listen to Christians in the poorest lands and to find ways truly to empower these sisters and brothers without dominating and maintaining control. We are called to find the will of God in empowering all those who are denied justice, who are poor and abused.

Because the Christian story is being read differently in our postmodern world, we have new opportunities as followers of Jesus to understand and to use power. The Spirit of God is moving with power within these different readings and interpretations. It will not be easy for us to grasp what the Spirit is saying to our churches. It will take some deep thinking and feeling and a willingness to try things out. It will take listening to each other; it will take feeling with each other; it will take acting together. Men need to learn to trust their feelings and women to trust their thinking. And we all need to learn to trust our young people. As a whole people and as whole people, we can work toward making our faith communities places in which the power of Christ heals and liberates all who have suffered abuse of power, including our indigenous brothers and sisters, mother earth and each other.

Christian Communities in Earliest Christianity: The Church before Churches

Bill Loader

It was at least two centuries before Christians began to erect buildings called churches and meet in them. Before that people met in houses, house churches. Today, when in many parts of the world Christians are beginning to rediscover the value of small Christian communities, it is salutary to look again at the corporate forms of Christianity at its earliest stages.

It is a common cultural assumption, certainly in much of western Christendom, that the main community activity of Christians is a large gathering on a Sunday in a hall or specially constructed building. In the beginning this was not so, and it is worth asking whether something vital has been lost in the historical process of moving to large gatherings in large buildings. It is also worth pursuing the issue at a time when many congregations in remote areas are again becoming small Christian communities. Instead of using the occasion to explore new (and old) possibilities of experiencing Christian community, they often remain paralysed by the guilt of being reduced congregations. Shrinkage in rural areas and expansion in the cities mean that churches will increasingly face the crises of being viable with less and of providing spiritual nourishment without traditional models of corporate Christian life, in other words, finding hay without the traditional barn.

Of course, the earliest models are not always the best. It is naive to suggest that we should emulate biblical models simply because they are biblical. They may inspire us; but they may equally be irrelevant, for they belong to a different world. Yet it is worth knowing what they were like. They were, after all, so close to the beginnings and to the one who is at the heart of the gospel.

Small Christian community began with Jesus. Jesus actually called some to leave their families, possessions and jobs to follow him, to join an itinerant group with a shared simple lifestyle and to live off local support. Why? It had to do with Jesus' vision of God's reign, the kingdom of God. In this vision Jesus looked to the realisation under

God of an inclusive community of transformed individuals living together in justice and peace, symbolised by shared feasting in the presence of God. He looked forward to the day when Abraham, Isaac and Jacob would be joined by many from east and west, north and south, reclining at table in the kingdom of God (Mt 8:11). During his final supper with the disciples Jesus declared that this would be his last such meal with them until he drank the cup with them in the kingdom (Mk 14:25). His parables, like the Wedding Feast or Great Feast, represent the call to the kingdom as a call to the great future community feast of the kingdom (Mt 22:1-14; Lk 14:15-24). Jesus' vision of the community of the kingdom had its roots in the prophets, who spoke of a gathering of the peoples at Mount Zion in peace to hear God's Law and to share food and wine together (Isa 2:2-4; 25:6-10).

This was a hope; but it was also an agenda for living now and thus became an emerging reality. No one can seriously pray, 'Your kingdom come', and mean it in this way without letting that vision govern present lifestyle. It was certainly the case with Jesus. The kingdom hope became his present agenda. This shows in Jesus' inclusiveness, his healing, his forgiveness and acceptance. It shows also in his celebratory lifestyle (in contrast to John the Baptist) and in his teaching, preaching and image-making. Already during his lifetime Jesus' meals came to represent a fulfilment of that future vision in the present. Radical inclusiveness in community, particularly at meals with people like Zacchaeus, made Jesus notorious and sparked Jesus' creative response in parables like the story of the Prodigal Son, where the feasting imagery is central. Such meals came to symbolise the breaking through of God's kingdom into the present and, like the Last Supper, also became a way of celebrating that future vision. More broadly, community in the here and now became a sign of God's kingdom.

The Jesus community of the kingdom was also a provocative statement about traditional cultural values, including some religious values. People abandoned wealth and possessions. The family system no longer ruled; people left house and home. Outcasts (on racist, sexist and 'healthist' grounds) found a place. Religious structures, enshrined in the biblical law, became democratised. Servant leadership models replaced competitive and hierarchical ones. Nature, life and story, accessible to all, became the fount of theology; official stories and cult remained, but were seen in a different perspective. Here was a fringe movement laying claim to the heart of Israel's tradition while calling into question the values of land, family and cult embodied in it. It was an alternative community, choosing as its alternative the agenda of the vision of the kingdom.

The Jesus movement belongs broadly within a tendency, present in movements of the Hellenistic world of the time, towards relativism. Traditional cultic and religious structures were breaking down. Alternative communities were developing. The so-called philosophical movements of the time focused on new ways of looking at life and of reappropriating (or abandoning) traditional religion. They sought to humanise the power structures, to put greater emphasis on human intimacy and to value egalitarianism. The meal, the symposium, was often the place where such new adventures found an audience and a following. Some of the earthiest of these teachers, such as the Cynic and Cynic-Stoic wandering preachers, were notorious for demonstrably living an alternative lifestyle that called the systems of wealth, family and status hypocrisy into question. These alternative communities were a mark of the age and took various forms also within Judaism, particularly among the Essenes and the Pharisees. In all, meals played a significant communal role.

Jesus' own movement was a radical manifestation of such communal life, but it was also wider than that. Not everyone who espoused the cause of Jesus left possessions and family to follow him. Many more remained where they were, in cities, towns and small rural villages. It was not that there were two standards, one radical and one rather lax. Nothing in the traditions about Jesus suggests that attitudes towards wealth or family should vary between the two. Whether taking to the road with Jesus or staying put, commitment to the kingdom of God meant that God reigned, and this called all other values into question. Wherever you were, saying 'Yes' to Jesus meant a radical break with prevailing values.

The two kinds of believers in Jesus not only shared the same values and the same vision. They were also interdependent. The itinerant group depended for their support on local believers, who retained power and possessions. When Jesus sent out his disciples, a model for later commissionings, he assumed that there would be people in cities and towns who would offer board and lodging to the emissary preachers (Mk 6:7-13). It was so much a pattern for the early missionaries to operate in this way that Paul found himself in trouble when as an apostle (an emissary) he opted for the alternative model of working to support himself (1 Corinthians 9). Thus both communities—those with Jesus, who later became itinerant missionaries in pairs, and those who stayed put—lived by the radical vision of the kingdom, which was a vision of community. Both groups were Jesus communities.

After Easter the infant church manifested the same forms of life: shared meals, an emerging eucharist, a common purse and property, worship and study together, teaching and preaching the kingdom; but in addition it told the story of Jesus' execution and vindication and baptised members into the community of the Spirit. This is clearly evident in the early chapters of Acts. Belonging within traditional religion, yet sitting loose to it, remained an early feature. But soon conflict emerged, first with the religious authorities once again (Acts 4–5), then within the communities themselves (Acts 6). Language, culture, distance, leadership and inadequate caring strategies compounded the difficulties of being community. Disputes (a) over the basis of entry for people not at first envisaged as members (Gentiles) and (b) over the extent to which Jews should remain bound to their laws governing contact with Gentiles threatened to tear the cohesion of communities apart (see Acts 15 and Galatians 2). What was biblical? What was Law? What does the Bible say? What was opportunistic compromise? Ultimately, wherein lay group identity?

Yet the communities continued to bubble into existence, now in new, pagan cities. If some survived the stringencies of synagogue life, most found that the house and the household was the community base. Church buildings were not built for some centuries. Christians mostly met in houses. The new house churches of the big population centres faced new opportunities and dangers of leadership. (Who, for example, is responsible and who leads, when it happens in my household?) Gratitude for visiting apostles easily became suspicion when itinerants overstayed. Outwardly, there would have been pressure for households to protect themselves against charges of disorder and subversion. That would have included the pressure to retain good order in the household: slaves should be good slaves, women submissive, and men, good citizens! Such pressures would compete with the radical egalitarianism of the kingdom vision. Frequently the communities seem to have espoused a compromise that surrendered to prevailing household patterns, yet enjoined each to love the other as Christ loved (see, for example, Eph 5:21–6:10).

Social revolution was probably far from the mind of those wealthy enough to own a house large enough to host a church. The best of contemporary morals of modesty and moderation would have informed their expositions. Those with a strongly Jewish background adapted Jewish versions of common social mores; others baptised them directly. Cardinal virtues were born. And yet they acclaimed Jesus as Lord, a confession that always carried the potential to subvert the stations.

Such were the failures and victories, the compromises and conflicts that must have characterised these scattered communities seeking to maintain their identity in the midst of the pressures of urban society. But new problems also arose from within these communities themselves. Enthusiasm produced its own uncontrollable outbursts of piety. What gave every member a sense of ministry gave others a sense of superiority and transcendence, which left the rest behind and sometimes became the basis of new communities where spiritual self-fulfilment became an agenda (networks of ladder-climbing ecstasy) all in the name of Jesus! Corinth was probably not alone in these tendencies. Transforming the earthy, whether here or at the resurrection, became irrelevant. *Diakonia* (service) is a drag if all one wants is 'celebration'. Irksome apostles and teachers struggled to bring such groups down to earth. Paul's correspondence with Corinth reveals the passion and pain of such an endeavour. 2 Corinthians shows it was complicated by the intrusion of a super-breed of outstanding speakers and spiritual whizzes who knew how to extend their support base at (the less spectacular) Paul's expense. Even then, techniques, especially rhetorical techniques, determined much consumer appeal.

In the face of faith that had lost its moorings and was on the way to becoming Christian gnosticism, the frustration of caring about structures and writing memoirs became the required strategy. The real Jesus and his message had to be rescued. The pragmatics of developing leadership patterns, with elders and overseers, later romanticised and gilded into potencies, became a necessity. People wrote persuasive letters (for example, those addressed to Timothy and to Titus) and composed accounts of a Jesus rewarded only after a shameful death (for example, Mark). Such structures and scriptures made survival possible; communities connected with Jesus continued to flourish. In new worlds they still had to grapple with an appropriate sense of identity with the Jewish past and their own reason for existence, in short, how they came to be where they were. Thus Luke wrote both the Gospel of Luke and Acts. Their inclusive love was their evangelism;

their *diakonia*, a way of living together and expressing their life. This seems to have been especially characteristic of the community that read the Gospel of John and in a different, more Jewish and didactic way, also of Matthew's churches. They were cells of hope, not worth counting demographically, but they made the future possible.

We have inherited the legacy of their faithfulness mediated across centuries more of Christianity. Theirs is a foreign world. They would probably think we are odd the way we gather so formally in our edifices. I suspect they would miss the immediacy and intimacy that the house can give. They would be familiar, however, with the long sermon. That was more dangerous in a crowded house: as Luke tells us in Acts 20:7-9, a certain Eutychus fell asleep on a window ledge and soon found himself on the street three floors below!

Yet the kingdom vision and the presence of the one who made it his agenda need to continue as the basis of all Christian communities. From the first they took various forms. Their life was a gospel statement. One form of this life was a particularly visible statement. At the same time their early history exposes a wide range of challenges. Most of the 'viruses' have remained active in the Church's life, and we have developed many new strains. It seems to me that we need to take our bearings afresh from the radical nature of the kingdom community of Jesus. For them it meant remaining connected to and earthed in the gospel of Jesus through the historical community. We remain connected to, and earthed in, the gospel of Jesus through scripture and church. Perhaps for us it is harder, for we look back on our heritage with both pride and shame. Jettisoning our cumbersome inheritance for some kind of free-lance community individualism is a path of deceptive freedom, exposing us afresh to viruses without antibodies and denying the inclusiveness and belonging that is at the heart of the gospel. Christian cells need contact with each other and above all they need the body of Christ, the whole Christian community. But perhaps the larger connection in the large building will cease being weekly as groups are encouraged to emerge and regain central place.

Freedom and flexibility in developing new forms of corporate discipleship appropriate for living out that connection in new contexts characterised the earliest stages of Christian community, and they remain essential. They made possible the survival of the Jewish fringe group centred on Jesus, which rose to new life in the smelly, congested houses of Hellenistic cities. It is the risen Lord who opens new possibilities.

Perhaps the day will come when unaffordability will provoke alternatives to the present 'large gathering/large building' form of Christian corporate life. Already in some emptying churches there is a rattling new sense of friendship and fellowship as small groups find themselves, not least in rural areas. Mission, evangelism and identity seem to mean something different in the house setting. Yet ultimately it is not the location that matters. Houses then were so different from ours. To try to recycle the first centuries is naive. We are, however, called more to community than to congregation, more to intimacy than to formality, more to modelling justice and equality than to patterns of authority and monopoly. We are still called to be the community of the kingdom.

To say such things is to call for a revolution in understanding ministry. The early Christian communities would probably have been mostly of a size to survive (sometimes without detection) in a house. Even in the richest houses, numbers were probably not large. They developed patterns of local leadership. The house churches would have been dependent upon each other for resources. Local leaders would have been linked to regional overseers to ensure coherence and connection. In earliest days, travelling apostles and teachers would have served the wider connection. In present-day parishes with smaller groups the role of the minister is closest to that of the overseer. The role of that overseer is also to teach and resource the local group leadership so that in each place the gospel is well preached and the sacraments celebrated. There is what one might call a 'devolution' taking place, a shift of categories. Traditional descriptions of bishops now best fit priests and ministers, and traditional descriptions of ministers and priests may best fit group leaders in time to come. Such a devolution must also entail a devolution of responsibilities, including sacramental responsibility. Practice, with regard to the latter, is already exerting pressure on inherited traditions and customs right across the spectrum of denominations, sometimes with ecclesiastical casuistry, sometimes with 'exceptions', sometimes in disobedience.

Later, of course, the overseer role expanded greatly. Its translation into English as 'bishop' evokes a task of greater proportions, but to recall the pragmatics of its origins is salutary. In effect, it is this role that will increasingly fall to the local minister or priest. They are becoming unaffordable as leaders of small churches and must develop more strongly educating, resourcing and supportive roles. In this they will be recovering an overseer role that probably played a significant part in the growth of the church in its most formative period. This means that the major connecting roles of apostles, prophets and teachers probably should have their modern equivalent in a wider leadership role in the churches, sometimes well represented in the regional bishop and certainly also in the roles assigned to moderators, presidents and the like. But equally significant are those who fulfil a more regional or national prophetic ministry and act as resource people and spokespeople, as well as those who bear the responsibility of the teaching ministry that maintains and develops the connection with the great historical tradition.

In all this the church, by what it is, is making a statement about the kingdom and its reality. The kingdom vision is in many senses far away and yet also always potentially at hand, especially where it is allowed to set the agenda for community. In our changing world the church faces new opportunities to grapple with what it means to be that community. That means taking the shape of present-day society seriously. It also means staying in touch with what it meant to be Christian community before church buildings and congregations became the norm.

The Boundaries of Freedom

Rick Strelan

In Galatians, the apostle Paul states categorically, 'For freedom Christ set us free . . . for you were called to freedom' (Gal 5:1, 13). Yet immediately he also defines, and so confines, this freedom by placing a boundary around it—the 'law of love' (5:13-14). This article explores the NT understanding of Christian freedom and indicates some implications for a Christian community both within itself and within the larger community of the world. It also explores that single, definitive boundary of Christian freedom, the 'law of love'.

It could be argued that freedom is a clear and constant theme in both Hebrew and Christian scriptures and that it is the action of God most celebrated in many of the festivals that mark both Jewish and Christian covenants. The celebrations of Passover and the Eucharist, for example, centre on God's liberating action to release from bondage, slavery and oppression. In turn, both these rituals have their foundation in the myth of God's creativity. When God creates, God liberates. The creation song of Genesis 1 depicts a God who frees earth from chaos and from the destructive beast. God sets the cosmos free. Yet God also establishes limits for the freed cosmos by setting boundaries between the earth and the heavens, the earth and the seas, day and night. So already in God's act of creation, freedom is defined and confined by boundaries. In this freed cosmos, the home for the human image of God is depicted as a garden, a paradise in which the two human creatures are 'at-one' in freedom, where God walks and talks freely with them, where the serpent and the ground are free from any curse.

It is well known, but worth repeating, that the Bible links God's creative activity and God's saving actions. Just as God created freedom for the cosmos from the diabolical chaos, so also the same creative God freed the Israelites from the diabolical anti-God powers of Pharaoh by making them pass through the chaotic waters of destruction and death. There is no freedom without passing through the waters that threaten to destroy and enslave. Israel remembered and celebrated that freeing creativity of its God and waited in hope for God to act in that way again. While being set free, Israel was called into a covenant with its liberating God, a covenant that placed boundaries around its freedom. To transgress those boundaries meant curses, loss and death.

The early Christian writers (nearly all, if not all, Jews) picked up this foundational theme and used it to sing their new song. In Jesus God had acted again to liberate God's people. Just as God created and liberated the earth from the chaotic monsters of the deep, and just as God freed Israel from the slavery of Egypt, so now God was acting creatively to liberate Israel again. This freedom, they understood, was not something offered only to Israel but to the whole creation, something that Jewish hope had expected 'on that day'. But Christian writers went beyond much traditional Jewish expectation by affirming that this freedom was offered not on the basis of faithfulness to Torah, with its ritual and purity demands, but on the basis of the faithfulness of Jesus the Christ, in whom God was offering freedom from the demands of tradition and the obligations of the Torah-covenant. This freedom, modelled by Jesus the Christ, was understood to be graciously given to the Christian community through the dynamic of the Spirit of Christ. It was seen as a freedom that creates new relationships between humanity and God, between humans themselves, and between humans and the rest of creation. These relationships are marked by, and move towards, harmony, 'at-onement', wholeness and peace.

The gospels portray a God who works through Jesus to liberate people from all that is oppressive and dehumanising and from all that threatens life, even from that which takes life. God in Jesus, the one 'who will save his people from their sins' (Mt 1:21), sets the blind, deaf and lame free from the demons of sickness; he even raises the dead and breaks the power of that prison. As God's verification that this announcement is good news for all, God also delivers Jesus from that final tyrant by raising him from the dead as the first fruit of the whole creation. Jesus himself passes through into the freedom of God only by passing through the agonies, desolation and loneliness of death. Just as the 'son of God', Israel, passed through the waters into freedom (to worship in the desert, interestingly enough), so this son of God passes through the deep waters and is raised to life and freedom by God. The death and resurrection of Jesus is God's sign to the world that freedom is a gift to all humanity. It is the sign that God's grace has been set loose in the world as God's dynamic power to save. Freedom comes through this graceful action for God's people and for God's creation. It is a freedom that has been won by the creating Word who entered into the imprisoned creation, passed through the diabolic chaos of death and was raised to freedom.

The gospels provide numerous examples of the freedom that Jesus brought, each of which has obvious implications for Christians and the church. One example is the curiously ignored story in Lk 13:10-17. A woman appears in the synagogue where Jesus is teaching. She is bent over, literally unable to stand up to her full height. It is the Sabbath, the day of hope and liberation for all creation. Not surprisingly, Jesus heals the woman. The male synagogue official is indignant because Jesus was willing to heal on the Sabbath; he does not know the joy of freedom, the celebration of God's rest. He wants the traditional, twisted, male-determined boundaries to remain in place. Those who enforce demands and obligations cannot be free and will not free others. Jesus crosses the boundaries and dismantles them to free this woman. As such, the story is one of liberation for the woman. Her freedom takes on added poignancy if, as has been suggested by an experienced psychiatric nurse, she was a victim of sexual abuse, perhaps incest. For eighteen long years this woman had kept this terrible secret; for eighteen years she had been crippled 'by a spirit', perhaps the spirit of male domination and abuse.

Today the church is challenged constantly to review the boundaries it has established in light of the liberating gospel. Boundaries drawn along gender lines, imposed by the powerful over the weak, are warped and need to be replaced by the single boundary that the Spirit of the church draws, the 'law of love'. Love within the church frees women (and others) to stand up to their full height within the community of the liberating Spirit. The church needs to confess that in many ways and for many people it has been a 'crippling spirit' because it has established boundaries of obligation and of a righteousness dictated by moral behaviour. The good news the church is to offer all cripples is that they can be freed from those demands and liberated to stand up straight in their own eyes, in the eyes of the community and, above all, in the eyes of God.

Another example from the gospels is the well-known parable of the Good Samaritan in Lk 10:25-37. Here again, distorted boundaries are removed and replaced with the single line of love. This time boundaries drawn along ethnic and cultural lines are dismantled. Every society constructs boundaries between clean and unclean, insider and outsider, acceptable and unacceptable. Many communities justify these boundaries by their theology and their reading of sacred scriptures. Jesus tells this shocking and socially disruptive story to dismantle such barriers. Prejudice based on ethnicity and social behaviour is abandoned when a community takes on the mind of Christ. In this story the new boundary of love is epitomised by a single action: the despised Samaritan 'went to him' (10:34a). In doing so the Samaritan broke through the boundary-line of race, religion and culture. The line between priest and laity was also broken. Jesus told the parable to explain what it means to love one's neighbour. Love is more than having compassion (10:33). Love is 'going to the other', transgressing established norms and prejudices that divide one from another and standing alongside the other who lies in one's path.

This incident takes place 'on the road', that is, in the world rather than within the community of believers. Christian freedom calls Christians to love in the world, to push against and even to dismantle boundaries within society. In Australia this clearly includes cultural and religious boundaries between Aboriginal and non-Aboriginal, Asian and European, Muslim and Christian, homosexual and heterosexual. Any line drawn between these and other groups that discriminates, marginalises or oppresses is to be challenged and replaced by the single limit of love. The law of love will not draw a line because lines divide. The law of love transgresses all lines and stands 'at-one' with the other. As a result, the role of Christians and the Christian community is to mediate between groups who have drawn lines separating each other.

Using the language of the gospels, the Christian community is free to transgress boundaries that class people as clean or unclean, insider or outsider, those who belong or those who do not. It is called to model that freedom in which there is neither Jew nor Greek, male nor female, slave nor free because 'you are all one in Christ' (Gal 3:28). The strongest boundaries Jesus himself challenged were those set along family or blood lines and those drawn on the basis of wealth and power. Disciples of Jesus are to lead the way in crossing boundary lines that divide people so that only love stands as any kind of law or boundary. To change the analogy, disciples of Jesus are called to make the transition across the waters, across the demon-filled, chaotic sea. They are to go over to the other side where it is unclean. They are to leave the security of 'their side' and cross over to the other. In doing so they may experience fear as they stare death and the monsters of the deep in the face. But in their transition to freedom they hear the words, 'Don't be afraid', and witness the appearance of 'I am' (Mk 6:50). The implication of this call of Jesus is obvious: Christian freedom comes with the limit and the challenge to love—to cross over to, and stand with, the other.

The one whom Protestants hold to be the champion of freedom is the apostle Paul. Paul's understanding of freedom is fundamentally the same as that of Jesus in the gospels, but it is expressed differently. For Paul, the Christian is freed from the tyranny of sin, which has the power of self-alienation as well as the destructive potency to drive a wedge between the self and God and between the self and another. The good news is that in Christ the prisons of slavery and alienation have been torn down, and the reconciled, 'at-oned' person is placed within the limits of love, which frees that new person to live as a child of God. The Christian, for Paul, is also freed now from the limits of death, which is the wage of sin, and is placed now within eternal life, the life-to-come, which knows no boundary except that of love. Finally, for Paul the Christian is freed from the demands, requirements and conditions of the law, which kill, confine, limit, demand and enslave. Paul insisted that righteousness is not gained by observing Torah; nor are the demands of Torah to be placed on those who wish to enter into the covenant with God. Righteousness comes as a free and freeing gift of God through the faithfulness of Jesus Christ. It is a righteousness and a freedom that knows only one boundary, that of love, which is the fulfilment of the law. All boundaries established on the basis of gender, class, status and wealth enslave, cripple and dehumanise because they distort the boundary of love by turning it into a barb-wire fence electrified by power and authority. Christ establishes a new liberating authority based not on power but on free, liberating grace, which provides the dynamic for free and liberating love and service to another, thereby abolishing all dehumanising boundaries.

I have said that Christian freedom is not infinite. Being in Christ is not to be released from prison into the vacuum of free choice. Christian freedom has a boundary. Paul can speak of the 'law of faith' (Rom 3:27), the 'law of Christ' (Gal 6:2) and the 'law of the Spirit' (Rom 8:2). These limits to Christian freedom exist between us and God, between ourselves and between us and creation. Freedom does not allow the transgression of those boundaries, the abuse of those limits. Even in Eden a tree marks the boundary between humanity and God. To transgress that boundary is to enter the domain of sin and death. To distort that boundary and shift the markers is characteristic of dehumanising and destructive power, which leads to the murder of another. Boundaries to freedom protect against abuse and the distortion of relationships. People need protection against the violence of another who transgresses the boundaries or who distorts the boundaries in order to control, manipulate or dominate. The new tree that stands between oneself and another is the boundary of love demonstrated on the cross. Love is the limit to Christian freedom, the boundary that defines and confines freedom. Augustine understood this limit well. 'Love and do what you will', he wrote.

The Christian is freed to love another. This implies that Christians are free to be vulnerable, free to take on the pain and death of another, free to restore the creature from brokenness and fragility to the image of God. Christian freedom is the freedom to suffer. This understanding of freedom derives from the centrality of the gospel, namely, that God was in Christ reconciling the world to God (2 Cor 5:18-19). The cross is God's liberation of the world from the powers that dehumanise, marginalise and destroy. Freedom comes through that action of God in Christ. The Christian community is called to model that suffering of Christ; it is free to suffer for and with others. That is its commission. As Dietrich Bonhoeffer reminded us, the call to discipleship is the call to die. Jesus himself said, 'As the Father sent me, so I now send you' (Jn 20:21). The Father sent the Son to die! To cite Bonhoeffer again: 'Freedom is not something that one has for oneself but something one has for others . . . It is not a possession, a presence, an object . . . but a relationship and nothing else . . . Being free means "being free for the other" because the other has bound me to him/her. Only in relationship with the other am I free.' Bonhoeffer may well have learnt this from Martin Luther, who wrote, 'The Christian is free to be the servant of all.' Luther also said, 'Suffering is what makes a true theologian, not reading and praying.' By suffering he did not mean self-denial, although that is not excluded, but taking on the pain and injustices that others experience on their behalf.

Finally, Christian freedom is not yet complete. Christians groan together with the whole of creation waiting in hope for the liberation of all things (Rom 8:19-25). Within the life of the individual Christian and of the Christian community there is a continuous struggle to become free. To paraphrase Luther, the Christian is simultaneously free and a slave. That is not to say that sometimes the Christian lives as a free person and at other times not, but that every step of the Christian's life is marked simultaneously by freedom and imprisonment. Strictly speaking, Christians are not free but freed. Christians have been freed from the powers of sin, death and the law, to use Paul's language, but they are not free because these powers continue to influence life and behaviour. Christian freedom, in this sense, is believed in and hoped for. Life without the dialectical tension between freedom and slavery, between being freed yet not free, will only come when God finally acts to bring all things together with Christ as head. Now is the time before God's final act. There is still a future freedom, a promised and awaited freedom. This means that for now freedom is lived out and enjoyed in a sinful and broken world by sinful and broken humans. That is a liberating thing to know because it means that one is free to fail. Freedom is the daily listening and hearing of the word of grace, the good news that daily liberates. Freedom is lived out in hope.

This hope has good foundations and is not simply a pipe-dream. God's resurrection of Jesus from an unjust death is God's guarantee that injustice, brutality, murder, oppression and all the destructive powers of evil imprisoning God's creatures will not have the last word. God will set creation free as surely as God raised Jesus from the dead. This Easter good news is the motivating factor in the thinking and action of the Christian community. This community has hope and that hope stirs it into action. Because of Easter, Christians are called to announce to the world that God will destroy all prisons (in both the narrow and broad sense of that word) and set the cosmos free. Christians announce this not only as a future action of God but as a present activity of God through themselves. To use NT language, the kingdom of God is here, and it is seen wherever and whenever injustice, oppression and abuse of power are challenged and where and when justice, life, freedom and love are experienced. Easter freedom draws the Christian community into the political arena in which it proclaims the free and living Lord. The resurrection of the body of Jesus has direct implications for the involvement of the body of Christ in the struggle for freedom from sexual abuse and violence and from all forms of sexual immorality. It also compels Christians to be concerned for health and for the daily struggle against starvation by millions in the world. Such action is driven by hope.

In conclusion, Paul understood Christian freedom well and expressed it this way: 'All things are yours, and you are Christ's, and

Christ is God's' (1 Cor 3:21-23). God's graceful, dynamic presence in the life of the Christian and the church provides the stimulus for the exhilarating freedom to explore the boundaries of love, moving towards and hoping for the time when Christ will fill all things. The call and the challenge is to live in and for the world as witnesses to this gospel of freedom.

Part II

Theological Perspectives and Resources

Open Heaven/Closed Hearts: Theological Reflections on Ecumenical Relations

Graeme Garrett

My title alludes to the story of Stephen's stoning in Acts 7. During the course of his martyrdom, the dying Stephen looked up to heaven and, in his mind's eye, saw the glory of God. 'Look', he said, 'I see the heavens opened and the Son of Man standing at the right hand of God!' (Acts 7:56). This ecstatic vision served only to enrage his opponents further. With increasing ferocity they rained stones upon his head. His dying words were, 'Lord, do not hold this sin against them.' Presuming that his prayer, like the similar prayer of Jesus from the cross (Lk 23:34), was heard in heaven, we have here a picture of heaven's generosity, acceptance and forgiveness, while on earth we religious people throw rocks at each other in suspicion and anger. Open heaven/closed hearts!

Stanley Hauerwas, a Methodist who has been influenced by the Mennonite theologian John Howard Yoder and who taught theology for many years at the Roman Catholic University of Notre Dame, tells the story of how he once pinned to his office door a Mennonite peace poster that read:

A Modest Proposal for Peace:

Let the Christians of the world agree
that they will not kill each other.

He relates how numerous students responded angrily: How dare you say Christians should refrain from killing other Christians? This is just another example of Christian self-centredness, as if you're the only ones who count! To which Hauerwas's standard response was, 'I agree that it would be a good thing for Christians to stop killing anyone. But you have to start somewhere. After all, it is a modest proposal for peace!'[1]

Thinking about ecumenical relationships, this Mennonite stand on peace seems a good place to begin:

A Modest Proposal for the Church in the 21st Century:
Let the Christians of the world agree that they will stop refusing to speak to each other.

Or to sharpen it up a bit:

A Modest Proposal for the Church in the 21st Century:
Let the Christians of the world agree that they will stop excluding each other from the Lord's Table.

No doubt there will be some angry responses to such a proposal, as there were to the peace poster: How dare you restrict the issue to Christians only? It is high time Christians began speaking respectfully with traditions other than their own. We live in a pluralist world. Other religious and non-religious perspectives must be given their rightful place. I agree. Such wide ecumenical dialogue is vital in our time. To hammer out a responsible 'theology of religions' is one of the urgent tasks facing the contemporary church. But for the sake of today's agenda, I might say, with Hauerwas, 'We have to start somewhere.' Mine is a modest proposal for current ecclesiology, so I will confine my remarks to inter-Christian fellowship.

By the same token, however, the increasingly pluralist context of our present world necessarily throws into sharp relief the importance of better fellowship and understanding amongst those of us who call ourselves Christians. The divisions that threaten to tear the world asunder (race, class, gender, culture, religion) are bad enough without those who ostensibly share basic faith assumptions being at each other's throats. Given our increasingly marginal status as Christians in Australia, if we are going to achieve anything beyond the cultivation of individual piety in the next century, it will have to be in co-operation, not competition, with each other.

But it is not merely the pragmatic argument that counts. I want to make the case that *koinonia*, fellowship, mutual respect and acceptance

1. See *St Mark's Review*, Number 150 (Winter 1992): 29.

of our fellow travellers in the faith is an integral part of what it means to be the church of Jesus Christ. We cannot claim to be a part of the one, holy, catholic and apostolic church without taking seriously the call to be one body, the body of Christ in the world. We know enough of Paul's ironic discussion of parts of the body mistaking themselves for the whole (eyes dismissing ears as irrelevant and the like) to be alert to this matter (see 1 Corinthians 12). The arrogant assumption that we alone represent the true body of Christ, and the careless attitude that regards the issue of catholic *koinonia* with indifference, are both theologically and ecclesiologically dubious.

Reconciliation is one of the central moral issues facing our society. The recent behaviour of some political leaders has made us squirm: an inability to tell the truth; an unwillingness to admit fault; an incapacity to say, 'We're sorry'; an absolute determination to avoid reparations at any cost. It has not been a pretty sight. Reconciliation is a central motif of the gospel. We believe the nature of God to be defined in God's act of reconciling our hostile world to Godself in the life, death and resurrection of Jesus. We, of all peoples, ought to know the importance of telling the truth, of accepting responsibility, of repenting old ways, of opening new paths to fellowship and friendship. We see the destructiveness that follows the failure of this process in black/white relations in Australia. Can we not see the importance of living this theology in our own Christian communities? How can we speak of reconciliation as central to our knowledge of God and God's will for the world, but not enact it in our church communities? The unity of the church is, or ought to be, a parable of the God-willed unity of humankind. The community of reconciliation is, or ought to be, a parable of the God-willed reconciliation of all humans, including God's enemies.[2] If we wish to have any credibility in the world, we cannot preach one thing and act another.

1. A personal perspective

I want now to make a few observations from personal experience. There is a risk in this, of course. One's own journey is idiosyncratic, full of the foibles of personal biography, and so not easily generalised to the problems and opportunities of ecclesial policy in ecumenical

2. See Martin Walton, *Marginal Communities: The Ethical Enterprise of the Followers of Jesus* (Kampen: Kok Pharos Publishing House, 1994), 61.

affairs. We all know that ecumenical relations can and do operate widely and creatively at the grassroots level. We can deal with individual believers and even local groups from other traditions for limited conversation, specific action and even occasional worship. But the lumbering dinosaurs of broad ecclesiastical structures are another matter.

On the other hand, personal experience is a crucial dimension of all theological understanding and faithful living. It is comparatively easy to be indifferent or hostile to the idea of ecumenical action if it is all kept in the realm of theological theory and institutional debate. How do you and your group interpret the presence of Christ in the bread and the wine of the Lord's Supper? What is the meaning of apostolic succession in the formation of the ministry as you understand it? Does your mission praxis lean toward justice or evangelism? And so on. We can easily find ourselves forever at loggerheads on such matters and give up. It is harder if we personally come up against the genuine reality of faith, hope and love in the lives of real people whose theologies of the Eucharist, the ministry or whatever, are different from our own. Likewise, it is easy to feel relatively unmoved by the scandal of our fragmentation as Christians if we never personally feel the raw pain of being regarded as an outsider and deliberately excluded from the place of grace and mercy, just because we don't have the right ecclesiastical union card. This personal stuff counts.

I have had a chequered denominational history. I grew up in the Plymouth Brethren Assembly, became a Baptist and worked as an ordained minister in the Baptist Church for twenty-seven years, and now am an Anglican priest. Some unkind souls think I am on my way to Rome! This is not a course of discipleship I recommend. I didn't plan it; it happened that way. But of the many things I have learned from the experience, I will mention two: one is a look at the Anglican tradition from a Baptist background; the second a look at the Baptist tradition from an Anglican standpoint.

1.1 The Sacramental imagination

First, I want to speak about what Nathan Scott once called the 'sacramental imagination'. By this he meant, I think, the kind of spirituality that is sensitive to the mediation of the grace of God with, through and under finite elements of the natural world, especially, but by no means only, the experience of divine mediation through the ritual use of bread, wine and water in the major sacramental rites of the church.

All of us know from history and experience the hesitation, suspicion and even outright hostility of the radical wing of the Reformation toward the practice of sacramentalism in the worship life of the liturgical churches, especially the mystique that surrounds the celebration of the Lord's Supper. Two criticisms stand out. The first is a tendency toward what we might call 'sacramental objectification', that is, the propensity to identify the sacramental media (bread and wine) with the reality of Christ's presence, even the physicality of Christ's body and blood. Moreover, this sacramental objectivism is often accompanied by what seems to the outside observer to be a kind of *ex opere operato* theology in which divine grace is automatically mediated to participants through the official performance of the rite. The quality of life, faith and discipleship of both officiant and participant are of secondary significance, if significant at all. My description is a caricature, of course. From a Protestant perspective, the sacramental imagination can look suspiciously like mistaking the creature for the creator, which is the essence of idolatry.

The second criticism has to do with ecclesiastical control of grace. Sacramental mediation lies in the hands of the official hierarchy of the church. Its operation is ontologically unavailable to rank and file believers. The Eucharist can only be celebrated by the appropriately authorised persons. This can appear to introduce another mediator, church officials, between God and ourselves, which seems to fly in the face of the one sufficient mediation of the death and resurrection of Jesus Christ.

We know all this theological stuff, and it is not without its real point. But there is another side. By regular participation in a disciplined sacramental community, I have found what a powerful and deeply moving quality of Christian spirituality is cultivated by the nurturing of the sacramental imagination. I have been forced to acknowledge that my former tradition did not teach me the discipline and hence the meaning of this sacramental approach to God, or better, this sacramental approach of God to us. A whole understanding and appreciation of the doctrines of creation and redemption is implicit in the sacramental sensitivity. You cannot simply talk about it, even with the most subtle of theology. You have to learn it, practise it, live it and pray it in community with others. In recent years I have watched, felt, learned and tried to imitate what sacramental imagination means to those whose lives are shaped by it. In the process I have gained a profound respect for it. I regret I was not introduced to it earlier. It is not something you step into, like a river. It is something you learn, like a language. Looking back at my experience in Baptist communities, I feel that the sacramental imagination was unnecessarily cramped. In some places it almost disappeared altogether, with the exception, perhaps, of a reverence for Scripture and preaching, in other words, a sense of the sacramental mediation of grace in the word.

I think this is spiritual impoverishment, especially in the current circumstances of global ecological crisis. Unless we can recover a greater respect for nature, for the presence of God in and through God's creation, our rapacious and selfish destruction of the natural order of the world is likely to proceed apace. I agree with Paul Tillich about the decline of the sacramental dimension of Protestant worship: 'A complete disappearance of the sacramental element (not the same thing, be it noted, as the particular sacraments) would lead to the disappearance of the cultus and, finally, the dissolution of the visible church itself.'[3] I am not suggesting that the whole Baptist tradition is in danger of losing the sacramental element in the extreme way that Tillich spoke about. But I do think we have a lot to learn from other traditions of faith in this regard. Not to avail ourselves of it by genuine ecumenical sharing is to cut ourselves off from dimensions of God's dealings with the world that are, in my view, of great value at every level.

1.2 The dissenting tradition

Since becoming involved with the Anglican community, I have been able to see the value of the Baptist tradition in a new light. It is rather like the experience of leaving the country of your birth for the first time. Travelling in a foreign land enables you to see the life, values, attitudes and limitations of your own society much more sharply. You have a real point of comparison, a perspective not available to those who never venture out. Ecumenical engagement is the ecclesiastical equivalent of delightful, perhaps occasionally terrifying, travel in other lands.

I could say many things about church polity, the theology of the word, the priesthood of all believers, the community of committed discipleship and so on. But the issue I want to highlight is the strength

---

3. Paul Tillich, *The Protestant Era*, trans. James Luther Adams (Chicago: Phoenix Books, 1957), 94.

within the Baptist community of 'the dissenting tradition'. The Baptist community was born in the crucible of dissent, the living expression of what Tillich called the 'Protestant principle'. Alternatively, we might call it the prophetic stance of the church, or the practical application of a theological hermeneutics of suspicion. It is a spirituality acutely aware of the dynamics of what in doctrinal terms is referred to as 'original sin', the seemingly inevitable tendency to place ourselves and our own interests in the position that should only ever be occupied by God, that is, at the centre of reality. 'Idolatry' is the sharp word for it.

In the Anglican church where I often worship, there are many plaques on the walls commemorating the life and work of former members of the community. It is interesting how many names are those of establishment figures: Sir somebody this; Lady somebody that; Lt General the other; Mr Justice whoever. They are, or were, movers and shakers in the military, bureaucratic, political and business arenas. Anglicanism is, or, at any rate, has been, the church of the establishment. That is important. The church needs to be able to speak and act at the macro-level of society, in and through the corridors of official power. The hope and the critique of the gospel ought to be brought to bear in places where crucial decisions are made about the way our society shapes and orders its life.

But the dissenting voice, the voice that speaks not from the side of power but from the side of powerlessness, the voice that Bonhoeffer said comes from below, not above, the voice of the poor, the outcast, the marginalised, the oppressed (which is often silenced, muted, neglected, and increasingly so in our present political climate) is heard more clearly in word and deed in the Baptist community than in the Anglican. A whole tradition of symbols, ecclesial practices and personal discipleship better suited to this aspect of Christian witness in the world is available within the Baptist community than in many other branches of the church. I am not saying it is totally missing in other communities, but I am conscious of how much it is present in the Baptist tradition. The rest of the church needs to learn about this dissenting tradition, to be in conversation with it and to be challenged by it. I think we are derelict in our Christian duty and untrue to our Baptist view of discipleship if we don't bring this gift to the ecumenical table and share it.

2. The *status confessionis*

At this point I want to float a theological proposition. I am not sure that I am fully convinced of it, but something in me responds to it. I want to use a term that Bonhoeffer introduced, or reintroduced, into contemporary theological discussion. If the historians are to be believed, its usage can be traced back at least to Reformation times. But in more recent days it has fallen into disuse. Bonhoeffer reclaimed it. The term, rather dauntingly set out in Latin, is *status confessionis*, which, literally translated, means 'confessional standing' or 'confessional situation'. Bonhoeffer applied the term to the circumstances facing the church in Germany in the 1930s, particularly when the infamous Aryan paragraph was enacted into law in April 1933. That law was directed in the first instance against Jewish people in the civil service. But its net quickly spread wider and even challenged the right of non-Aryans (especially Jews) to hold office in the church. Bonhoeffer, Barth, Niemöller and others who were responsible for drafting the Barmen Declaration in May 1934 argued that the Nazi regime had placed the church in a situation in which its very being as church—its ground, substance and proclamation—were at stake. The church could not capitulate to the government's demands in this instance without ceasing to be the church. In November 1933, Martin Niemöller wrote:

> Under these circumstances a church law that excludes non-Aryans or not full Aryans, to the extent that they belong to the Jewish people, from church offices is contrary to the confession, because it fundamentally negates the communion of saints as confessed in the third article; for precisely with regard to the converted Jews it must be seen *if the church of Jesus Christ is serious about the communion which reaches beyond natural bonds*.[4]

In response to the issues then confronting the church in Germany, the Barmen Declaration was a courageous *actus confessionis* (act of confession). On one hand, it resisted the interference of the state in the ordering of the church's life and ministry; on the other, it challenged those factions of the church that went along with the Aryan paragraph.

4. Quoted in Walton, *Marginal Communities*, 11 (emphasis added).

It did so on the basis of the church's confession of faith in Jesus Christ as the sole source of authority in the church.

The *status confessionis* flags a crisis in the church, but not just any crisis. It flags a crisis in which the church might cease to be the church in the true sense if it is not careful. It is a crisis to which the church must respond, not because there is some pragmatic advantage to be gained but because its foundation in the act of God in Christ requires it to act. Since the Barmen crisis there have been a number of occasions in various parts of the worldwide church that a *status confessionis* has been invoked: the situation of racial apartheid in South Africa; the development and deployment of nuclear and biological weapons in Europe; and the issue of the church's relation to the poor and disadvantaged in Latin America. In each case the appeal to a *status confessionis* has been controversial. For example, in the racial debate, those who argue that the church faces an issue of faith, not merely justice, appeal to creation (all people are made in the image of God), redemption (all people are recipients of the grace of God in Christ), ecclesiology (all believers are an equal part of the new community in Jesus Christ) and eschatology (all people are invited to the final feast of life in the presence of the eternal God). On all confessional counts, apartheid is an unacceptable offence against the faith of Christ; the church cannot be the church and countenance it. Opponents, of course, develop arguments that aim to undercut this kind of confessional appeal. For example, it is not that some people are not created in the image of God, they maintain, but that racial segregation is the will of God for different manifestations of that image in history. Similar debates rage over issues of nuclear and biological warfare and questions of poverty and wealth. Perhaps we are facing new crises of this magnitude in relation to ecological questions.

But my question is this: Is ecumenical fellowship with Christians of other traditions a *status confessionis* issue or not? Is the foundation of the church itself at stake in the challenge of ecumenical *koinonia*? I have a feeling that it is. There is a sense in which a divided church is a contradiction in terms. It is a theological nonsense and a discipleship scandal.

Those who oppose ecumenical involvement are also able to appeal to the *status confessionis* argument. Indeed, they can be adamant about it. The reason why we cannot be involved in such *koinonia*, they say, is that other groups who claim the title of 'Christian' and of 'church' have abandoned the true faith. For this reason, those who have maintained the true basis of faith (namely, us) cannot, precisely as a *status confessionis* issue, have Christian fellowship with them. We are not breaking the unity of the true church; we are defending it against those who have betrayed it.

This is the point of engagement. The appeal to a *status confessionis* always signals a crisis in the church. There is always disagreement as to what constitutes the true situation of faith in given circumstances. The Barmen Declaration of the Confessing Church challenged the German church's reading of the situation in the 1930s, and was challenged in return. Are we in a similar, if somewhat less extreme, situation? Is the question of how we relate to (that is, how we speak to, work with, befriend and participate in the life of those who call themselves fellow believers in Christ) a matter of the *esse* (the being) and not merely the *bene esse* (well being) of the church? Can we make a case like that of Barth, Bonhoeffer and Niemöller that excluding others from our Christian conversation and eucharistic fellowship fundamentally threatens our adherence to the third article of the creed? Does it violate the confession concerning the communion of saints? Does it, in the final analysis, deny the doctrine of justification by grace through faith alone? Does it fly in the face of the freedom of the Spirit to blow where it wills? Can we seriously claim that the table of Christ is our own ecclesiastical table? Looking at the life of Jesus, his table fellowship with outcasts and sinners, his free feeding of the 5,000 persons of all ages, and especially remembering that at the table of the last supper both Peter and Judas were included by him in the feast, can we continue to exclude those who wish to be with us there simply because they differ from us in theology or denominational allegiance?

The theologian Robert Osborn argues for the church as a genuinely open community:

> The Church, the local Church as a member of the ecumenical (ie catholic) Church, includes Israel as its presupposition and the world as its promise. The love in which the Christian community has its reality is grounded in its faith in the God of Israel and in His Messiah Jesus, and is sustained and given its life by its hopeful participation in the universal community whose redemption is promised with the coming of Christ. In community with Israel, the

> Church has its faith; in community with the world, it expresses its hope; sustained by this faith and hope it finds itself as a community of love.[5]

If this is a reasonable statement of the nature of the church, it means that to be true to its own story, to be the church locally, regionally and globally, the church needs to be in deliberate friendship and conversation with Israel as God's elect on the one hand, in deliberate debate and political engagement with the world as the object of God's saving compassion on the other and in loving dialogue and fellowship with the ecumenical Christian community in the middle. Failure or dereliction in any of these three involvements is a distortion of the fundamental life of the church in faith and hope and love. If this is so, then the ecumenical issue is a *status confessionis* issue. We must deal with it because not to do so is to put at risk the integrity of the church in terms of its own theological identity.

3. Three theological considerations

Whether we regard ecumenical *koinonia* as a *status confessionis* issue or not, I want to conclude by raising three theological considerations that are worth pondering as we deliberate on the ecumenical policy of our denomination: the mystery of God, the meaning of courtesy and the importance of conversation.

3.1 The mystery of God[6]

We can never be reminded too often that, as Søren Kierkegaard put it, God is in heaven and we are on earth, or, in another of his famous phrases, there is an infinite qualitative distinction between God and our apprehension of God. These expressions have been etched into twentieth century theology through the work of Karl Barth. But they reflect the age-old Jewish and Christian assumption that despite the reality of revelation and, in Christian thought, even of incarnation (indeed, *because* of these things) God remains the Lord, God remains God, God remains a mystery to our comprehension. That is why

5. Quoted in Walton, *Marginal Communities*, 75.

6. On what follows, see Nicholas Lash, *Easter in Ordinary: Reflections on Human Experience and the Knowledge of God* (London: University of Notre Dame Press, 1990), 231ff.

idolatry stalks human religiosity so closely. We find it hard to admit and to live with the mystery that surrounds us. We try endlessly to domesticate it, to clip the wings of infinity to accommodate the finite cages of our thoughts.

The Roman Catholic theologian Karl Rahner places what he calls 'holy mystery' at the heart of all his theological investigations. Here is a typical statement by Rahner:

> Man is he who is always confronted with the holy mystery, even when he is dealing with what is within hand's reach, comprehensible and amenable to a conceptual framework. So the holy mystery is not something upon which man may 'also' stumble, if he is lucky . . . Man always lives by the holy mystery, even if he is not conscious of it.[7]

Rahner is well aware that the doctrines of grace, revelation and incarnation qualify this powerful emphasis on divine transcendence. The gospel declares that the holy mystery has drawn near to us, so near that the mystery is found, as the Holy Spirit, in the midst of our communities of faith and in the depths of our own human spirits. And in Jesus Christ the holy mystery has entered fully our space and time and bodily existence with all that implies for an understanding of our material world, our living, our suffering and our dying. But even in this gracious presence, God's reality as God is never delivered into our keeping. To be touched by this history of revelation in Christ is to know that faith in God is a journey into the immensity, inexhaustibility and infinity of a holy mystery that surpasses all understanding. To be drawn into the operation of the Holy Spirit is to be precipitated into a love that breaks open anew every apprehension of that love we may presently have reached.

---

7. Karl Rahner, *Theological Investigations*, Vol 4, 53-54; quoted in Lash, *Easter in Ordinary*, 237. (I refer to Rahner to remind ourselves that whatever our particular institutional attitude to ecumenical co-operation may be, it is now simply a matter of fact that we all draw on the theological work of others in the wider church. This is true in biblical studies, pastoral theology, spirituality, liturgy and systematic theology. Any theological library that is solely confessionally based is impoverished. Whatever the institutions say officially, theology is a thoroughly ecumenical enterprise throughout the world. And the church everywhere has been the richer for it.)

The consequences of such a theology of holy mystery is that all our knowledge, especially our knowledge of God, must be qualified by reticence and humility. We are privileged to know something of God, but that very knowledge brings with it the further knowledge that we know that we don't know. This does not mean that we will not think and argue as strongly as we possibly can for the theological truth that grasps us. But it does mean we must never confuse our apprehension of God with the reality it reaches for. I am reminded of the words of Barth, no slouch when it came to putting his theological point of view strongly:

> The angels laugh at old Karl. They laugh at him because he tries to grasp the truth about God in a book of Dogmatics. They laugh at the fact that volume follows volume and each is thicker than the previous one. As they laugh, they say to one another, 'Look! Here he comes now with his little pushcart full of volumes of the *Dogmatics*!'—and they laugh about the men who write so much about Karl Barth instead of writing about the things he is trying to write about. Truly, the angels laugh.[8]

If the angels laugh, perhaps God is in stitches! Ecumenical *koinonia* often founders on a theology that does not know it should laugh at itself.

If one consequence of a theology of holy mystery is that we know the limits of our knowledge in face of the limitlessness of God, another is that we feel the limits of our love in face of the boundless grace of God's love toward the world. 'In this is love, not that we loved God but that he loved us and sent his Son to be the atoning sacrifice for our sin' (1 Jn 4:10). That text applies not only to us and our kind. It applies also to the 'other'. Peter as well as John was at the Last Supper. Matthew as well as Judas was at the table of the Lord. This means that

8. Ernst Wolf (ed), *Antwort* (Zollikon-Zürich: Evangelischer Verlag, 1956), 895, trans. Robert McAfee Brown in his Introduction to *Portrait of Karl Barth* by Georges Casalis (Garden City: Doubleday, 1963), 3, and cited in John Godsey's Introduction to *Karl Barth 1886–1968: How I Changed My Mind* (Edinburgh: Saint Andrew Press, 1969), 14. I owe this quotation to a paper presented by a student of mine, Mr Peter Wild.

our relationships with others, especially with others who wish to be at the Lord's table, must be qualified by genuine reverence before the holy mystery of God, which is present in them and for them, as for us.

This theology of the holy mystery, which seems to require of us reticence in knowledge and reverence in love, means that as Christians we are never in possession of final answers or ultimate explanations. To quote Karl Rahner one last time: 'The Christian has less "ultimate" answers which he could throw off with a "now the matter's clear" than anyone else.'[9] For this reason alone, we cannot afford to exclude from the *koinonia* of the church those who wish to see themselves as part of it. To live with theological reticence towards ourselves and theological reverence towards the other is to be open to the truth that transcends us all and open to the love that embraces us all. It is to see our participation in the faith of Christ as a gift of grace to be celebrated, not a possession of mind to be paraded. It is to understand ourselves not as a politico-theological party in competition with enemies, but as a pilgrim community on a common journey with companions who, like ourselves, know and love the mystery of God and walk beside us in reticence and reverence. This is the ecumenical task. Or, to put it the other way, to be unecumenical is to know too much about God's intentions and to live too little from God's love.

3.2 Courtesy

What I mean by theological reticence and reverence can be summed up by the quaint term 'courtesy'. Perhaps it would be better to use a more contemporary or better known term: fellowship, communion or love. These are the categories in which we need to think if Christian ecumenical action, to say nothing of inter-religious dialogue, is to be taken seriously. But I want to explore the word 'courtesy', if only because it is less familiar and for that reason may help us to examine the question with fresh eyes.

Put bluntly, to cut ourselves off from conversation, prayer and action with our fellow travellers in the community of Christ is to behave discourteously when courtesy is called for. It is to behave inhospitably when hospitality is called for. The word 'courtesy' derives from a Middle English term (I think!) *cortesia,* which was originally associated with the romantic ideal of courtly love, the sort of ideal we

---

9. Karl Rahner, *Christian at the Crossroads*, quoted in Lash, *Easter in Ordinary*, 240.

probably all imbibed in rough form in our memories of the stories of the knights and ladies of King Arthur's Round Table. The word gathered into itself all the connotations of the appropriate way in which people of grace and dignity were to order, arrange and pursue their meetings with each other, whether those meetings were with a beloved or an adversary, with one familiar or with a stranger. Courtesy is the style of interaction with the 'other'. It is characterised by thoughtfulness, respect, graceful speech and attentive listening. In circumstances of love, it is reverence; in situations of enmity, it is respect. Courtesy is a 'letting be' of the other and a willingness to be there with and for the other. The Jewish critic George Steiner describes it thus:

> We lay a clean cloth on the table when we hear the guest at the threshold . . . We light the lamp at the window. The implicit impulses in such acts are precisely those in which the yearning towards and fear of the other, the motions of feeling and of thought which would, at the same time, guard and open outward their particular, individual dwelling, come together. Such impulses are known in immediacy. They cannot be formalised or 'proved' (no significant act of spirit can be). But they are of the essence, which is to say, essential.[10]

Steiner is well aware of the Passover and Eucharist echoes of table fellowship that sound through this description of the courteous attitude and action. Courtesy has to do with hospitality, with welcome, with taking in others and sharing the nourishment of our lives with them. Notice that it is not a *sentimental* emotion. Steiner captures the ambivalence involved in courtesy. The reaching out to the other, 'yearning', he calls it, is inextricably bound up with 'fear' of the other. Courtesy needs to guard its dwelling place but simultaneously open that dwelling place to the other. Ecumenical courtesy means that we guard our traditions, our faith, doctrine, worship and prayer. These are a sacred dwelling place for us, the home of our spirit. There is a risk in inviting others to our table. They may challenge the rules of the feast. They may introduce strange food to our menu. They may bring with

---

10. George Steiner, *Real Presences* (London: Faber and Faber, 1989), 149.

them still others whom we fear more. We do not abandon our dwelling place to the other. But neither do we board it up like a fortress against the other. Ecumenical courtesy is the table deliberately laid. We cannot do that if we are not prepared to yearn and fear in our connections with others.

In the writings of Julian of Norwich, courtesy plays an essential theological role. Courtesy for Julian is the name for God's attitude and action towards us. In Christ God sets the table and lights the lamp for us. God yearns for communion with us, the 'other'. God opens God's dwelling place for us and seeks to live with us. It is a risk, as we know. There is a cross at the heart of the divine gesture of courtesy. God is treated by us with discourtesy in the extreme. But that does not deter God in action or attitude. In the words of Julian:

> And this is a supreme friendship of our courteous Lord, that he protects us so tenderly whilst we are in our sins . . . And then our courteous Lord shows himself to the soul, happily and with the gladdest countenance, welcoming it as a friend, as if it had been in pain and in prison, saying: My dear darling, I am glad that you have come to me in all your woe. I have always been with you, and now you see me loving, and we are made one in bliss.[11]

Divine courtesy is the expression of God's welcoming and liberating love. God courts us; God receives us; God dwells with us. In our dealings with others, others to whom the courtesy of God has likewise been extended, can we treat them discourteously? Can we refuse to lay the cloth, light the lamp in the window and, while guarding, yet also open our dwelling to others? If we do turn away, are we not turning away from the very action of God we claim to live by?

3.3 Conversation

My third point concerns conversation or, to use the more technical term, conciliarity. Courtesy cannot be enacted at a distance. It finds concrete expression, or it is nothing. Courtesy means meeting the other. At minimum, that means conversation and hospitality. It means

---

11. Quoted in Kerrie Hide, *Gifted Origins to Graced Fulfillment: The Soteriology of Julian of Norwich* (Collegeville, MN: The Liturgical Press, 2001), 50-51. The original comes from Julian's 13th Revelation, chapter 40.

listening and speaking, with all that implies for the risk of confronting otherness and the possibility of having to change. It means sharing the table with others, with all that implies for a clash of strange spiritualities. But there is no other way. There is no way to be courteous but by doing the courteous thing. To put it in the words of Martin Walton:

> There is no way to an ecumenical movement; the ecumenical movement is, as movement, the way. The way to unity is the practice of unity (as interrelatedness of variety). The way to conciliar relations is the praxis of conciliarity (as the committed and conflictual interaction of diversities and divisions). The way to eucharistic community is not that of exclusive conditions, but eucharistic hospitality. The way to inclusive community is inclusion.[12]

The ecumenical movement is the church actively seeking the unity that is both its gift and its call in Christ. It is a search that takes place in a divided world and a divided church. The unity in question is more than mere coexistence, a willingness to let the other be. As Walton suggests, it is a deliberate exchange of views, a commitment to interaction that, given our diversity and division, will no doubt sometimes entail conflict. But this is the dynamic of *koinonia*, a common pursuit of the truth of Christ in reticence and a common search for the fellowship of the Spirit in reverence. There is a risk, of course, but it is a risk taken in the context of the holy mystery of God. It trusts that the reconciliation of the world undertaken by God in Jesus Christ is a real possibility that, even if it will only be fully realised eschatologically, can be more fully realised here and now. Ecumenical conciliarity believes that apartheid, the assertion that Christian diversity implies irreconcilable difference, is in the final analysis a heresy, a contradiction of the confession of faith.

Open heaven needs to invade our closed hearts. It is a modest proposal for the church in the twenty-first century:

That the Christians of the world
stop refusing to speak to each other.

---

12. Walton, *Marginal Communities*, 91-92.

And that the Christians of the world
stop excluding each other from the Lord's Table.

Both things are needed. Baptists are more likely to agree to an open table, but refuse to take part in conciliar conversation. Other groups are likely to be happy with conversation, but jealously guard the guest list of the table. But until both exclusions, and the fears that underlie them, are overcome, the ecumenical movement will remain a deep theological challenge to the church of God in our time.

Jesus Christ and Spirituality

Thorwald Lorenzen

The term 'spirituality', like the word 'religion', can be the bearer of good news or bad news. It can build up, and it can tear down. It can liberate, and it can oppress. The quest for spirituality is booming. Talk of spirituality is no longer a strange phenomenon in our so-called secular world; it occurs in the doctor's surgery, the boardroom and the public bar. In the search for meaning and comfort, gazing at stars, feeling the warmth of the earth, hugging trees, yoga meditation and tarot card readings have for many become alternatives to church, sermons, liturgies, sacraments and creeds. Within Christian churches there is also an intensive search for a spirituality that is holistic, celebrative and life-enhancing.

We should welcome this search to uncover spiritual dimensions to life. It unmasks the fact that the idols of consumerism, materialism and militarism have clay feet and are unable to satisfy the longing of the human soul for truth, freedom and meaning.

Nevertheless, in these days no spirituality or religion can claim the luxury of being inherently true and life-enhancing. Too much has happened; too many terrible things have been caused by spiritual people and have been validated by religious sentiments. Christian fundamentalists deny equality to women, permit torture, support the death penalty and are willing to fight wars against 'infidels'. Islamic radicals attack, persecute and kill Christians, Jews and Hindus in the name of Allah. Hindus and Muslims maim and kill each other and destroy each other's sacred places.

Even if it is true that spirituality and religion have not directly caused these and legions of other conflicts and atrocities (which have ethnic, political and economic origins), it remains a fact that spirituality and religion have been functionalised by allowing themselves to be used to fuel conflicts and to validate atrocities. From an historical perspective, spirituality and religion are ambiguous, to say the least! They have brought healing *and* destruction, liberation *and* slavery, selflessness *and* selfishness. Therefore, every claim to a life-enhancing spirituality, whether Christian or not, needs to be *measured,* and it needs to name the *norms* used for such evaluation.

1. Ground and norm

Christian faith is clear on this point. This does not imply that Christian spirituality actually echoes such clarity, but it does mean that at least in theory Christians name both the *ground* and the *norm* by which their spirituality must be measured. The ground deals with the question of *ontology,* and the norm deals with the question of *content*. The ground identifies where Christian spirituality is anchored and from which wells Christians drink, while the norm indicates those values and virtues that shape Christian spirituality.

Both the ground and norm of Christian faith are anchored in the confession that God raised Jesus from the dead. For our purpose, this entails a twofold message. On one hand, this confession addresses the ontological question by affirming that in raising Jesus from the dead, God broke the estranging power of death. Death separates; death isolates; death destroys relationships; death is active in the midst of life. On the basis of the resurrection of Jesus, Christians affirm that at the centre of reality there is not death but life, not hatred but love, not war but peace, not injustice but justice.

On the other hand, it is important to realise that it was the *crucified* Christ who was raised from the dead. Jesus did not die a natural death. He did not die of a heart attack. He was not even the victim of judicial error. Jesus was opposed, betrayed, captured, tortured and killed for discernible reasons. Against the religious, political and economic interests of his contemporaries, Jesus fleshed out his understanding of God as love. That implied a passion to value human life above institutions like Torah, Sabbath and temple, and it entailed a partiality that manifested itself in his passion to heal the sick, to liberate the oppressed and to provide space for those who had been pushed to the margins. Consequently, when God raised Jesus from the dead, God did not only destroy the power of death but also confirmed and validated Jesus' interpretation of God's being and nature.

2. Jesus Christ—the *one* word we are to hear, trust and obey[1]

Christian faith and the Christian church began when God raised the crucified Jesus from the dead. Through the appearances of the risen Christ, it was revealed that by raising Jesus from the dead God shared God's life with the dead Jesus and thereby provided the ground for the confession that *nothing*, not even death, can separate us from the love of God (Rom 8:31-39). By raising Jesus from the dead, God bound God's very being to the world and its future. Thereby not only God but also the world has been *changed.* With Jesus, part of humanity, part of us, has reached its ultimate destiny. God affirmed Jesus' humanity, his vision, his struggle, his temptation, his doubt, his obedience. God has graced our world and its future with the unconditional promise that God will be with us to the end of the age.

For the early Christians, the fact that God raised Jesus from the dead resulted in glorious certainty, filling their lives with creativity, vision and meaning. They knew that nothing could separate them from the love of God, and this knowledge resulted in the confessions that have since been at the core of the church's faith: 'The Word', that great mediator between God and God's creation, '*became flesh* and dwelt among us, full of grace and truth'. And how does the confession continue? '*We* have beheld his glory, glory as of the only Son from the Father' (Jn 1:14). The Pauline tradition makes the same point: 'In him [in Christ] *the whole fullness of deity dwells bodily* . . .' And how does the text continue?

> . . . and *you* have come to fullness of life in him, who is the head of all rule and authority. In him also *you* were circumcised with a circumcision made without hands, by putting off the body of flesh in the circumcision of Christ; and *you* were buried with him in baptism, in which *you* were also raised with him through faith in the working of God, who raised him

1. This formulation is an allusion to the 'Barmen Theological Declaration' of 1934, with which the Confessing Church in Germany delimited itself from the ideology of German National Socialism. The 'Barmen Declaration' is reproduced in many books and liturgical resources, for example, Robert McAfee Brown (ed), *Kairos: Three Prophetic Challenges to the Church* (Grand Rapids, MI: Eerdmans, 1990), 156-58.

> from the dead. And *you*, who were dead in trespasses and the uncircumcision of your flesh, God made alive together with him, having forgiven us all our trespasses, having cancelled the bond which stood against us with its legal demands; this God set aside, nailing it to the cross. God disarmed the principalities and powers and made a public example of them, triumphing over them in him. (Col 2:9-15)

This reality of God in Christ sharing divine life with God's creation without being dissolved into creation was classically formulated at the Council of Chalcedon in 451 CE:

> . . . we . . . confess the one and only Son, our Lord Jesus Christ. (He) . . . is perfect both in deity and also in humanness, truly God and truly human . . . He is of the same 'reality' (*homoousios*) as God as far as his deity is concerned and of the same 'reality' as we ourselves as far as our humanness is concerned; thus like us in all respects, sin only excepted . . . We apprehend this one and only Christ—Son, Lord, only-begotten—in two 'natures'; without confusing the two 'natures', without transmuting one 'nature' into the other, without dividing them into two separate 'categories', without contrasting them according to area or 'function'. The distinctiveness of each 'nature' is not nullified by the union. Instead, the 'properties' of each 'nature' are conserved and both 'natures' concur in one 'person' (*prosopon*) and in one *hypostasis*. They are not divided or cut into two *prosopa*, but are together the one and only and only-begotten *Logos* of God, the Lord Jesus Christ.

Here the community of faith confesses to whom it belongs and what the ground and content of its faith is.

Two points have emerged. First, by raising Jesus from the dead, God laid the foundation for our faith, hope and love: 'No other foundation can anyone lay than that which is laid, which is Jesus Christ' (1 Cor 3:11)! Second, God's act in raising Jesus from the dead extends to shape *us, our world, our future*. The apostle summarises: 'If the Spirit of him who raised Jesus from the dead dwells in you, he who raised Christ Jesus from the dead will give life to your mortal bodies also through his Spirit which dwells in you' (Rom 8:11). Or, in different words, the apostle speaks of 'always carrying in the body the death of Jesus, so that the life of Jesus may also be manifested in our bodies' (2 Cor 4:10).

What does this actually mean, that Christ, his cross and resurrection, is present in the existence of the apostle? Here is Paul's answer in 2 Cor 4:8-12:

> We are afflicted in every way, *but not crushed;*
> perplexed, *but not driven to despair;*
> persecuted, *but not forsaken;*
> struck down, *but not destroyed* . . .
> For while we live we are always being given up to death for Jesus' sake, *so that the life of Jesus may be manifested in our mortal flesh.*
> So death is at work in us, *but life in you.*

Before we can speak about values and virtues, morality and ethics, church, Bible and experience, we must be clear about the ground of our being—Jesus Christ, his life, death and resurrection.

3. Witness

We have seen (in John 1 and Colossians 2) that by raising Jesus from the dead, God includes us, those who believe and are baptised, in the sphere where Jesus Christ is heard, trusted and obeyed. Christians are called not only to be bearers and proclaimers of the word but also to be *witnesses* for Jesus Christ. Witnesses testify to the givenness of an event; by doing so they become part of the event itself. They keep the event alive. Without witnesses, events have no ongoing history; they are forgotten. As a result of the appearances of Jesus to his disciples and their obedience of faith, these witnesses were drawn into the resurrection event. Jesus Christ is the 'first fruit' of the divine process leading to God being 'all in all'. Witnesses are important links in the historical process. They receive and pass on in word and deed the good news that God raised Jesus from the dead and is thereby in the process of reclaiming what has become estranged or separated from God.

This 'receiving' and 'passing on' is more than the communication of theoretical information. The nature of the event requires not only the juridical dimension *that* God raised Jesus from the dead, but also the existential dimension that with God's raising of Jesus from the dead our being and the being of the world have been *changed*. This new being can only be understood, demonstrated and communicated in a holistic way. Christian spirituality, therefore, has a kerygmatic thrust; it reveals to whom the believer belongs.

4. Agents of change

Since Jesus Christ came into the world to bring life, Christians are therefore agents of change, and Christian spirituality must empower Christians to change things in the direction of truth, freedom and justice. Christian spirituality derives from the awareness that Jesus Christ in the power of the Spirit is impinging upon us, drawing us into the truth, freedom and justice that God has established by raising Jesus from the dead. Not our religious needs, not popularity and success, not the status quo (however comfortable and convenient it may be), but the 'dangerous memory of Jesus'[2] shapes Christian spirituality.

So, we are not speaking of arbitrary change, but change that has focus and direction. It is made possible by God's activity in Jesus Christ. In Jesus Christ, God has fleshed out the promise for our world and the purpose for our lives. In Christian spirituality (there are other spiritualities!), it must therefore be clear that Jesus Christ is the ground and content of our faith; that Jesus Christ is the one word we are to hear, trust and obey; that for us there is no other foundation on which to build our lives and future. In that sense, the early interpretation of the Nicean-Constantinopolitan Creed of 381 CE (the *filioque* addition) is theologically and scripturally correct: 'the Spirit proceeds from the Father *and the Son*'.[3] This does not deny that the Spirit has her own

2. This helpful concept is adopted from Johann Baptist Metz, *Faith in History and Society: Toward a Practical Fundamental Theology* (New York: Seabury Press, 1980), chaps 5 (pp 88-99), 6 (pp 109-15), 11 (pp 184-99) and the 'Excursus: Dogma as a dangerous memory' (pp 200-204).

3. This does not exclude the possibility of restoring the original wording of the creed, without the *filioque* clause. What is important is not the wording, but the interpretation of the text.

centre of identity.[4] But it does mean that as with the Father and Son, the identity of the Spirit must be seen in relation to, not apart from, both Father and Son. The early church wanted to confess what is most clearly expressed in the Johannine farewell discourses (John 14–16) that the Spirit who dwells in Christian believers (14:17) does not speak on his ('paraclete' is masculine) own authority (16:13), but glorifies and bears witness to Jesus (16:14; 15:26) and will bring to their remembrance all that Jesus had said to them (14:26).

What does it mean *today* to make room for Jesus Christ and for the Spirit in our lives and in our churches? What kind of spirituality is worthy of Jesus Christ? That spirituality is important can hardly be doubted. Do not we all yearn for oases in the deserts of our lives? Do not we all need moments of truth and inspiration in the everydayness of our world? No wonder that spirituality workshops and encounter groups spring up everywhere, promising to bring some life, warmth, touch and acceptance into the otherwise cold humdrum of life.

Within the Christian view of reality, the Holy Spirit ensures that we do not relegate Jesus Christ to the past, that we do not freeze Jesus Christ into a doctrine, that we do not lock Jesus Christ into church structures, hierarchies and bureaucracies, that we do not imprison Jesus Christ within the Bible, and that we do not dissolve Jesus Christ into our experience. Spirituality gives structure to the foundation and content of our faith, Jesus Christ.

Perhaps we need to take stock with reference to our spirituality. Perhaps we need to ask whether contemporary spirituality needs to discover new wells from which to drink. Perhaps we need to depart from our traditional spirituality. Is there any way to understand the grammar of traditional spirituality so that we may evaluate it in light of the ground and content of our faith in Jesus Christ?

---

4. The word for 'Spirit' in the OT, *ruach*, is feminine; 'Spirit' in the NT, *pneuma*, is neuter. In Latin and modern languages, 'Spirit' is generally masculine. Given the limitations of language to conceptualise the divine, it is entirely appropriate to refer to the Spirit as 'her'.

5. Traditional spirituality

Traditional spirituality tended to *compartmentalise life* into sacred and profane, holy and secular. We felt that we must withdraw from the profane and secular life to enter a holy and sacred realm in which we could receive energising fuel, then return to the struggle of life. God was not out there in the marketplace of life, we thought; God had to be sought elsewhere, away from life. We felt that the inward journey led towards God, while the outward journey led away from God. We felt that on Sundays we needed to replenish our spirituality to keep us going from Monday to Friday.

Traditional spirituality showed *docetic and gnostic tendencies*. I use the terms 'docetic' and 'gnostic' because they immediately raise flags of caution and danger. From the beginning the church had to struggle with docetism and gnosticism; both were rejected as heresies. Docetism denies that in Jesus Christ God's being has really been shared with the world. Docetists claim that God only *appeared* to have shared his life with Jesus. To this gnostics add that human beings possess an inner light or *knowledge* that either cannot be touched by the evil world or needs protection from the evil influence of the world. In either case, the 'world' has a negative connotation; it is 'fallen', so God is not to be found in the world. Consequently, we have to withdraw from the world to feed our spirituality. This view is not Christian because it denies that the world is God's good creation, that God loves the world and that in Jesus Christ the world has been reconciled to God. Christians are called to be the salt of the earth and the light of the world. They are to let their 'light shine before others, so that they may see your good works and give glory to your Father in heaven' (Mt 5:13-16).

Traditional spirituality displayed *individualising and privatising tendencies*. Conversion and sanctification play an important role in the Christian life. But they have become mixed up with both the individualism of our culture and the tendency to regard religious convictions as merely private matters. Bible-reading and prayer are mainly practised for personal edification. Participating in the sacraments is understood as strengthening individual spirituality. The possibility that reading the Bible, prayer, being baptised or participating in the Eucharist can be subversive acts, that they can lead the believer into the peace movement and fuel protest against racism and torture, has hardly ever been entertained as part of our *spirituality*. That 'knowing God' implies doing justice, as the prophetic tradition (Jer 22:13-17), Jesus himself and the early church (Mt 25:31-46) emphasised, has usually been linked with 'social ethics' rather than with 'spirituality'.

Traditional spirituality also tended to be *self-centred rather than community-centred.* Although many Christians honour the Lutheran pastor and theologian Dietrich Bonhoeffer and the Roman Catholic Archbishop Oscar Romero as twentieth-century saints, we often fail to recognise that their spirituality, like the spirituality of Jesus, led them to violent deaths. Bonhoeffer was murdered in a concentration camp, and Romero was gunned down in front of an altar by a death squad. Both lost their lives because the political powers of their day considered that they were meddling in community affairs.

Have we perhaps fallen prey to the ancient Greek idea, which is a persistent spiritual temptation, of seeing the body as the prison of the soul, of playing off 'heaven' against 'earth', of glorifying 'spirit' and devaluing 'matter'? Indeed, is not our refusal to recognise the ministry of women on equal terms with that of men a result of the historical development in which a male-dominated church too willingly took on board the ancient but non-Christian idea of equating maleness with 'heaven' or 'spirit' and femaleness with 'earth' or 'matter'? Has not this compartmentalisation of life so deeply influenced us that we no longer hear that the Lord claims the *earth* for Godself (Psalm 24)? Have we not failed to affirm the *goodness of creation*? Have we forgotten that God in Christ has reconciled the *world* to Godself (2 Cor 5:17-21)? Is God not a God who 'makes the sun rise on the evil *and* on the good, and sends rain on the just *and* on the unjust' (Mt 5:45)? In our anthropology and eschatology, why have we rejected the doctrine of the immortality of the soul and affirmed the resurrection of the body, if not to show the value of the *body*?

If in our spirituality we want to bring to expression that God in Christ has said 'Yes' to the world and graced the world with a promise, perhaps we need to start again at the beginning. What grammar should underlie and shape a contemporary spirituality? What structure and content should such a spirituality have? Where do we find wells from which to drink? Of what dangers should we be aware? Below are some preliminary considerations, realising of course that within certain parameters spirituality will be different for each one of us.

6. Towards a contemporary spirituality

6.1 We must retrieve a theology that *rejects the compartmentalising of life* into holy and profane, sacred and secular. We must retrieve what the early Christians meant when, in light of the resurrection of the crucified Christ, they confessed that the Word had become flesh (Jn 1:14); when they rejected the immortality of the soul and affirmed the resurrection of the body; when they confessed that God's life had been shared with the dead Jesus; when they insisted that the cross is not a prelude to the resurrection, but the very content and meaning of the resurrection; when they formulated the confession that Jesus Christ is *vere deus* and *vere homo*, truly God and fully human.

In Mk 7:15 the Markan church confesses that in Jesus Christ the gulf between sacred and profane is overcome: '. . . there is nothing outside someone which by entering can defile that person; but the things that come out of a person are what defile'. When Paul heard that in Corinth Christians were celebrating the Lord's Supper without waiting for the nannies, servants, slaves and wharf labourers, he exclaimed that, with all their spirituality, it was not the *Lord's* supper they were celebrating (1 Cor 11:20-22). The Lord, he had to teach them, is the crucified One ('the Lord Jesus, on the night when he was betrayed, took bread . . .'), and he was crucified because he spent his life *with and for* 'latecomers'. How, then, could they celebrate the *Lord's* supper while forgetting about latecomers?[5] For the believer in Christ and for the community of faith, it is not possible to divide life into holy and profane. That must be the theological basis for our spirituality.

6.2 Within the wider context of the church, *theology has the constructive and critical function* of continually reminding the church that apart from a living relationship with Jesus Christ and faithful obedience to his ways, the church is nothing but a noisy gong and clanging cymbal. Theology must refuse to be an instrument of the church's leadership or the church's majority; it must refuse simply to reflect what people believe. Instead, it should be so overwhelmed by the *joy* of the gospel that it fearlessly examines the faith and practice of the church in light

5. For further elaboration of this point, see Thorwald Lorenzen, 'The Crucified Christ as Lord of the Church: Theological Reflections on 1 Corinthians 11–14', in David Neville (ed), *Prophecy and Passion: Essays in Honour of Athol Gill* (Adelaide: ATF Press, 2002), 83-125.

of the gospel and courageously accepts its function of being a thorn in the flesh of the church.

6.3 Christian spirituality knows an *'inward journey' and an 'outward journey'*. Given the frailty and brokenness of human life, how can we remain open to God? We know that even the most pious and righteous people have skeletons in their cupboards; we know of our unbending self-will; and we know that we don't even shy away from using the word 'God' for our own schemes and interests. It is important, therefore, to have sacred times and safe places for reflection and meditation. We need to create space and time to review our lives in light of the story of Jesus. Just as a marriage-enrichment weekend is not withdrawal into another world, but a creative interruption of life to ask who we are and who we want to be, so our Bible study, prayer life and communal worship are not withdrawals from life. They are the reminders, the celebration, the worship that the life of faith is a gift whose meaning increases as we share it with others.

6.4 Towards a holistic anthropology

The three points above have set the stage for self-understanding. We have been given a body with which we kneel in prayer and with which we touch in love. With our bodies we change instinct into culture and we participate in the ecological process. With our bodies we are interwoven into an interlocking network of relationships: to ourselves, to others, to nature, to history and to God.

In these relationships our faith in Christ adds a specific thrust. The Spirit who points us to Jesus Christ as the well from whom to drink points us in two directions. The first direction is towards heaven, seeking God and thanking God for the wonderful gift of life and its promises. In a secular world with its ongoing human experiment to live without God, Christian spirituality offers an alternative. Prayer, reflection, meditation, Bible study, community worship, fellowship and discipline become ways in which the awareness of God in our lives and in our world is kept alive.

The second direction in which the Spirit leads is discerned in the conviction that heaven is found on earth, where much healing needs to take place, where the lost need to be found, where the hungry need to be fed, where the oppressed need to be liberated and where the tortured need to be freed. Faith in Jesus Christ knows a specific orientation *towards the below.* It places the promise in our hearts that the torturer will ultimately not triumph over his innocent victim and that we cannot bypass Lazarus in our worship of God.

6.5 Community

A holistic anthropology implies that we acknowledge and retrieve the *communal nature of the human person.* In our individualistic and competitive culture, we tend to forget that we have been created as communal beings. God created the human being as male *and* female (Gen 1:27). When unbending selfishness centred human interest on the self, our perception of reality became individualised. When the 'other' was no longer seen as a medium of grace, but as a competitor and potential enemy, and when our communal nature was denied and distorted, our identity and relationship to God also suffered. Through faith and baptism, as in the confession of the apostle Paul (Gal 3:24-28), the communal nature of the human person has been re-established, so that 'in Christ' we recognise that we need each other for the journey ahead.

Here the importance of the church as a community of faith comes into its own. It is an important part of the Baptist tradition that we emphasise the soteriological importance of the *church as the social manifestation of faith.* Are we able and willing to shape alternative communities in which people feel warmly accepted and are empowered to take their place in the marketplaces of life?

6.6 Faith as restlessness and anticipation of the victory of the crucified Christ

Faith is anchored in the Christ-event. By raising the crucified Jesus from the dead, God foreshadowed the reality by which this world will be measured. Since the world is not as it ought to be and since the church is not what it ought to be, the believer who is focused on Jesus Christ becomes an *agent of change*: not arbitrary change, nor change for the sake of change, but change arising from a radical commitment to Jesus Christ and a willingness to prepare the way of the Lord. On the road we are sustained by the Spirit who deeply speaks the promise into our lives that ultimately the lamb is stronger than the lion and it is therefore worthwhile to follow Jesus.

6.7 Spirituality and justice

Spirituality has to do with knowing God, and knowing God has to do with implementing *justice* (see Jer 22; Isa 58; Rom 12:1-2). In Jeremiah 22 we read:

> Thus says the LORD: Act with justice and righteousness, and deliver from the hand of the oppressor anyone who has been robbed. And do no wrong or violence to the alien, the orphan, and the widow, or shed innocent blood in this place. For if you will indeed obey this word, then through the gates of this house shall enter kings who sit on the throne of David, riding in chariots and on horses, they, and their servants, and their people . . . Are you a king because you compete in cedar? Did not your father eat and drink and do justice and righteousness? Then it was well with him. He judged the cause of the poor and needy; then it was well. *Is not this to know me?* says the LORD. But your eyes and heart are only on your dishonest gain, for shedding innocent blood, and for practising oppression and violence.

The struggle for justice is not the result or consequence of faith. It is part of our faith and therefore belongs to our spirituality. Let us not forget that Jesus Christ does not only meet us in the Word and in the Sacrament, but also in the stranger, the refugee, the asylum-seeker, the orphan and the prisoner in our midst (Mt 25:31-46).

6.8 The preacher as priest and prophet

For those of us who are ministers, we may need to remind ourselves that, to use a sporting analogy, our function is not only to counsel, inspire and massage the players; it is also our task to interpret the game and to lead the players on to the field to play, with the risk, of course, that they will get bruised, make a mess of things and lose!

On this point Baptist ecclesiology is not very helpful. We are too close and too dependent on those who call us and pay us. How many ministers have left the ministry because they felt quenched and limited by the expectation of people to preach a gospel of cheap and comfortable grace? Perhaps a way out of this dilemma is to re-emphasise the importance of *ordination.* To ordain is not to create a spiritual elite, but to set apart women and men to interpret the word and administer the sacraments as the word *of Christ* and the sacraments *of Christ*. By ordaining a person, the church confesses that Jesus Christ stands *over against* the church in grace and judgment; and the preacher whose conscience is bound to Jesus Christ is expected to speak those words of grace and judgment. The preacher must claim this freedom to be not only a balm for body and soul, but also a thorn in the flesh of the church.

6.9 Worship as awareness of the 'dangerous memory' of Jesus

I sometimes have the uncomfortable feeling that our only interest in planning a worship service is to entertain people and make them feel good; to withdraw from life for a moment of solitude and forget about the pain, injustice and frustration around us. There is a need for such withdrawal, but it cannot be the sole aim of a *Christian* worship service. What is important is not our feelings nor our wishes, but whether we worship God for God's own sake and whether we meet Jesus in grace and judgment.

7. Conclusion

My aim has been twofold. I have said, firstly, that all our thinking and doing, our talk of values and our engagement for justice, need to have a ground, a basis, a foundation, something that was there before and that outlasts the ambiguity and uncertainty of the moment, something stronger than our fears and inability to understand, something that transcends our experience and commitments. For Christians that something is someone, *Jesus Christ*, whom God raised from the dead to give structure and meaning to our living and our dying. I have tried to explain what the apostle Paul meant when he said: 'No other *foundation* can anyone lay than that which is laid, which is *Jesus Christ*' (1 Cor 3:11).

My second point is that we need a spirituality that sustains, energises and empowers us on the journey. How does Jesus Christ, whom God raised from the dead, flow into our lives and open windows, break chains and lead us to wells of refreshing water? In dialogue with traditional spirituality, I have suggested how a contemporary spirituality may historically and experientially manifest the Christ who is the focus of our lives.

King, Merton and Barth: Their Abiding Significance

David Neville

On the evening of 4 April 1968, the Baptist minister and civil rights activist Martin Luther King, Jr, was murdered on a motel balcony in Memphis. On 10 December that same year, the Catholic contemplative Thomas Merton perished in Bangkok during the first extended trip granted to him since joining a Trappist monastery twenty-seven years earlier. And in the early hours of that same day, the Swiss Reformed theologian Karl Barth died in his sleep.

King and Merton are among a handful of American Christians who will be remembered well into the twenty-first century and perhaps beyond. Barth was one of the most creative Christian theologians of the twentieth century. But is there anything more than the coincidence that these three died in the same year to justify commemorating them together? Apart from some superficial connections between them, three common features form part of their enduring legacy. First, each was a Christian whose faith was central to his understanding of himself and of the world in which he lived. Each took his bearings from Jesus Christ, albeit in different ways. Second, because of their Christian faith, all three demonstrated a profound sense of responsibility to and for the world; their faith motivated them to work responsibly within society. Finally, enlightened by Christian faith, King, Merton and Barth each adopted a radical stance on the issue of peace.

In the 1960s, Merton's writings were replete with references to King. Like King, he was influenced by Gandhi, and he supported King's nonviolent campaign for social change. In addition, through a Quaker couple active in both the civil rights and peace movements, Merton was in touch with the Kings. Indeed, through this liaison Coretta Scott King was attempting early in 1968 to organise a date for her husband to spend time on retreat with Merton. The two never met, however, because King was assassinated before the retreat could be arranged.

Merton was an avid reader and during the 1960s became familiar with the major theological voices of his time, so he was familiar with Barth. Whether Barth knew of Merton is difficult to know. However, he was certainly familiar with King. Indeed, while in Princeton during 1962 to deliver the Warfield Lectures, Barth heard King preach and was photographed with him afterwards. He later bemoaned the fact that '. . . my relationship to the courageous Negro pastor Martin Luther King was confined to being photographed together in front of a church door'.[1]

King knew of Barth but was not significantly influenced by him. In 'Pilgrimage to Nonviolence' (1960), he noted that by the time he graduated from Crozer Theological Seminary he was 'a thoroughgoing liberal'. He recalled, 'I was absolutely convinced of the natural goodness of man and the natural power of human reason.'[2] Clearly Barth had had little impact on his thinking at this stage in his life! During his doctoral studies at Boston University, however, King became more familiar with Barth's thought and came to accept neo-orthodoxy's corrective to liberalism. Nevertheless, he continued to regard neo-orthodoxy, and therefore Barth as well, as too pessimistic about human nature and excessively emphatic about God's transcendence.

1. Martin Luther King, Jr (1929–1968)

In 1962, while King was speaking at a Southern Christian Leadership Conference convention in Birmingham, Alabama, a young white man jumped on to the stage and punched him. King refused to strike back, and after his assailant had been restrained he asked that the young man be permitted to rejoin the audience. He later remarked, 'This system that we live under creates people such as this youth. I'm not interested in pressing charges. I'm interested in changing the kind of

---

1. Karl Barth, *Evangelical Theology: An Introduction* (Grand Rapids, MI: Eerdmans, 1979), ix. George Hunsinger, *Disruptive Grace: Studies in the Theology of Karl Barth* (Grand Rapids, MI: Eerdmans, 2000), 1-4, describes this photographic record of Barth's and King's chance encounter as symbolic of his own dream of a merger between the legacies of Barth and King.
2. Martin Luther King, Jr, 'Pilgrimage to Nonviolence', in James Melvin Washington (ed), *A Testament of Hope: The Essential Writings of Martin Luther King, Jr* (San Francisco: Harper & Row, 1986), 35. Where possible I have referred to this collection of King's writings.

system that produces this kind of man.'[3] This incident illustrates King's commitment to nonviolence, his compassion for enemies and his insistence that the movement of which he was the symbolic figurehead aimed to create a harmonious society for *all* Americans. Most importantly, however, it reveals his commitment to bring about a radical transformation of the structure of American society, which he perceived as inculcating racism, poverty and violence.

King is remembered primarily as a civil rights activist. But he was first and foremost a Christian whose faith commitment was both tested and toughened within the context of the black freedom struggle. King was a Baptist minister whose formative years were spent in the black church and whose training was, after initial indecision, geared towards serving the black church.[4] He preached on most Sundays and occasionally was absent from significant developments in his civil rights campaigns because he had returned to preach in his home church. For example, King was absent on 'Bloody Sunday', the day black freedom marchers were brutalised by Alabama state troopers on the Edmund Pettus Bridge in Selma, because he was preaching at Ebenezer Baptist in Atlanta.

Until his involvement in the Montgomery bus boycott, King's faith was what he described as an 'inherited religion'. But in the early stages of the boycott two incidents forced him to recognise his dependence on God. The first occurred on 5 December 1955, the first day of the boycott, after King had been elected president of the newly formed Montgomery Improvement Association (MIA). As president he was naturally burdened with the task of giving the main address at a mass meeting that evening. After returning home and briefing his wife of developments during the day, he was left with twenty minutes to pre-

3. See Stephen B Oates, *Let the Trumpet Sound: The Life of Martin Luther King, Jr* (New York: Harper & Row, 1982), 198.

4. For further reflections on the importance of King's faith for understanding his historical significance, see James Wm McClendon, Jr, *Biography as Theology* (Philadelphia: Trinity Press International, 1990), 47-66 ('The Religion of Martin Luther King, Jr'); Stanley Hauerwas, *Wilderness Wanderings: Probing Twentieth-Century Theology and Philosophy* (Boulder, CO: Westview Press, 1997), 225-37 ('Remembering Martin Luther King Jr Remembering'); John Howard Yoder, *For the Nations: Essays Evangelical and Public* (Grand Rapids, MI: Eerdmans, 1997), 125-47 ('The Power Equation, the Place of Jesus, and the Politics of King').

pare his address. Feeling inadequate and anxious he 'turned to God in prayer'. Later, after concluding his extemporaneous address, King '. . . realized that this speech had evoked more response than any speech or sermon I had ever delivered, and yet it was virtually unprepared. I came to see for the first time what the older preachers meant when they said, "Open your mouth and God will speak for you."'[5]

The second incident occurred nearly two months later. By this time white citizens of Montgomery had launched a vicious intimidation campaign against King. He and his wife were receiving numerous abusive and threatening letters and telephone calls every day. On 26 January 1956 King was arrested and jailed for allegedly travelling thirty miles an hour in a twenty-five-mile-per-hour zone. While being driven to jail King feared he would be killed. The following night he returned home late only to receive another threatening call. Unable to sleep, he went to the kitchen to make himself a cup of coffee and to think of a way to relinquish his MIA leadership without appearing a coward. Leaning over the kitchen table he prayed out loud, asking God for strength. He later recalled:

> At that moment I experienced the presence of the Divine as I had never before experienced him. It seemed as though I could hear the quiet assurance of an inner voice, saying, 'Stand up for righteousness, stand up for truth. God will be at your side forever.' Almost at once my fears began to pass from me. My uncertainty disappeared. I was ready to face anything. The outer situation remained the same, but God had given me inner calm. Three nights later, our home was bombed. Strangely enough, I accepted the word of the bombing calmly. My experience with God had given me a new strength and trust. I knew now that God is able to give us the interior resources to face the storms and problems of life.[6]

---

5. Martin Luther King, Jr, *Stride Toward Freedom*, in Washington (ed), *A Testament of Hope*, 436.
6. Martin Luther King, Jr, 'Our God Is Able', in Washington (ed), *A Testament of Hope*, 509.

Throughout the Montgomery bus boycott, which catapulted King into public prominence, King insisted on conducting the boycott on the basis of Christian love. In *Stride Toward Freedom* he wrote:

> From the beginning a basic philosophy guided the movement. This guiding principle has since been referred to variously as nonviolent resistance, non-cooperation, and passive resistance. But in the first days of the protest none of these expressions was mentioned; the phrase most often heard was 'Christian love'. It was the Sermon on the Mount, rather than a doctrine of passive resistance, that initially inspired the Negroes of Montgomery to dignified social action. It was Jesus of Nazareth that stirred the Negroes to protest with the creative weapon of love.[7]

Even after consciously embracing Gandhi's method of nonviolent direct action, King claimed that 'Christ furnished the spirit and motivation' for his and others' involvement in the struggle for freedom and justice. Indeed, in a March 1956 interview he asserted, 'I have been a keen student of Gandhi for many years. However, this business of passive resistance and nonviolence is the gospel of Jesus. I went to Gandhi through Jesus.'[8]

Throughout his brief life King conducted his civil rights campaigns in accordance with what he understood to be Christian ideals. Equally important was his commitment to a public life that conformed to the life and teaching of Jesus. For example, during the Birmingham demonstrations he required each volunteer to sign a commitment card that contained ten commandments for the nonviolent movement. The first of these was to 'meditate daily on the teachings and life of Jesus'. In addition, King's sermons were full of references to the example and instruction of Jesus as the basis for understanding how things should be, both spiritually and socially. A fine example is 'The Drum Major Instinct', one of his last sermons. Taking as his text the story in Mk

---

7. King, *Stride Toward Freedom*, in Washington (ed), *A Testament of Hope*, 447.
8. David J Garrow, *Bearing the Cross: Martin Luther King, Jr, and the Southern Christian Leadership Conference* (New York: William Morrow, 1986; London: Jonathan Cape, 1988), 75.

10:35-45 of James and John's request for positions of authority in the coming messianic kingdom, he reflected:

> What was the answer that Jesus gave these men? It's very interesting. One would have thought that Jesus would have said, 'You are out of your place. You are selfish. Why would you raise such a question?' But that isn't what Jesus did. He did something altogether different. He said in substance, 'Oh, I see, you want to be first. You want to be great. You want to be important. You want to be significant. Well you ought to be. If you're going to be my disciple, you must be.' But he re-ordered priorities. . . And he transformed the situation by giving a new definition of greatness.[9]

King's social commitment needs no vindication. His life was literally expended in his persistent confrontation with injustice. But an aspect of his social commitment that is inadequately emphasised was his campaign for a more equitable economic system for *all* Americans. King's concern for poverty did not become publicly noticeable until his 'war on slums' in Chicago in the summer of 1966, but ever since his seminary days he had regarded Western-style capitalism as dehumanising. In 'Pilgrimage to Nonviolence' he wrote, 'I had also learned that the inseparable twin of racial injustice is economic injustice.'[10] And in *Stride Toward Freedom* he asserted, 'Any religion that professes to be concerned with the souls of men and is not concerned with the slums that damn them, the economic conditions that strangle them, and the social conditions that cripple them is a dry-as-dust religion.'[11]

In the final years of his life King became more and more outspoken against capitalism. Following the successful campaign in Selma, which led to the Voting Rights Act of 1965, and the Watts riot, he announced a direct-action initiative in Chicago and in doing so indicated his fundamental concern for economic, as well as racial, justice: 'The nonviolent movement must be as much directed against the violence of poverty, which destroys the souls of people, as against the

9. Martin Luther King, Jr, 'The Drum Major Instinct', in Washington (ed), *A Testament of Hope*, 265.

10. King, 'Pilgrimage to Nonviolence', in Washington (ed), *A Testament of Hope*, 37.

11. Martin Luther King, Jr, *Stride Toward Freedom* (New York: Harper & Row, 1958), 36.

violence of segregation.'[12] In October 1966 King issued a statement declaring that 'America's greatest problem and contradiction is that it harbors 35 million poor at a time when its resources are so vast that the existence of poverty is an anachronism.'[13] In his final presidential address to SCLC staff he said, 'We must develop a program that will drive the nation to a guaranteed annual income.' He also urged

> . . . that we honestly face the fact that the movement must address itself to the question of restructuring the whole of American society. There are forty million poor people here. And one day we must ask the question, 'Why are there forty million poor people in America?' And when you begin to ask that question, you are raising questions about the economic system, about a broader distribution of wealth. When you ask that question, you begin to question the capitalistic economy.[14]

During the final months of his life, King and SCLC were planning a massive campaign aimed at confronting the nation's leaders in Washington with the brutal reality of American poverty. Named the Poor People's Campaign, it demonstrated King's commitment to raise the living conditions of all America's poor, whether black, white, native American or Hispanic. It was because he saw a connection between his Poor People's Campaign and the concerns of striking sanitation workers in Memphis that he agreed to address them and subsequently to lead a march on their behalf. On a return visit to Memphis he was shot. During the years that he challenged racial injustice, King's life was continually threatened, but he was eventually killed only after he publicly challenged economic injustice. As James Melvin Washington bluntly observed, 'His dream proved to be too

---

12. Oates, *Let the Trumpet Sound*, 369.
13. Garrow, *Bearing the Cross*, 533.
14. Martin Luther King, Jr, 'Where Do We Go from Here?', in Washington (ed), *A Testament of Hope*, 247, 250.

threatening. It implied a massive redistribution of wealth and resources. He was murdered.'[15]

In the final few years of his life, King was not only preoccupied with the issue of economic justice. Against the advice of many close to him, he spoke out with increasing stridency against American involvement in Vietnam. After winning the Nobel Prize for Peace in 1964 he regarded himself as an ambassador for peace not only on the stage of American race relations but also in the international arena.

King's commitment to peace and nonviolence stretched back to his Montgomery days when the newly formed MIA adopted the motto, 'Justice without Violence'. During the Montgomery bus boycott of 1956, King was at first unaware that he had applied Gandhi's principle of nonviolent direct action to end the indignity of racial segregation. But as he learned more about the principles of nonviolent direct action from pacifist advisers, his own commitment to nonviolence grew until it became more than a social tactic. In 'Pilgrimage to Nonviolence' he wrote,

> The experience in Montgomery did more to clarify my thinking on the question of nonviolence than all of the books that I had read. As the days unfolded I became more and more convinced of the power of nonviolence. Living through the actual experience of the protest, nonviolence became more than a method to which I gave intellectual assent; it became a commitment to a way of life. Many issues I had not cleared up intellectually concerning nonviolence were now solved in the sphere of practical action.[16]

King went on to say that although he was no 'doctrinaire pacifist', he was convinced that twentieth century weapons made the principle of nonviolence a practical necessity in the sphere of international relations. As he was to repeat on numerous occasions, 'The choice today is no longer between violence and nonviolence. It is either nonviolence or non-existence.' He also stated that 'occasionally in life one develops a conviction so precious and meaningful that he will stand on it till the

15. James M Washington, 'Editor's Introduction', in Washington (ed), *A Testament of Hope*, xxi.
16. King, 'Pilgrimage to Nonviolence', in Washington (ed), *A Testament of Hope*, 38.

end. This is what I have found in nonviolence.'[17] King accepted one's right to self-defence if attacked, but he discarded his own gun in the early stages of the Montgomery bus boycott because he considered it incompatible with his leadership of a nonviolent movement.

Though for a time King called his method of provoking social change 'passive resistance', he did not mean it to be understood as passive. As numerous passages in his early writings demonstrate, King regarded 'passive' and 'nonviolent' resistance to be synonymous. Nevertheless, '*passive* resistance' was a misnomer. What he meant to emphasise was that nonviolence is neither physically aggressive nor destructive: 'The method is passive physically but strongly active spiritually. It is not passive nonresistance to evil, it is active nonviolent resistance to evil.'[18] Complementing the commitment not to cause bodily harm to another human being, nonviolence also avoids what King described as 'violence of spirit'. By this he meant that the non-violent person refuses to meet hatred with hatred, but rather breaks the 'chain of hate' with love.

King liked to call love the 'regulating ideal' of nonviolent resistance, but he was always careful to clarify that when he spoke of love he meant a Christian understanding of love. He often noted that he was not referring to romantic, sentimental, emotional or even reciprocal love, but rather to disinterested, redemptive good will. He meant a love that expects nothing in return, with the possible exception of suffering, which King believed had redemptive potential. He also noted that this kind of love arose in response to people's *need*. One cannot help but wince on behalf of white segregationists when reading this line from *Stride Toward Freedom*: 'Since the white man's personality is greatly distorted by segregation, and his soul is greatly scarred, he needs the love of the Negro.'[19] Furthermore, King was genuinely concerned to knit together rather than to tear apart. For King, the objective of nonviolent resistance motivated by Christian love was neither to defeat nor to humiliate but to create bonds of

17. Martin Luther King, Jr, *Where Do We Go from Here: Chaos or Community?*, in Washington (ed), *A Testament of Hope*, 595.

18. Martin Luther King, Jr, 'An Experiment in Love', in Washington (ed), *A Testament of Hope*, 18.

19. King, 'An Experiment in Love', in Washington (ed), *A Testament of Hope*, 19. ('An Experiment in Love' was excerpted from *Stride Toward Freedom*.)

mutual understanding and friendship between people formerly at loggerheads, in short, to bring people together into community. In a paragraph of shimmering profundity he wrote:

> *Agape* is love seeking to preserve and create community. It is insistence on community even when one seeks to break it. *Agape* is a willingness to go to any length to restore community. It doesn't stop at the first mile, but it goes the second mile to restore community. It is a willingness to forgive, not seven times, but seventy times seven to restore community. The cross is the eternal expression of the length to which God will go in order to restore broken community. The resurrection is a symbol of God's triumph over all the forces that seek to block community. The Holy Spirit is the continuing community-creating reality that moves through history. He who works against community is working against the whole of creation. Therefore, if I respond to hate with a reciprocal hate I do nothing but intensify the cleavage in broken community. I can only close the gap in broken community by meeting hate with love. If I meet hate with hate, I become depersonalized, because creation is so designed that my personality can only be fulfilled in the context of community.[20]

Because nonviolence springs from indiscriminate love and is directed towards the 'creation of the beloved community', one who chooses the way of nonviolence cannot be opposed to people but must be opposed to social and institutional structures that both perpetrate and perpetuate racism and injustice. Furthermore, if sacrificial love lies at the heart of nonviolence, faith in God's resolve towards justice is its undergirding foundation. King believed that the person who resisted injustice nonviolently had 'cosmic companionship'.

---

20. King, 'An Experiment in Love', in Washington (ed), *A Testament of Hope*, 20.

2. Thomas Merton (1915–1968)

'Merely to have someone like Merton take our side would have been enough, but we could not have asked for a more effective statement of the case.'[21] The 'case' was racial justice, and the speaker was Martin Luther King. Thomas Merton never participated in a lunch counter sit-in, never walked in a freedom march, never withstood police brutality for the cause of racial equality; nevertheless, his life was an articulate protest against violence and injustice.

Born during World War I on 31 January 1915, Merton spent most of his childhood in France and England. His mother died when he was six, his father when he was fourteen. He spent his first year of university at Cambridge, then left England for New York and entered Columbia University. While at Columbia he flirted with communism and was known as someone who livened up a party. He aspired to write and during his time at Columbia had a number of book reviews published. While writing his Master's thesis on 'Nature and Art in William Blake', he became a Catholic.

Not long after this reversal in his life, Merton began toying with the idea of joining a religious order. He considered the Jesuits but eventually applied to and was initially accepted into the Franciscan order. During a subsequent interview, however, he related his life's story more fully, including the detail that he had fathered a child during his reckless year at Cambridge, after which he was asked to withdraw his application. At Easter-time in 1941 he spent a week on retreat at a monastery in Kentucky. That summer he did volunteer work in Harlem and came face to face with the twin realities of poverty and racial injustice. He considered devoting his life to volunteer work among the poor in Harlem, but on 10 December 1941, two days after Congress declared war on Japan, he entered the Abbey of Our Lady of Gethsemani in Kentucky, the monastery of the Order of Cistercians of the Strict Observance, otherwise known as Trappists.

Although he had always wanted to write, Merton now tried to suppress this impulsion. His abbot encouraged him to write, however, and even assigned him a number of writing projects. Alongside these projects he began to write poems and to work on his autobiography, *The Seven Storey Mountain,* which was published in 1948 when Merton

---

21. Cornelia and Irving Süssman, *Thomas Merton*, rev ed (Garden City, NY: Image Books, 1980), 126.

was 33.[22] During the next decade he wrote numerous books, including *The Waters of Siloe* (a history of the Trappists), *Seeds of Contemplation* (a collection of short meditations), *The Ascent to Truth* (a book on 'mystical contemplation', with reference to Saint John of the Cross), and *The Sign of Jonas* (selections from his journals). He once confessed,

> It is possible to doubt whether I have become a monk (a doubt I have to live with), but it is not possible to doubt that I am a writer, that I was born one and will most probably die as one. Disconcerting, disedifying as it is, this seems to be my lot and my vocation . . .[23]

In 1958, when he was 43, he had an experience that changed his outlook on what it meant to be a monk. Merton had joined the monastery over seventeen years earlier to escape the world and to put it behind him. But on 18 March 1958 he found himself on a street-corner in Louisville, Kentucky, watching people passing by. The following day he wrote in his journal about the impact of this simple experience. Some years later, after he had dramatically increased his contact with people outside Gethsemani through letters and visits, he recalled the incident as follows:

> In Louisville, at the corner of Fourth and Walnut, in the center of the shopping district, I was suddenly overwhelmed with the realization that I loved all those people, that they were mine and I theirs, that we could not be alien to one another even though we were total strangers. It was like waking from a dream of separateness, of spurious self-isolation in a special world, the world of renunciation and supposed holiness. The whole illusion of a separate holy existence is a dream. Not that I question the reality of my vocation, or of my monastic life: but the conception of 'separation from the world' that we have in the mon-

22. Thomas Merton, *The Seven Storey Mountain* (New York: Harcourt, Brace and Company, 1948).

23. Monica Furlong, *Merton: A Biography* (Place: Harper & Row, 1980), 237. Cf Jim Forest, *Living with Wisdom: A Life of Thomas Merton* (Maryknoll, NY: Orbis Books, 1991), 100.

astery too easily presents itself as a complete illusion: the illusion that by making vows we become a different species of being, pseudoangels, 'spiritual men', men of interior life, what have you.

. . . [T]hough 'out of the world' we are in the same world as everybody else, the world of the bomb, the world of race hatred, the world of technology, the world of mass media, big business, revolution, and all the rest. We take a different attitude to all these things, for we belong to God. Yet so does everybody else belong to God. We just happen to be conscious of it, and to make a profession out of this consciousness. But does that entitle us to consider ourselves different, or even *better*, than others? The whole idea is preposterous.

This sense of liberation from an illusory difference was such a relief and such a joy to me that I almost laughed out loud. And I suppose my happiness could have taken form in the words: 'Thank God, thank God that I *am* like other men, that I am only a man among others.' To think that for sixteen or seventeen years I have been taking seriously this pure illusion that is implicit in so much of our monastic thinking.

It is a glorious destiny to be a member of the human race, though it is a race dedicated to many absurdities and one which makes many terrible mistakes: yet, with all that, God Himself gloried in becoming a member of the human race. A member of the human race! To think that such a commonplace realization should suddenly seem like news that one holds the winning ticket in a cosmic sweepstake.[24]

Whether or not this incident had the immediate impact that Merton ascribed to it when he reworked his journal entry for publication, it was around this time that he began to take greater interest in what was going on in the world outside the Trappist monastery, not only the

24. Thomas Merton, *Conjectures of a Guilty Bystander* (Garden City, NY: Image Books, 1968), 156-57.

disturbing problems of racism and war but also literature, politics, psychology and sociology. He began a voluminous correspondence with people from all walks of life. He also began to write 'meditations' like *Original Child Bomb*[25] and articles like 'Nuclear War and Christian Responsibility' (1962), which later appeared in a book of essays edited by Merton entitled *Breakthrough to Peace*.[26] In a letter to Dorothy Day in August 1961 he wrote,

> I don't feel that I can in conscience, at a time like this, go on writing just about things like meditation, though that has its point. I cannot just bury my head in a lot of rather tiny and secondary monastic studies either. I think I have to face the big issues, the life-and-death issues: and this is what everyone is afraid of.[27]

On 23 October he wrote in his journal:

> I am perhaps at the turning point in my spiritual life, perhaps slowly coming to a point of maturation and the resolution of doubts—and the forgetting of fears. Walking into a known and definite battle. May God protect me in it. . . I am one of the few Catholic priests in the country who has come out unequivocally for a completely intransigent fight for the abolition of war and the use of nonviolent means to settle international conflicts. Hence by implication not only against the bomb, against nuclear testing, against Polaris submarines, but against all violence. This I will inevitably have to explain in due course. Nonviolent action, not mere passivity. How am I going to explain myself and defend a definite position in a timely manner when it takes at least two months to get even a short

---

25. Thomas Merton, *Original Child Bomb* (New York: New Directions, 1962); reprinted in *Thomas Merton On Peace* (London and Oxford: Mowbray, 1976), 7-15.
26. Thomas Merton (ed), *Breakthrough to Peace: Twelve Views on the Threat of Thermonuclear Extermination* (New York: New Directions, 1963).
27. Forest, *Living with Wisdom*, 135.

> article through the censors of the Order, is a question I cannot attempt to answer.[28]

Merton was soon advised to discontinue writing on peace and war. In a letter to Dan Berrigan in December 1961 he wrote,

> My peace writings have reached an abrupt halt. Told not to do any more on this subject. Dangerous, subversive, perilous, offensive to pious ears, and confusing to good Catholics who are all at peace in the nice idea that we ought to wipe Russia off the face of the earth. Why get people all stirred up?[29]

Nevertheless, he was able to let people know what was on his mind by correspondence, by circulating mimeographed materials and by publishing the occasional article pseudonymously. Shortly after the beginning of the Second Vatican Council in October 1962, he sent all his writings on peace and war to the secretaries of the International Fellowship of Reconciliation who had been granted permission to circulate them among the theologians drafting the text of the Catholic church's position on social responsibility. In April 1963 Pope John XXIII published *Pacem in Terris* ('Peace on Earth'), an encyclical that along with Merton's writings changed the direction of Catholic social thinking. However, in response to being awarded a medal by Pax, a Catholic peace group, Merton responded: '. . . to say these things seems to me to be only the plain duty of any reasonable being'.[30]

In November 1964 Merton hosted a four-day ecumenical retreat on the 'Spiritual Roots of Protest' for a number of pacifists and peace activists, including Abraham J Muste of the Fellowship of Reconciliation, John Howard Yoder, Dan and Phil Berrigan, and James Forest of the Catholic Peace Fellowship. Such meetings and his willingness to interact through correspondence with people involved in nonviolent social action led Forest to call Merton a 'pastor to peacemakers'. His books *Seeds of Destruction* (1964), *Gandhi on Non-violence* (1965) and *Faith and Violence* (1968) reveal the depth of his feeling about the

---

28. Forest, *Living with Wisdom*, 138.
29. Forest, *Living with Wisdom*, 142.
30. Forest, *Living with Wisdom*, 147.

problems of racism and violence. Nevertheless, Merton's thinking and writing on peace caused him considerable consternation in more ways than one. Not only was he prohibited from publishing on the topic by his superiors, but he over-reacted by temporarily withdrawing his support for the peace movement when a Catholic Worker volunteer self-immolated in front of the United States Mission to the United Nations on 9 November 1965 in protest against American involvement in Vietnam. Merton seems to have had grave misgivings about the rightness and effectiveness of certain forms of civil disobedience and direct action, particularly those that might create misunderstanding and antagonism in the minds of those who supported the status quo.

Despite Merton's enthusiasm in the 1960s for grappling with social problems, these were not wholly new concerns. He had been sensitive to these same issues during his Columbia days in the late 1930s. Moreover, he had not entirely ceased to think about them in the interim. One of the first articles he published on the question of war in Dorothy Day's *Catholic Worker* was 'The Root of War is Fear'. This was also the title of one of his brief reflections in *Seeds of Contemplation*, in which he wrote:

> I have very little idea of what is going on in the world: but occasionally I happen to see some of the things they are drawing and writing there and it gives me the conviction that they are all living in ash-cans. It makes me glad I cannot hear what they are singing.

This is Merton the world-denier. In the very next paragraph, however, he presages the impact his writing will have once he reaffirms his commitment to the world:

> If a writer is so cautious that he never writes anything that cannot be criticized, he will never write anything that can be read. If you want to help other people you have got to make up your mind to write things that some men will condemn.[31]

---

31. Thomas Merton, *Seeds of Contemplation* (Norfolk, CT: New Directions, 1949), 70-71.

'The Root of War is Fear' was considerably enlarged for *New Seeds of Contemplation* (1961) and given a further lengthy preamble for publication in the October 1961 issue of the *Catholic Worker*. Whereas the original meditation is discursive and general, the later version is finely focused and concrete. Here one catches a glimpse of the clear-sighted Merton who comprehends the big picture:

> It does not even seem to enter our minds that there might be some incongruity in praying to the God of peace, the God Who told us to love one another as He had loved us, Who warned us that they who took the sword would perish by it, and at the same time planning to annihilate not thousands but millions of civilians and soldiers, men, women and children without discrimination, even with the almost infallible certainty of inviting the same annihilation for ourselves![32]

Merton is by now also less didactic, less prone to hand out advice. Gone for the most part are the distancing words, 'men', 'they', 'them' and 'you'. In their place one reads 'our' and 'we', words almost totally absent from the original.

Another characteristic of the revised version of 'The Root of War is Fear' is Merton's insistence that we can only hope and work effectively for peace if we are prepared to deal first and foremost with our own aggression, prejudice, fears and obsessions rather than pointing the accusing finger at others:

> Thus we never see the one truth that would help us begin to solve our ethical and political problems: that we are *all* more or less wrong, that we are *all* at fault, *all* limited and obstructed by our mixed motives, our self-deception, our greed, our self-righteousness and our tendency to aggressivity and hypocrisy.[33]

32. Thomas Merton, *New Seeds of Contemplation* (Norfolk, CT: New Directions, 1961), 120.
33. Merton, *New Seeds of Contemplation*, 115-16.

This willingness to recognise and to honour the humanity and dignity of one's enemies, real or imagined, appears frequently in Merton's latest writings. In 'Toward a Theology of Resistance', for example, Merton echoes both Gandhi and King:

> . . . nonviolence seeks to 'win' not by destroying or even by humiliating the adversary, but by convincing him that there is a higher and more certain common good than can be attained by bombs and blood. Nonviolence . . . does not try to overcome the adversary by winning over him, but to turn him from an adversary into a collaborator by winning him over.[34]

And in 'Blessed are the Meek' Merton avers that one important condition for the honest implementation of nonviolent resistance is a willingness to learn from adversaries. Against the dishonest and cowardly tendency to dehumanise our enemies, Merton insisted that we must genuinely love and respect them.[35]

Among other important insights on peace and nonviolence, Merton emphasised that nonviolence is not the same as nonresistance. In 'Nonviolence and the Christian Conscience' he wrote, 'Not only does nonviolence resist evil but, if it is properly practised, it often resists evil more effectively than violence ever could. Indeed, the chief argument in favor of nonviolent resistance is that it is, per se and ideally, *the only really effective resistance to injustice and evil*.'[36]

Whether Merton would allow that what I have identified as being of abiding significance in his thinking and writing corresponds to what he thought to be of lasting value is hard to know. He may well have specified something more existential or simple or mysterious or funny—such as friendship or the flight of a bird overhead or a walk in the woods or rain.[37]

---

34. Thomas Merton, *Faith and Violence* (Notre Dame, IN: University of Notre Dame Press, 1968), 12.
35. Merton, *Faith and Violence*, 14-29.
36. Merton, *Faith and Violence*, 38-39.
37. See, for example, Merton's evocative essay, 'Rain and the Rhinoceros', in his *Raids on the Unspeakable* (New York: New Directions, 1966), 9-23.

3. Karl Barth (1886–1968)

Karl Barth is sometimes named alongside Augustine, Anselm, Thomas Aquinas, Luther, Calvin and Schleiermacher as one of a select number of truly great Christian theologians. However, Barth was unimpressed with the word 'great' as an epithet for a theologian. 'There may be great lawyers, doctors, natural scientists, historians, and philosophers', he wrote in *Evangelical Theology*. 'But there are none other than *little* theologians . . .'[38]

Barth was largely instructed in the liberal theology of his day, but events associated with World War I convinced him that theological liberalism, with its faith in human progress, was bankrupt. He therefore explored the Bible afresh, beginning with a careful study of Romans, which by 1918 formed an unusual 'commentary' whose central message was a clarion call to recognise God as God, the 'Wholly Other'.[39] This book provoked strong reactions in Germany and touched off a movement called 'dialectical theology' or 'theology of crisis'. In 1921 Barth was invited to become a professor of theology at Göttingen. In 1925 he moved to Münster and in 1930 to Bonn, where he played a significant role in the church's opposition to Hitler. It was he who drafted the 'Barmen Declaration', the manifesto of the Confessing Church in which it refused to offer allegiance to the Führer of the Third Reich. Barth was dismissed from his teaching post in 1935 and forced to return to Basle, his home city, where he taught until his retirement in 1962.

Between the first and second editions of *The Epistle to the Romans,* Barth hung above his desk a sixteenth-century painting of Jesus on the cross by Matthias Grünewald. In this painting John the Baptist stands impassive, apart from a trio of mourners on the other side of the cross, with the forefinger of his right hand pointed resolutely at the distorted and discoloured figure of Jesus. Above his arm are the words, 'He must increase, but I must decrease.' Of this painting Barth wrote:

> John the Baptist . . . can only point—and here everything is bolder and more abrupt, because here all

38. Karl Barth, *Evangelical Theology: An Introduction* (Grand Rapids, MI: Eerdmans, 1979), 77.

39. Karl Barth, *The Epistle to the Romans* (London: Oxford University Press, 1933). The first edition was published in 1919, the second in 1922.

> indication of the revelation of the Godhead is lacking—point to a wretched, crucified, dead man. This is the place of Christology. It faces the mystery. It does not stand within the mystery. It can and must adore with Mary and point with the Baptist. It cannot and must not do more than this. But it can and must do this.[40]

It is commonplace but nonetheless apposite to speak of Grünewald's 'Crucifixion' as an image of Barth's theology. Barth was a twentieth-century John the Baptist in more ways than one. In his early period he sounded a blast of judgment on the 'culture theology' of his day, in much the same vein as John's diatribe against the religious elite of his time (see Mt 3:7-12). But Barth was most like John the Baptist in his insistence on the primacy and centrality of Jesus, Messiah and Son of God.

Shortly before the outbreak of World War II, the editor of the *Christian Century* asked Barth to reflect on how his thinking had changed in the previous decade. In response, Barth noted that although his thinking had not changed in one important respect, nevertheless:

> in these years I had to learn that Christian doctrine, if it is to merit its name and if it is to build up the Christian church in the world as she must needs be built up, has to be exclusively and conclusively the doctrine of Jesus Christ—of Jesus Christ as the living Word of God spoken to us . . .[41]

He then went on to say, with reference to his thinking and writing, 'My new task was to take all that has been said before and to think it through once more and freshly and to articulate it anew as a theology of the grace of God in Jesus Christ.'[42]

---

40. Karl Barth, *Church Dogmatics* I/2 (Edinburgh: T&T Clark, 1956), 125. A picture of Grünewald's 'Crucifixion' from the Isenheim Altar in Colmar appears as the Frontispiece to Eberhard Busch, *Karl Barth: His Life from Letters and Autobiographical Texts* (London: SCM Press, 1976; Grand Rapids, MI: Eerdmans, 1994).
41. Karl Barth, *How I Changed My Mind* (Edinburgh: The Saint Andrew Press, 1969), 43.
42. Barth, *How I Changed My Mind*, 43.

One could illustrate what Barth called his 'christological concentration' by referring to almost any of his writings. A good example is his 1956 essay, 'The Humanity of God'. He had already developed the theme of this essay in his *Church Dogmatics,* but for many it was evidence of a shift in his thinking. He began by reflecting on what had led him forty years earlier to emphasise the deity of God. According to the prevailing theology of that period, Barth noted, '. . . to think about God meant to think in a scarcely veiled fashion about man, more exactly about the religious, the Christian religious man'.[43] Barth reaffirmed his original insight but conceded that he had been only partly right to insist on the 'wholly other' God. By stressing God's *otherness,* he recalled, he had overlooked God's *togetherness* with humanity. He had intended to safeguard God's sovereignty and freedom, but he had failed to acknowledge that the sovereign and free God has chosen to be humanity's partner. So, Barth did not affirm the 'humanity of God' by repudiating, but by refining and clarifying, his earlier insight that God is not the projection of human ideals but the sovereign and free Lord of all.

How, one asks, can anyone know that God's being as God includes humanity? Barth posed the same question himself and replied:

> It is a *Christological* statement, or rather one grounded in and to be unfolded from Christology . . . Certainly in *Jesus Christ,* as he is attested in Holy Scripture, we are not dealing with man in the abstract: not with the man who is able with his modicum of religion and religious morality to be sufficient unto himself without God and thus himself to be God. But neither are we dealing with *God* in the abstract: not with one who in his deity exists only separated from man, distant and strange and thus a non-human if not indeed an inhuman God. In Jesus Christ there is no isolation of man from God or of God from man.[44]

Here Barth affirmed and built upon the insight distilled in Jn 1:18 that we know God only in so far as God is revealed to us in Jesus Christ.

43. Karl Barth, *The Humanity of God* (Atlanta: John Knox Press, 1960), 39.

44. Barth, *The Humanity of God*, 46.

Jesus reveals God's humanity by demonstrating God's unwillingness to be God without humanity.

Describing Barth's work on his *Doctrine of Reconciliation,* Eberhard Busch noted that 'Barth was now preoccupied with the subject he believed to be at the heart of all theology, the knowledge of Jesus Christ.' He also observed that 'of the criticisms directed against him Barth took seriously only those concerned with his concentration on Jesus Christ'.[45] To be a theologian, for Barth, was not simply to concern oneself with Christian doctrine or church dogma, but to be oriented in a special and specific way towards a deeper understanding of who Jesus is and what he means for us. In 1952 he explained in a letter, 'I have no christological principle and no christological method. Rather, in each individual theological question I seek to orientate myself afresh—to some extent from the very beginning—not on a christological dogma but on Jesus Christ himself *(vivit! regnat! triumphat!).*'[46] During a radio interview in the last year of his life, Barth was asked to explain the meaning of 'grace'. He acknowledged that he had used the word often but that for him:

> Grace itself is only a provisional word. The last word that I have to say as a theologian or politician is not a concept like grace but a name: Jesus Christ. He is grace and he is the ultimate one beyond world and church and even theology. We cannot lay hold of him. But we have to do with him. And my own concern in my long life has been increasingly to emphasize this name and to say: 'In him'.[47]

This emphasis on Jesus Christ is Barth's principal legacy to the church and to the world.

To the world? Paradoxical as it may seem, Barth's 'christological concentration' made him more, not less, concerned with the world. Despite his stature as a theologian, many are critical of his theology, or of what they understand to be his theology. There is, however, far less criticism of his social commitment. It was Barth who affirmed the importance not only of the Bible but also of the daily newspaper. Despite

---

45. Busch, *Karl Barth*, 379-80.

46. Busch, *Karl Barth*, 380.

47. Karl Barth, *Final Testimonies* (Grand Rapids, MI: Eerdmans, 1977), 29-30.

the misleading caricature sometimes drawn of Barth as a 'theologian of the Word of *God*', he was anything but aloof from the pressing social and political concerns of his day. He never understood his theology to be a negation of the world, even in his most 'dialectical' phase.[48] For Barth, to affirm the God revealed in Jesus Christ was also to affirm the world of human beings precisely because Jesus reveals *both* God's unwillingness to accept human alienation *and* God's determination to remain humanity's partner.

As early as January 1906 Barth delivered a lecture, 'Zofingia and the Social Question', in which he urged that the Zofingia student association, of which he was an energetic member, discontinue handing down what he called 'honourable ancient student customs' and become instead 'filled with a new spirit, with the spirit of social responsibility towards the lower strata of society and above all towards ourselves'.[49] Busch reports that during his time as assistant pastor in Geneva (1909–1911), Barth '. . . spent a great deal of time in relief work with the poor. He deliberately made acquaintance with real poverty, with the strong feeling that he was quite incapable of coping with it'.[50] After moving to Safenwil in 1911, Barth became more and more involved in social issues, so much so that he became known as the 'red pastor of Safenwil'. Reflecting late in life on his early years, Barth recollected that 'when I moved to the industrial village of Safenwil, my interest in theology as such had to step back noticeably into second place . . . Because of the situation I found in my community, I became passionately involved with socialism and especially with the trade union movement'.[51] No sooner had Barth arrived in Safenwil than he began to give lectures to the local Worker's Association. In December 1911 he gave an address on 'Jesus Christ and the Social Movement', in which he impressed upon his audience 'the inherent connection be-

48. In a 'Letter to the Editor', in Donald K McKim (ed), *How Karl Barth Changed My Mind* (Grand Rapids, MI: Eerdmans, 1986), Barth's son Christoph wrote of his father: 'You can hardly imagine how "secular" this giant theologian actually was. He loved the world, in spite of all its obvious misery' (7).

49. Busch, *Karl Barth*, 37.

50. Busch, *Karl Barth*, 55.

51. Karl Barth, *The Theology of Schleiermacher* (Grand Rapids, MI: Eerdmans, 1982), 263.

tween Jesus and socialism'.[52] For the duration of his time in Safenwil, Barth's social and political involvement created tension among his parishioners, some of whom were so disturbed that they left his church.

There has been considerable debate over whether Barth's theology was dominated by his socialist leanings. It seems fairly clear that although he was not ideologically committed to any particular form of socialism, he was nevertheless socialist in a practical sense.[53] Barth was no 'armchair theologian', but perhaps his acute sense of social responsibility was the result of his pastoral duties and disappeared once he became a university professor of theology. After 1921, when he left pastoral work and began to teach at the University of Göttingen, he devoted almost all his energy to theology. Nevertheless, despite (Barth would say, because of) his theological focus, he stood at the forefront of the church's opposition to Hitler.

When the National Socialists seized power early in 1933, Barth was teaching in Bonn. He was not slow to understand the ramifications of Hitler's accession to power, particularly for the church. Within a short time the 'German Christian Movement' in the Protestant churches began to identify church aims with those of National Socialism and committed itself to assimilating the church to the Nazi state. In response Barth wrote an essay entitled 'Theological Existence Today', in which he denounced the position of the 'German Christians' as heresy. It turned out to be 'the first trumpet blast of the "Confessing Church,"' which based its opposition to Hitler and the 'German Christians' on

---

52. An English translation of this lecture can be found in George Hunsinger (ed), *Karl Barth and Radical Politics* (Philadelphia: Westminster Press, 1976), 19-37, and in Clifford Green (ed), *Karl Barth: Theologian of Freedom* (London: Collins, 1989), 98-114. Cf Bruce L McCormack, *Karl Barth's Critically Realistic Dialectical Theology: Its Genesis and Development 1909–1936* (Oxford: Clarendon Press, 1995), 78-83, who contends that during Barth's student years he knew little about the socialist movement.

53. When I wrote the preceding sentences a decade ago, I had in mind the collection of essays edited by George Hunsinger, *Karl Barth and Radical Politics*. In 'Karl Barth and the Politics of Sectarian Protestantism: A Dialogue with John Howard Yoder', Hunsinger also describes Barth's socialism as practical rather than ideological. Written in 1980 in response to Yoder's unpublished lecture on 'The Basis of Barth's Social Ethics' (1978), Hunsinger's essay was first published in his *Disruptive Grace: Studies in the Theology of Karl Barth* (Grand Rapids, MI: Eerdmans, 2000), 114-28.

confession of faith in Jesus Christ as its *sole* Lord. Barth even sent a copy of the essay to Hitler. It was later banned but not before 37,000 copies had been printed. Throughout this period, Barth's central themes were the theological and political relevance of the first commandment and his denial of natural revelation. Early in 1934 Barth refused to open his lectures with the Hitler salute, though all university professors were required to do so.

The high point of Barth's resistance to Nazi ideology, for this was how he understood all his teaching, preaching and writing at this time, was his drafting of the Barmen Declaration. Barth wrote it prior to the first Confessing Synod of the German Evangelical Church in May 1934, which met in Barmen. In it he made the following affirmations, each of which made it absolutely clear that the church could not accept Hitler as a Führer alongside, not to mention above, Jesus Christ:

> Jesus Christ, as he is attested to us in Holy Scripture, is the one Word of God whom we have to hear, and whom we have to trust and obey in life and in death. We reject the false doctrine that the church could and should recognize as a source of its proclamation, beyond and besides this one Word of God, yet other events, powers, historic figures, and truths as God's revelation. . . We reject the false doctrine that there could be areas of our life in which we would belong not to Jesus Christ but to other lords . . .[54]

Barth later regretted that he did not make the mistreatment of Jews a feature of the text. In November 1934 he refused to sign an oath of loyalty to Hitler required of all state-appointed officials unless he could add a qualifying clause. As a result, he was suspended from his teaching duties but continued to live in Germany. In March 1935 he was informed by the Gestapo that he was no longer permitted to speak in public, and in June he was formally dismissed from his teaching post.

---

54. An English translation of the Barmen Declaration is in Green (ed), *Karl Barth*, 148-51. Busch, *Karl Barth*, contains a facsimile of part of the original draft of the Barmen Declaration (Illustration 48).

Much has been written about Barth's role in the Confessing Church's resistance to National Socialism. Here the point is that while Barth's deliberations and public statements were unfailingly theological, he was always socially and politically relevant, even if (at times) indirectly.[55] Barth refused to hide behind his faith and standing as a professor of theology.

Barth's political activism during his Safenwil years and his forthright resistance to Hitler in 1933-34 testify to his sense of social responsibility. A feature of Barth's social commitment, however, was his thinking on peace and war. A decisive event was the outbreak of World War I in August 1914. Although Barth had already broken away from political liberalism by associating himself with socialism, World War I precipitated his break with theological liberalism. Reflecting on this event, Barth later remarked:

> One day in early August 1914 stands out in my personal memory as a black day. Ninety-three German intellectuals impressed public opinion by their proclamation in support of the war policy of Wilhelm II and his counsellors. Among these intellectuals I discovered to my horror almost all of my theological teachers whom I had greatly venerated. In despair over what this indicated about the signs of the time I suddenly realized that I could not any longer follow either their ethics and dogmatics or their understanding of the Bible and History.[56]

Barth's recollection of this occasion was faulty and exaggerated. The declaration supporting the Kaiser's war policy was released not in

---

55. In 1968 Barth recalled, 'The theology in which I decisively tried to draw on the Bible was never a private matter for me, remote from the world and man. Its theme is God for the world, God for man, heaven for earth. This meant that all my theology always had a strong political side, explicit or implicit.' See Barth, *Final Testimonies*, 24. For an overview of Barth's social and political involvement throughout his adult life, see Frank Jehle, *Ever against the Stream: The Politics of Karl Barth, 1906–1968* (Grand Rapids, MI: Eerdmans, 2002).

56. Karl Barth, 'Evangelical Theology in the 19th Century' (1957), in Barth, *The Humanity of God*, 14.

August but *October* 1914,[57] and only two of the twelve theologians among the ninety-three intellectuals had influenced Barth to any significant extent. Nevertheless, they were two of the most important theologians of the day, Adolf von Harnack and Wilhelm Herrmann, and each had had a decisive impact on Barth. Another factor also caused Barth consternation. He was as dismayed by the socialists' capitulation to nationalism and war as by his former teachers' support for war. In an autobiographical sketch, Barth recalled:

> A change came only with the outbreak of World War I. This brought concretely to light two aberrations: first in the teaching of my theological mentors in Germany, who seemed to me to be hopelessly compromised by their submission to the ideology of war; and second in socialism. I had credulously enough expected socialism, more than I had the Christian church, to avoid the ideology of war, but to my horror I saw it doing the very opposite in every land.[58]

There were also other incidents, meetings and conversations (such as Barth's encounter with Christoph Blumhardt in April 1915) that contributed to Barth's break with liberal theology. He seems to have 'telescoped' the outbreak of the war, the manifesto of support for Kaiser Wilhelm II, his disenchantment with socialism and various personal encounters into a single cause for his break with liberalism. Nevertheless, the war and support for the war by at least some of Barth's mentors were decisive.[59]

It is striking how confidently Barth judged an entire theological tradition, nineteenth century liberalism, by its adherents' support for the war. According to Barth, 'Their "ethical failure" indicated that "their exegetical and dogmatic presuppositions could not be in or-

---

57. Perhaps Barth was thinking of the Kaiser's call 'To the German Nation!' (6 August 1914), whose composition benefited from Adolf von Harnack's presence 'in an advisory capacity'. See Jehle, *Ever against the Stream*, 36-37.

58. Bernd Jaspert (ed), *Karl Barth—Rudolf Bultmann: Letters 1922–1966* (Grand Rapids, MI: Eerdmans, 1981), 154.

59. For a fuller discussion of Barth's break with liberalism, see McCormack, *Karl Barth's Critically Realistic Dialectical Theology*, ch 2.

der."'[60] In other words, by their fruits you will know them! What particularly annoyed Barth was the confidence with which theologians appealed to God in support of the war. The ease with which they mustered support from above for such a dubious enterprise no doubt influenced Barth's sharp rhetoric in *The Epistle to the Romans* where he identified God as the crisis confronting *all* human activity.

However, anyone familiar with Barth knows that he defended the war against Hitler on theological grounds. Indeed, Barth's insistence that both ideological and, if necessary, military resistance to Hitler were imperative even for his native Switzerland placed him in conflict with the official interpretation of Swiss neutrality. Despite being in his early fifties, in 1940 Barth reported for military service and served in the Swiss armed auxiliary. For Barth, Nazi ideology and expansionism were worse than war and had to be halted by military means. In his 'Letter to Great Britain from Switzerland', written in April 1941, Barth distinguished World War II from World War I and the majority of all previous wars by saying, '. . . we do not just accept this war as a necessary evil, but . . . we approve it as a righteous war, which God does not simply allow, but which He commands us to wage'.[61] He disallowed regarding the war as a 'crusade' or 'war of religion' but defended his unequivocal statement, 'The obedience of the Christian to the clear will of God compels him to support this war',[62] on the basis of the past resurrection, future return and present reign of Jesus Christ. Not surprisingly, 'Barth, who had long endured charges of "pacifism," now had to hear accusations of "militarism," even from some of his friends.'[63]

In *Karl Barth and the Problem of War* John Howard Yoder argued that Barth's theological defence of war violates his own strict method of doing theology, particularly because of his willingness to import justifications not grounded in God's self-disclosure in Jesus Christ. Yoder was careful not to criticise Barth himself or his decisions, but rather critiqued his defence of war in extreme cases from within the framework of Barth's own theology. Despite his critique of Barth on this point, Yoder noted that Barth's negative appraisal of warfare as

---

60. Busch, *Karl Barth*, 81.
61. Karl Barth, *A Letter to Great Britain from Switzerland* (London: The Sheldon Press, 1941), 3-4.
62. Barth, *A Letter to Great Britain*, 9.
63. Busch, *Karl Barth*, 303.

the worst and least justified form of killing is 'unique in the history of mainstream European Protestant theology'.[64] In *Church Dogmatics* III/4 Barth goes so far as to say that the pacifist refusal to go to war 'has almost infinite arguments in its favour and is almost overpoweringly strong'.[65] According to Yoder, 'Karl Barth is far nearer to Christian pacifism than he is to any kind of systematic apology for Christian participation in war.' As a result, he perceived his debate with Barth as follows:

> The discussion with Barth is therefore not a debate between pacifism and militarism, nor even between pacifism and non-pacifism. It is rather a debate to be carried on within the pacifist camp, between one position which is pacifist in all the general statements it can make but announces in advance that it is willing to make major exceptions, and another position, nearly the same in theory, which is not able to affirm in advance the possibility of the exceptional case.[66]

Moreover, Yoder detected signs in Barth's latest writings of a further move towards a pacifist position. In *Church Dogmatics* IV/2 Barth wrote, 'In conformity with the New Testament one cannot be pacifist in principle, only practically. But let everyone give heed whether, being called to discipleship, it is either possible for him to avoid, or permissible for him to neglect becoming practically pacifist!'[67]

---

64. John H Yoder, *Karl Barth and the Problem of War* (Nashville: Abingdon Press, 1970), 38. For a critical response to Yoder's argument in *Karl Barth and the Problem of War*, see Dennis Okholm, 'Defending the Cause of the Christian Church: Karl Barth's Justification of War', *Christian Scholar's Review* XVI/2 (January 1987): 144-62.
65. Karl Barth, *Church Dogmatics* III/4 (Edinburgh: T&T Clark, 1961), 455.
66. Yoder, *Karl Barth and the Problem of War*, 52.
67. Yoder's translation of Karl Barth, *Die Kirchliche Dogmatik* IV/2 (1955), 622, in Yoder, *Karl Barth and the Problem of War*, 116-17. According to Yoder, Geoffrey Bromiley's translation of this passage in *Church Dogmatics* IV/2 (Edinburgh: T&T Clark, 1958), 550, 'considerably softens the thrust' of Barth's claim.

In an appendix to his book, Yoder surveyed the dispute within the German church in the 1950s over whether West Germany should rearm with atomic weapons. Claiming to stand in the tradition of the Confessing Church of the 1930s, some informal 'church brotherhoods' protested German rearmament with atomic weapons. This protest culminated in a petition to the Synod of the German Protestant Churches in March 1958, calling upon it to recognise that the issue of atomic weapons required a definite stand and that to avoid doing so placed the very being of the church at stake. The petition also asked the Synod to affirm ten propositions spelling out in unambiguous terms why the church could not remain neutral on the question of atomic warfare, but should formally declare participation in, or preparation for, atomic warfare to be 'under all circumstances sin against God and neighbour'. In Switzerland Barth was a member of a theological commission that drafted a statement similar to that of the German church brotherhoods. He was invited to attend a meeting of his German counterparts in October 1958 for further discussion of the issues raised by the earlier meeting. Although unable to attend, he wrote an open letter in which he affirmed his agreement with all ten theses in the March petition:

> What was the rumor spread about in Germany's newspapers, 'that Professor Barth is not theologically in agreement with the Ten Theses of the Petition'? You may say to all and to everyone, that I am in agreement with these Theses (including the 10th!), as if I had written them myself . . .[68]

Yoder noted that according to a reliable source, Barth helped to draft the original theses. According to Busch, however, Barth did more than this; as with the Barmen Declaration, he was the anonymous author himself![69] Like King and Merton, Barth was a 'nuclear pacifist'. He put it succinctly in a letter in June 1958: 'Atomic war cannot be a just war in any sense; it can only be universal annihilation.'[70]

---

68. Yoder, *Karl Barth and the Problem of War*, 137.

69. Busch, *Karl Barth*, 430-31. Cf Paul Matheny, 'Barth on Atomic War', and his translation of Barth's 'Ten Theses Concerning the Question of Atomic "Armament"' in the *Karl Barth Society Newsletter*, Number 9 (Spring 1994); reprinted in *Faith and Freedom: A Journal of Christian Ethics* 4/1 (March 1995): 26-27.

70. Busch, *Karl Barth*, 431.

Whether or not one agrees with Barth's earlier position on the theological legitimacy of violence and war in extreme circumstances, his readiness to confront such questions, not to mention the thoroughness of his deliberations, must be acknowledged. Barth was no quietist. If thinking on such issues was necessary in Barth's time, it is no less necessary in our own. In addition to the threat of terrorism and the many mid- to large-scale armed conflicts around the globe, we also face armed and unarmed hostilities within our inner-cities and suburbs, including domestic and drug-related violence. Barth would be the first to say that we should not resort to his arguments, but that in our own situation we should strive to find means of confronting violence, injustice, nihilism and despair that reflect our faithfulness to Jesus Christ.

* * *

Christian faith, social responsibility and commitment to peace are important legacies, but they do not exhaust all that King, Merton and Barth bequeathed to those willing to learn from them. One could do worse than to conclude by noting the importance of humour for all three men. A sense of humour allowed each one to carry on with the demands and sacrifices associated with his particular work and vocation; it also reflected his sense of freedom to be himself, despite his failings, because of the conviction that he lived by God's grace or experienced what King called 'cosmic companionship'. Introducing a series of essays to celebrate the one hundredth anniversary of Barth's birth, Daniel Migliore devoted considerable space to an analysis of Barth's theology of humour, then concluded: 'We are suggesting that one of Barth's lasting contributions to church and theology may just be this spirit of play and humor born of confidence in God's grace.'[71] This is no less true of Martin Luther King, Jr, and Thomas Merton.

71. Daniel L Migliore, 'Editorial', *Theology Today* XLIII/3 (October 1986): 314. Markus Barth wrote of his father: 'If I have learned anything from him in theology, it is this: that we all are fellow learners of the free grace of God, and that grace gives [one] a ground to live upon as a free and happy child.' See Markus Barth, 'My Father: Karl Barth', in McKim (ed), *How Karl Barth Changed My Mind*, 1.

Three Unfinished Pilgrimages

John Howard Yoder

The coincidence that three different men died in the same year is an odd reason for seeking to juxtapose their ministries or their thought. Each of them was important, but Thomas Merton, Karl Barth and Martin Luther King, Jr, lived and served in utterly different worlds. Yet in the perspective of a quarter-century one can discern some commonalities.[1] That is the way hagiography properly works; memory sifts and illuminates what resonates with the gospel.[2]

1. Reform

Each of these men understood himself to be restoring or renewing a normative vision that stood in judgment on the present, yet without being an outsider. Their resources for positive change were not radical, but classical.

Merton's path from ordinary student life into the Trappist lifestyle was radical for him, yet what he reached back to when he went to Gethsemani was what he took to be the classical heritage of the Christian West. His *Seven Storey Mountain* (1948) made Trappism attractive to a broad stream of ordinary American young men. The vision of renewal through withdrawal into contemplation was as old as the desert fathers whom Merton interpreted. It drew upon the neoplatonic vision of a deeper reality behind the surface of things, which it assumed one could be trained to discern through the discipline of contemplation. It led not only him but also a goodly number

1. 1968 was a landmark year in other ways as well. The collapse of the Johnson presidency, the death of Robert Kennedy, student uprisings in European and American cities, and the Tet offensive in Vietnam changed the terms of public life in ways not dealt with in this article.

2. Classic, that is, medieval hagiography made all the saints look more or less the same, since what it meant to be a saint was a timeless ideal. Thus one could not easily think of a saint growing or changing. Since two of these three men were cut off before finishing the path they had set out on, it is particularly fitting here to understand sainthood as a direction rather than a destination.

of others in his train into the monastic life. His role as novice master consisted in inducting young men into the otherworldly Trappist disciplines of silence, labour and prayer. Most of his writings until the 1960s were devoted to retrieving the contemplative tradition.

Karl Barth's path from the liberal Protestantism of the early years of the twentieth century through the 'theology of crisis' of the 1920s to the 'theology of the word' in the 1930s was likewise a renewal drawn from the resources of the establishment. In the face of the dilution imposed by two centuries of post-enlightenment humanism, Barth reached back to the agenda of the Reformation, and through the Reformers to the Scriptures, to revitalise what Christians had always believed. He undertook, and almost finished, the most massive encyclopedic *Summa* of the century, incarnating the claim that he represented the classic middle of normative Christianity, even though his idiosyncratic approach fit no one else's model. He resuscitated the term 'Dogmatics' to replace 'doctrine' or 'religious thought', thereby testifying that he was interpreting the mainstream of the Christian heritage. He spent the last thirty-five years of his full and honoured life as a University professor within the state-church structure of one of Europe's most comfortable and bourgeois cities.

Martin Luther King's path from his youth within the leadership elite of Atlanta's black Baptist culture to the personalism of Boston University Methodism and back combined in a privileged way two establishment visions. To be black in the USA in the 1940s and 1950s was no picnic. But there was no better way or place to be black than as a Baptist minister's son in Atlanta and a graduate of Rockefeller-funded Morehouse College. There was no better running start into a career on the interracial border areas where the white establishment admitted a few gifted blacks than earning a doctorate from Boston.

Nor was there a better issue to go into battle against than segregation, whose demise had been prepared for by two generations of patient legal struggle by the NAACP and the Urban League. There was no more apt appeal to use as leverage against Jim Crow than the 'American dream' of liberty for all. While smaller than the gospel of Jesus, this vision was negotiable in the streets, the media and the courts, with the help of the Kennedys and the Belafontes. The charisma of King drew on the resources for renewal offered by both sides of his elite identity, each with its own strengths and raised to a higher power by their coinciding. The Southern Christian Leadership Conference was the uniquely American 'voluntary association' instrument to channel moral and financial support from the white liberal establishment to the black-led movement.

Thus, in his own way, each of these three men saw himself as an agent of renewal of the mainstream of his respective church and culture, drawing on the resources of its unchallenged middle. Yet each was led by events and by his charisma (admirers might say by God the Spirit) to a far-reaching redefinition of the substance of his message. For each of them, three further changes had to come—and did.

2. Christ the fulcrum

In his own way, each of these three men moved beyond a reformation vision by appealing to the best resources within the mainstream tradition, for example, 'natural law' or 'reasonable consensus', to a substantially more critical renewal vision, which gained its leverage from an appeal to a higher moral authority.

In Barth's case the 'higher leverage' was the most directly named: 'Jesus Christ, as he is attested for us in Holy Scripture, is the one Word of God which we have to hear and which we have to trust and obey in life and in death. We reject the false doctrine, as though the church could and would have to acknowledge . . . other events and powers, figures and truths, as God's revelation.'[3] The challenges that provoked this radical recourse were multiple and markedly different from one another, but similar in the way they provoked this response from Barth. The most respectable provocation was that of Emil Brunner, whose 'apologetic' concern for making sense to the church's modern public led him to postulate a 'point of contact' (*Anknüpfungspunkt*) by virtue of which the gospel, without renouncing its claim to be revelatory authority and saving grace, would avoid seeming alien to the contemporary addressee. Barth's answer was a resonant *Nein!*[4] Only the Word of God itself makes the Word of God accessible; there is no

3. 'Barmen Declaration', Article 1 (May 1934), often reproduced.

4. *Theologische Existenz Heute*, No 14 (1934); ET *Natural Theology* (Geoffrey Bles, 1946). Brunner began to speak of theology as having 'a second task', which he called 'eristics'. Barth's tension with Brunner on this theme surfaced before he wrote *Nein!* See Eberhard Busch, *Karl Barth: His Life from Letters and Autobiographical Texts* (London: SCM Press; Philadelphia: Fortress Press, 1976), 195.

bridge or contact-point that makes the grace of divine initiative less absolutely indispensable or the scandal of grace more palatable.

On the other hand, the least respectable provocation was the claim of many German Protestants that the growing momentum of the Nazi movement was revelatory, a kind of divine guidance for the nation. That notion of a different, more direct word from God was the immediate adversary targeted by Barmen Article I; although politically the opposite, it was formally analogous to Brunner's 'point of contact'.[5]

Barth had already made that point in the most intellectual and academic way when he began his doctrinal corpus with his neo-reformation understanding of the Word of God as the presupposition behind which there is no other presupposition.[6] The coincidence between the theological parting with Brunner and the political severance from the 'German Christians' rounded out the wholeness of the new stance.

Thomas Merton was in no way a systematic theologian. He had a sharp eye for basic issues but little interest in sustained argument. Yet he was aware that he needed to be sure of his footing when he began moving beyond support for the nation's best ideals concerning civil rights into significant dissent concerning Vietnam. In November 1964 he invited to Gethsemani a group of peace movement people for a 'retreat' on the 'Spiritual Roots of Protest'.[7] Merton was aware, it seemed, that his viscera were more independently critical of Amer-

---

5. This parallelism is clear in Busch, *Karl Barth*, 195-207, 236-50.

6. In fact, it was a second start. He had begun with the title *Christian Dogmatics*, then started over with *Church Dogmatics* to honour more directly the substance of theology in the community's history.

7. Abraham J Muste was the grand old man of the Fellowship of Reconciliation (FoR). John Oliver Nelson had not yet left Yale Divinity to found the Kirkridge retreat community; he was also head of the ecumenical Association Press and of the Church Peace Mission (CPM). The CPM co-sponsored the event, though its archives have since been lost and its then Secretary, Paul Peachey, does not remember his share in the plan. There were five Roman Catholic activists, all from the Catholic Worker movement. Wilbur H Ferry, from Robert M Hutchins's Center for the Study of Democratic Institutions, was an old friend of Merton's who was soon to have a large share in giving public attention to Pope John XXIII's *Pacem in Terris*. I was the only person invited from an historic pacifist denomination who could attend. Both planners, John Heidbrink of FoR and Paul Peachey of CPM, were unable to attend.

ica's sense of vocation than his mind.[8] His own introductory talks at the retreat confirmed that:[9] he sensed a deepening discrepancy with the dominant culture, which his culture-critical book reviews (later gathered together in *Faith and Violence*) were spelling out in an occasional way. He sensed the need for a deeper rootage for his critique than was provided by the classical vision of the complementarity of the contemplative and lay callings.

In answer to his own question, 'What are the spiritual roots of protest?' Merton suggested such broad notions as that the origins of monasticism were rooted in social criticism. I was struck by his failure to reach for any of the usual gospel sources of ethical guidance. Assuming that 'we already know all of that', or perhaps that the church at large already thinks that is 'old stuff', Merton's contemplative angle on renewal seemed to prefer to look for critical leverage in some nonclassical formula or some hitherto unexploited depth dimension.

I had been invited to open one session by interpreting the older, more solidly dissident heritage of the 'peace churches', with some interest in comparison and contrast, yet not on the level of mere 'comparative ecclesiology', which sets all the traditions side-by-side but puts truth questions 'on hold'. My response to the assigned question was, 'Why not Incarnation?' Why, in other words, should persons seeking leverage to turn the world around, or (to switch metaphors) seeking energy to swim against the destructive currents of a violent culture, not give more weight to the words and the work of Jesus, especially when other more traditional renewal resources do not go deep enough? Of course, that was a protestant idea, but Merton did not immediately raise against it the screen he had already raised to fend off Barth's critiques.[10]

---

8. Elena Malits, *The Solitary Explorer: Thomas Merton's Transforming Journey* (San Francisco: Harper & Row, 1980), 78, describes this period in Merton's life as one of 'learning to take a position'.

9. A sketchy outline is preserved in Gordon Zahn (ed), *The Nonviolent Alternative* (New York: Farrar, Straus & Giroux, 1980), 259-60. Merton titled his preface to *Faith and Violence* (University of Notre Dame Press, 1968), 'Toward a Theology of Resistance', but its content is mostly directed toward interpreting the following occasional essays.

10. Merton's fullest statement of what he learned from the event, in the available correspondence, was: '. . . there is no hope to be placed in human or technological or political expedients . . .' See his Letter to Jean and Hildegard Goss-Mayr in William H Shannon (ed), *The Hidden Ground of Love: The Letters of*

Merton was and remained too 'catholic' (in the sense he himself defined) to give Jesus Christ the *kind* of centrality that he holds for the peace churches or for Barth.[11] His monastic (and monistic) anthropology, which finds God in the void within the contemplative process, has classically had less room (or less need) for either the historical particularity of Jesus the Jew or the epistemological centrality of Jesus the Logos. But since Merton was not a systematic writer, the place where we should look for a turning toward a christological fulcrum for protest is not in his theoretical moves (usually expressed only in offhand ways), but in his public ministry. In 1964 Merton moved dialogically toward the leaders of the pacifist movement, including those of the Catholic Peace Fellowship (Dorothy Day, Tom Cornell, James Forest, Daniel and Philip Berrigan, Gordon Zahn), the Fellowship of Reconciliation (represented in the November 'retreat' by Abraham J Muste and J Oliver Nelson),[12] and the historic peace churches. In his reading Merton was well acquainted with Protestant thought, but it was new that he should include a non-Catholic heritage in his churchmanship. I was never invited back to Gethsemani,[13] but for the next two years I received unsolicited numerous of his mimeographed non-imprimatured 'publications'.

Thomas Merton on Religious Experience and Social Concerns (New York: Farrar, Straus & Giroux, 1985), 335. This was the impact of the coinciding of (a) the criticism of technology in the terms of Jacques Ellul and (b) Pauline language about the principalities and powers. It confirms my inchoate impression at the time that neither my review of the minority peace church identity nor my christological appeal seemed particularly interesting to him.

11. This is what Merton held against Barth. In *Conjectures of a Guilty Bystander* (Garden City, NY: Doubleday, 1966; Image Books, 1968), Merton refers to Karl Barth several times, but contrasts Barth unfavourably with Bonhoeffer (see pp 201, 316). Many of the allusions use Barth only as a code reference to the systematic theological notion of the uniqueness of the Word of God, which (according to Merton's undocumented allusions) Bonhoeffer critiques in a more 'catholic' way. Bonhoeffer, he writes, is nearer to the Catholic view by being more open to general human wisdom and goodness.

12. Merton corresponded more frequently with John Heidbrink, FoR's church-relations secretary, but back surgery prevented Heidbrink from attending the November retreat. Merton was also in touch with Hildegard and Jean Goss-Mayr of the International FoR.

13. As his letters indicate, Merton's freedom for outside contacts was more limited from then on.

The other way in which Merton broke his mould was by his growing investment in communication. He remained committed to the practice and theory of mysticism, as dramatised by his final trip to Asia. He remained residentially solitary. Yet he never stopped writing, editing, commenting, investing his energy in the ephemeral, as if lay people would be helped more by his words than by his silence and intercession. What he wrote was intentionally ephemeral, not timeless: he wrote book reviews like the essays in *Faith and Violence* (1968) and fragmentary reflections on watching the world go by ('guilty bystander'). He may have done this partly on the grounds that commentary of that kind was less likely to be censored than would, for instance, a full-dress review of the just-war tradition.[14] Thus 'incarnation' entered the particularity of the contemporary, rather than preferring the generality of a universalizable nonviolent ethic.

The turns in Martin Luther King's life were his brushes with death: the bombing of his home, the stabbing in New York. His decision to move on in his public work unimpeded by the knowledge of danger was firm and in fact public. He spoke with increasing openness of his impending martyrdom, in a way that would have come to seem rhetorically overdone if it had not come true. The 'power of innocent suffering' had been part of his standard speeches at least since his visit to India, but to face one's own likely death raises that notion to a higher power. The concentration of attention on suffering, risk and having the faith to move on nevertheless drew on deeper roots in his black Baptist piety than he had needed before, although (since Jesus-language is already omnipresent in that culture) he did not belabour the point of defining that deepening as linked to Jesus' teachings and example.

---

14. He remained concerned to clarify that protest against the Vietnam war was not pacifism (cf *Faith and Violence*, 5). In two letters to *Commonweal* (printed on 2 April and 5 May 1965, pp 62 and 202 of vol 82), he made it clear that his rejection of the Vietnam war was an application of the just-war tradition.

3. War

Each of the three men moved farther than he had intended toward a principled Christian pacifism. None started there; none really arrived there; yet the directional movement was undeniable. Barth was explicitly opposed to pacifism and was on bad terms with the pacifists he knew. He considered pacifism to be a moralism and held Leonhard Ragaz, the pacifist he knew best, to be an erratic and rigid person. Hitler had to be defeated, although it was somehow acceptable that Switzerland, the nation most qualified to make war for the freedom of the church, did not have to enter the war.

Yet by 1950 Barth was making the burden of proof that war as *ultima ratio* must bear more demanding than any other Protestant ethicist.[15] Then in response to the rearmament of Germany and the impact of thinking about nuclear weapons, he became a categorical nuclear pacifist.[16] As his *Church Dogmatics* progressed from ethics in the context of the sanctity of created life (vol III) to the sanctification of the disciple in redemption (vol IV), he saw no way to exclude 'practical pacifism'.[17]

Merton's first decisive emergence into literary public life was in response to the civil rights troubles of the USA. He first appropriated nonviolence as a tactic and as a spirituality, but avoided dealing with it as an ethic. In his early reading of Gandhi and in *Faith and Violence*, nonviolence is primarily a matter of spirituality and lifestyle. Merton was disinclined to make it an ethical imperative. Only gradually did the escalation of the Vietnam tragedy oblige him to become firmer about war as a moral challenge for its own sake. As his condemnation of the war became more vocal, however, he was most concerned lest the protesters be impatient or self-righteous. Stopping the evil being done on the other side of the globe was less worrisome to him than the danger that the militants might forfeit their inner peace.[18]

---

15. See my *Karl Barth and the Problem of War* (Nashville: Abingdon Press, 1970).
16. See my *Karl Barth and the Problem of War*, 133-37.
17. Karl Barth, *Church Dogmatics* IV/2 (Edinburgh: T&T Clark, 1958), 550.
18. See his 'Letter to an activist' (Jim Forest), cited by Patricia McNeal, *Harder Than War: Catholic Peacemaking in Twentieth-Century America* (Rutgers University Press, 1992), 125f. Cf Zahn (ed), *The Nonviolent Alternative*, xxxv and 67: 'I am not a pacifist'.

King's commitment to nonviolence was principled from early on, then enriched and reinforced by what he learnt from his trip to India. Yet there were good reasons for him not to preach or argue aggressively in favour of nonviolence on the level of principled ethics. First, he was leading a multifaceted coalition, most of whose lieutenants accepted him as their figurehead, strategist, or co-ordinator, but did not accept his ethic.

Second, leadership demanded, or seemed to demand, certain 'manly' postures, for example, combativeness and confrontation. Especially does decisiveness in a leader appear to be spiritually indispensable when people long oppressed need to assume their God-given dignity. Authentic principled nonviolence is not contrary to decisiveness, but superficially many think that it is.

Third, the immediate practical political goals of black empowerment needed, and enjoyed to some extent, the support of the federal government. The Southern Christian Leadership Conference was a single-cause agency. If it were to take on all the other sins of the nation it might jeopardise its primary mission. Thus many of King's friends in the movement thought he should not speak out against the war in Vietnam, even though they also opposed it.

Nevertheless, after much slow struggle within himself and with his staff, King came out with a trumpet blast against the Vietnam war.[19] He thereby took on one more kind of innocent suffering, being punished from then on with ostracism by the Johnson government for forsaking the Great Society coalition.

4. The beloved community

None of these men stated expressly any preoccupation for measuring his work by the classical criterion of ecclesiology. Each of them began with the assumptions we associate with 'Christendom', that is, that moral discourse assumes the whole ('Christian') culture, not only as arena but also as agent. Each of them remained all his life in an establishment denomination. Yet at the edge of his thought each began to be aware of a need to discern the difference between the committed community of disciples and the wider society within which the church

---

19. On 4 April 1967, exactly one year before his assassination, King addressed an audience convened by Clergy and Laity Concerned in Manhattan's Riverside Church, part of the legacy of the same Rockefeller millions that created Spelman and Morehouse Colleges.

testifies and which the church calls to faith. A distinguishable believing community is the prerequisite for a pattern of moral thought in which Jesus Christ (rather than some lesser value like the well-being of the nation) is the norm, and for a nonviolent social ethic, even if none of these three men thought it through that way.

Although Dorothy Day was profoundly respectful of episcopacy and many things Roman, the Catholic Worker movement, where both Merton and the more active younger men who worried him found resources for thinking counter-culturally, was sociologically a 'believers' church'. Merton remained vowed to submissive symbiosis within the larger 'catholic' world; but he became increasingly restive in later years, and his ministry through the press and the mail gathered around him a different kind of supportive community.

The Confessing Church, which haltingly grew up around the Barmen Declaration, had the potential to be a 'free church', although its leaders were not equipped with the concepts nor blessed with the leisure to work through what it would have meant to be a free church.[20] When Karl Barth challenged infant baptism and the church's compact with western nationalism, he was moving toward a free-church vision.[21]

Since King was a Baptist and therefore belonged to a movement that is already theoretically and formally a free church, although sociologically established (in both black and white experience in the South), the criteria that would indicate his taking his distance from 'establishment' mentalities can not be the traditional ones such as adult baptism or the separation of church and state. Yet his readiness to

---

20. The one exception was Franz Hildebrandt, who left Germany for England (partly because of his clear difference with Bonhoeffer and others on the issue of creating a free church structure) and became a Methodist and a Wesley scholar. He was one of three surviving Barmen signatories when in 1984 he attended a commemorative conference at the University of Washington. In the 1930s 'Freikirche' did not mean a church enjoying evangelical liberty, but a small group without political status. The term designated Methodists, Baptists, Mennonites and Brethren, all of which were small and pietistic. Their effort to be apolitical made some of them uncritical of Nazi plans to take over the large churches.

21. See my essay, 'Karl Barth: How His Mind Kept Changing', in Donald K McKim (ed), *How Karl Barth Changed My Mind* (Grand Rapids, MI: Eerdmans, 1985), 166-71. In his final years Barth welcomed new contacts with Moravians and Mennonites.

jeopardise Lyndon Johnson's support for the sake of a moral stance and his entry into new arenas of conflict where his black Baptist culture had little clout (such as fair housing in Chicago) were indices of his growing awareness that the people of God whose dreams he spoke for was both smaller than and larger than America. He began to preach that 'We shall overcome' is not true without the cross. While ready to accept that some of his coalition partners made nonviolence a tactic rather than an integral aspect of faith, in his own leadership role he refused to let go of the deontological moral claim and the evangelical call to commitment.

When the three men died in 1968, they were no closer to each other's worlds, or to each other, than when they started out. Each had soon become aware of his own specialness, accustomed to finding easily a respectful hearing. Had they met they would not have found conversation easy. Yet in ways beyond the self-aware wisdom of any of them, they were on the same pilgrimage.

An Unmistakable Accent: Remembering Dietrich Bonhoeffer

Frank Nichol

Those of us fortunate enough to reach maturity during World War II found ourselves in a theological and church context characterised by dramatic developments, portentous events and intensive discussion and debate. The church, along with other groups, faced fundamental questions about the direction of, and prospects for, western civilisation, indeed, the human enterprise as a whole. This occasioned a searching reassessment of developments in Germany that had engendered the rise of Hitler and Nazism, as well as prompting wondering thoughts about the way forward from the ruins of Europe. The meaning of Christian faith and the viability of the church, both its product and bearer, seemed called into radical question, crying out once more for reformation and re-evaluation, contending again for its pertinence and integrity.

Onto this stage strode the then reputed giants of theology, regularly engaged in earnest and often bitter controversy over matters obscure yet evidently invested with profound significance for the Christian community. Some, like the protagonists of the ecumenical movement, conveyed a sense of practical urgency and exhilarating promise, while others who busied themselves with doctrinal and scriptural reinterpretation frequently succeeded in bemusing as much as enlightening. On one hand, the World Council of Churches came into being with resounding success and actual unions of churches were negotiated and brought to fruition. On the other hand, however, Karl Barth and Emil Brunner could be overheard quarrelling fretfully over whether the Word of God required a 'point of contact' with humanity. At the same time, Barth and Rudolf Bultmann were falling out over the question of hermeneutics, while Paul Tillich set about constructing his visionary and omnicompetent System, compiled with all the *gravitas* of an elder statesman who had been through it all before.

Yet, just as it began to appear that these voices would set the parameters for most future discussion, another began to be heard.

Speaking the same language, Dietrich Bonhoeffer's accent nevertheless differed distinctively from that of other partners in the conversation, compelling immediate attention. Bonhoeffer had shared as deeply and as critically as any other in the struggle for the soul of German Protestantism. Moreover, he had suffered the fate of a martyr at the hands of a Nazi hangman, a final sealing, were any needed, of his uniquely passionate and faithful involvement with his people and his Lord.

From his posthumous *Letters and Papers from Prison*,[1] Bonhoeffer emerged as a gentle, attractive, sensitive human being, deeply imbued with the highest values of the civilisation from which his aristocratic stock had sprung, and able to express himself with clarity and feeling in the moving verse to which he sometimes resorted. It was plain that here was a mind that had drunk as deeply at the same springs as his colleagues (as all the acknowledged 'great ones' were) and a heart that, out of a responsive natural compassion whetted by mutuality of membership in the Christian community with 'all sorts and conditions' of people, was able to appreciate, assess and understand the human state as it had to be endured by his contemporaries.

Those of us who began to read his writings as they became available felt ourselves drawn into the presence of one who shared uniquely in both church and world as we had experienced both, if only at a distance and as relative dilettantes, yet from a vantage point not dissimilar to his. In short, we encountered recognisable imperatives and commitments spelt out in his luminous and challenging pages.

It should be remembered, however, that while there were giants and 'mighty men of valour' in the land, there were also ogres, for the heyday was beginning of those critical philosophers (some in the clothing of theologians) who were asking whether there was any real sense to religious and theological language. We were all forced to wonder whether, in the end, all our 'God-talk' might not be empty sounds, signifying nothing, all our patient researches rendered pathetically void, or reduced at best to well-meant floral tributes on the grave of God or, worse, unmasked as the ideological posturings of self-serving lackeys of the political establishment.

---

1. Dietrich Bonhoeffer, *Letters and Papers from Prison*, ed Eberhard Bethge (London: SCM Press, 1953; enlarged edition, 1971). These *Letters and Papers from Prison* comprise vol 8 of the English edition of *Dietrich Bonhoeffer Works* published by Augsburg Fortress.

To this situation, too, the witness of Bonhoeffer spoke with telling effect. By no means the least attractive nuance of his writings was the directness, naturalness, robustness and unpretentiousness of Bonhoeffer's speech about God. No shrill cry here of the demagogue evangelist secure in his little, untroubled world of self-induced certitude; nothing either of the exaggerated caution of the chastened linguistic analyst gingerly picking his way through a minefield of possible existential commitments. Instead, borne through the very fires of hell, here was speech about God that did not hesitate to count on and evoke the divine presence in a powerful and persuasive way.

Paradoxically, Bonhoeffer also claimed our attention by the way in which he was able, from the depths of his own conviction, not only to acknowledge and measure the depth of the contemporary sense of God's absence but also to interpret it theologically. It may be that in this bold stroke and what flows from it is to be found his most positive and creative contribution to our theological and ethical thinking.

With no breath of self-contradiction, Bonhoeffer was able to speak of God deliberately withdrawing from human consciousness in such a way as to liberate us for authentic human existence before God, in the presence of God and for God. On 16 July 1944 he wrote to his friend, Eberhard Bethge:

> . . . we cannot be honest unless we recognize that we have to live in the world *etsi deus non daretur*. And this is just what we do recognize—before God! God himself compels us to recognize it. So our coming of age leads us to a true recognition of our situation before God. God would have us know that we must live as men who manage our lives without him. The God who is with us is the God who forsakes us (Mark 15:34). The God who lets us live in the world without the working hypothesis of God is the God before whom we stand continually. Before God and with God we live without God. God lets himself be pushed out of the world on to the cross. He is weak and powerless in the world, and that is precisely the

> way, the only way, in which he is with us and helps us.[2]

Alongside these daring thoughts, we see Bonhoeffer venturing his radical notion of 'coming of age', part and parcel of the entire vision of 'life before God' he was intimating. This aspect of his proposals, which occasioned a good deal of frowning and puzzled misgiving, probably directly provoked the lively 'secularisation' discussion of the 1960s, as well as sparking off the 'death of God' debate. How far he would have welcomed either must remain uncertain, and opinions as to the value of both will no doubt remain divided.

However, I would like to indicate where we might attempt to follow this seminal thinker in our time, a venture I feel sure he would wish us to take up. There are some points at which I believe him to have had more to say to us than we may have wished to hear and which could do with more development.

First, we should note the profound and radical development of Bonhoeffer's *Christology*, a continuing preoccupation from his earliest years. He gave seminal lectures on this topic at the beginning of his teaching career. Well aware though he must have been of the 'Quest for the historical Jesus', he appears to have shown little interest in the character and career of Jesus, just as he remained cool to other questions about Christianity's historical rootage and background. He had, it would seem, bigger fish to fry.

Steeped as he was in the Lutheran tradition, Bonhoeffer assumed an 'orthodox' Christology of the two natures in one person. Yet he developed it in characteristic ways, whose emphases continued to shape his writing to the end, where we find him striking out in noteworthy directions. For Bonhoeffer, Jesus Christ is primarily the one in whom no less than God has come to dwell among us human beings, and in whom God bestows unconditional divine fellowship upon us, claiming us for the privileges and costs attendant upon that blessed involvement. In one of his earliest works, *The Communion of Saints*,[3] he endeavoured to show that it is the church, a real, human, sociological reality, that is the *locus* of God's presence in our world. He coined the

2. Bonhoeffer, *Letters and Papers from Prison*, 360. See also Eberhard Bethge, *Dietrich Bonhoeffer: Theologian, Christian, Contemporary* (London: Collins, 1970), 772.
3. Dietrich Bonhoeffer, *Sanctorum Communio: A Theological Study of the Sociology of the Church*, *DBWE* 1 (Minneapolis: Augsburg Fortress, 1998).

provocative phrase, 'Christ existing as the Church', which drew Karl Barth's plaudits as he embarked on his own ecclesiology.

Thus we are pointed to the powerful role that Bonhoeffer's experience of the fellowship of the church, and his conviction of the mutual solidarity into which it binds us, played in his thinking. It was expressed when he championed the cause of Jewish pastors threatened by German Christian zeal, as well as in his deep sense of liturgical and ecclesiastical communion that informed the life of his underground seminary and pervades his little book, *Life Together*.[4]

Bonhoeffer saw clearly that Christian life is essentially communal life, participation in a reconciled and reconciling fellowship characterised by unconditional reciprocal acceptance, rooted in baptism and realised, renewed, expressed and received in the mystery of the Eucharistic feast and presence. If this indebtedness to the concrete society that is the actual 'visible' church led him to adopt a stance uncomfortably close to hard-nosed 'confessionalism', it also ensured that the 'hard nose' was unflinchingly applied to the grindstone of human reality as he pondered his sharpest question: Who is Jesus Christ for us today? This in turn led him to further depths of critical reflection, thereby producing his trenchant formulation, 'Jesus, the Man for others'.

Simplistic though such a formulation may sound, in Bonhoeffer's hands it was pregnant with all the depths of Reformation (especially Lutheran) Christology, which he inherited, explored and extended with the teeming insights of his last years. Luther's Christology emphasised the way in which the Incarnation gave us access to God, in so far as God gave Godself to us, pouring out (*kenosis*) the divine nature into a creature who is 'bone of our bone and flesh of our flesh'. In Jesus Christ God is God *for us* and *with us*, accessible and available to us. There is no 'hidden', 'majestic', 'transcendent' God beyond or behind this self-giving God, no obscure, possibly threatening, enigma somewhere in the background who might be different from this gracious God.

When we read the last writings of 'the man for others', this is what we should bear in mind. Bonhoeffer was not thinking primarily, or even at all, of the demeanour of the historical person, Jesus, and his

---

4. Dietrich Bonhoeffer, *Life Together and Prayerbook of the Bible*, *DBWE* 5 (Minneapolis: Augsburg Fortress, 1996).

purported 'openness to others', of which much is sometimes made homiletically. Rather should we paraphrase these words as something like: 'Jesus, the man in whom God is with us only for others'. What was rejected is any thought of a relationship with God that threatens to lure us into some 'special', 'spiritual', transcendent sphere in which spirituality may remain immaculate, untainted by contact with the concrete reality of the world. Or differently put, this God, in being *pro me* in Jesus Christ, thereby turns me around so that I dare not remain 'curved in upon myself', but am now claimed to exist for others, firmly directed outward from my own preoccupations. Still more, the implications for the church are revolutionary: the church is essentially a community whose doors are open to 'outsiders'. It is now, in principle and in essence, to use Hoekendijk's vivid phrase, 'The Church Inside Out'.[5]

In Jesus Christ God exists for the sake of the world, not (to put it too sharply) for God's own sake. But this existence 'for the other' is exactly the peculiar transcendence, the 'difference' that makes God God. Unlike us, God is 'free' to give Godself away, without thereby forfeiting Godhood, but rather thereby exhibiting and affirming it.

In contrast to Barth, whose account of God's transcendence emphasised 'wholly otherness', Bonhoeffer used the thought of God's freedom in a thoroughly positive way. In this respect Bonhoeffer considered Barth to be unduly negative and cautious. Whereas Barth had won a signal theological victory, and an urgently necessary one, by stressing God's 'freedom from' creation, for Bonhoeffer the time had come to speak up for God's 'freedom for' the creature, a line Barth later adopted in his celebrated essay of 1956, 'The Humanity of God'.[6] While Bonhoeffer approved and applauded Barth's theology as signalling God's liberation from servitude as the domestic idol of 'culture-Protestantism', he complained that Barth's apparently chilly scorn for human values and insights had the effect of 'leaving the world to its own devices'.

Further, we have noted that Bonhoeffer sprang from aristocratic stock and had learned to value the strengths of that background. In his conduct he manifested the costly self-discipline, fastidiousness, loyalty and patriotism (in 1939 he returned to Germany from New York to be

---

5. Johannes Christian Hoekendijk, *The Church Inside Out* (London: SCM Press, 1967).
6. See Karl Barth, *The Humanity of God* (Atlanta: John Knox Press, 1960).

among his people in their ordeal!) characteristic of his class, of whose bourgeois complexion he was well aware. In the 'religionless' world of which he was sharply and increasingly conscious, he was not willing to leave his struggling fellow humans with only a terrifying sense of an empty world and with no lights to guide them. No, he believed that God's being *for* human beings (real, concrete humanity) means that God cherishes, nourishes and upholds the person who stands by what he or she understands to be true, noble and right, and who implicates himself or herself in guilt in its implementation. Thus the churchman who took part in the 'July plot' against Hitler's life wrote with proleptic insight: 'Only now are the Germans beginning to discover the meaning of free responsibility. It depends on a God who demands responsible action in a bold venture of faith, and who promises forgiveness and consolation to the man who becomes a sinner in that venture.'[7]

In Bonhoeffer's thinking we have attractive suggestions for a Christian approach to ethical questions. These may preserve the integrity of ethical traditions, convictions and perceived obligations while at the same time drawing upon the critical and creative resources of Christian faith. The latter is not in competition with the former. Faith does not propose some divinely given, binding code or set of rules, some authoritative alternative strategy for problem-solving or an ultimate recipe, divinely sanctioned, for a 'better world'. Rather, faith brings the conviction of God's effective presence, inviting, calling for, human responsibility for humankind. God also offers support for those who step out into that responsibility and risk. This is the point, perhaps, to pick up John A Phillips's suggestion,[8] of the role of the church as it emerged in Bonhoeffer's earlier thinking: 'Christ existing as the church', the community in the midst of human affairs holding out the possibility and reality of *support and encouragement, fellowship and forgiveness* to moral agents at risk. The church is thus the sign and mediator of God's *renewing and effective presence* in the human situation. Bonhoeffer's ethic is thus one of *witness* rather than *prescription.*

---

7. Bonhoeffer, *Letters and Papers from Prison*, 6.
8. John A Phillips, *The Form of Christ in the World: A Study of Bonhoeffer's Christology* (London: Collins, 1967), 48-56.

Bonhoeffer was able to give a positive account of the values, obligations, imperatives and commitments we inherit from our cultural traditions. Barth seemed to fear they would intrude a human idolatry between us and the divine command. But Bonhoeffer saw how they are intrinsic to human creatureliness, expressions of the realisation of our freedom, our genuinely independent dignity before God, marks of our particular identity that God also savours. He was even able to conceive of God actively inviting, encouraging and fostering our admittedly critical reliance on them. Bonhoeffer was really interested in, and committed to, the possibility and the gift of genuine human integrity before God.

He readily acknowledged human responsibility for history and the future, which is to be effectively shaped for coming generations. However, it is not for us to mind God's business in God's 'absence'. Nevertheless, his keen sense of God's presence in no way leads to quietism or resignation; on the contrary, it is the spur and the prompt to responsible and effective action.

We may not leave our remembrances of Bonhoeffer without referring to his plainly central thoughts about *God's suffering*. This striking and distinctive theme points to the goal and shape of the Christian life, which is no less than 'to participate in the sufferings of God in a Godless world'. This is a role reversal, indeed, and one that not only casts an entirely different light on the Christian life, but also puts an end to triumphalism on the part of the church. The thought of God's suffering has been largely alien to traditional theology, but Bonhoeffer seems to have been forced to it by his determination to control his theology with radical Christology. If God in Christ became fully exposed to the realities of human life, then that meant exposure to all the tensions, weaknesses, claims and limitations amidst which humans must exist, without recourse to the 'escape route' available to the *deus ex machina*. The privilege of the Christian is to find fellowship *with* God *in* this situation, not beyond, above or removed and insulated from it. So Bonhoeffer dared to write:

Men go to God when he is sore bestead,
Find him poor and scorned, without shelter or bread,
Whelmed under weight of the wicked, the weak, the
  dead;
Christians stand by God in his hour of grieving.[9]

Christians who share in God's weakness may nevertheless 'live from the transcendent' by recourse to the 'secret discipline' whereby the foundational realities of Christian faith remain accessible to sustain endurance and persistence. For Bonhoeffer would have nothing to do with cheap, ham-fisted deployment of 'Christian truths' to brush off the challenges of this-worldly life.

There can be no doubt that the church was fortunate indeed to experience a theologian of Bonhoeffer's insight and creativity, even if his contribution has been largely forgotten and obscured. Necessarily fragmentary though his contribution is, it may be confidently expected to continue to challenge theologians and their kin for a long time to come. For the church will always need such as 'this astonishing, disturbing and comforting man'. He is before us in the inscription in the church at Flossenbürg, near the place of his execution:

> *Dietrich Bonhoeffer, a witness of Jesus Christ among his brethren. Born 4th February 1906 in Breslau. Died 9th April 1945 at Flossenbürg.*

9. Bonhoeffer, *Letters and Papers from Prison*, 348-49.

God of Compassion

Charles Birch

There are three creative acts that characterise God's compassion for the world. First, in every event we are addressed by God's compassionate love. Not only we, but all creation is also addressed by God's compassionate love. But how can we affirm this in the face of the agony and tragedy of the world?

Second, in every event we are ourselves to be compassionate. One translation of Mt 5:48 reads: 'Be you compassionate as your heavenly father is compassionate.' But what does that mean for Australia, which in the mid-1990s had the largest gap between the 'haves' and 'have-nots' of any OECD country and in which one million people were unemployed, fifty thousand cases of child abuse occurred each year and the Aboriginal child death rate was the highest in the world?

Third, in every event what we do makes a difference to God. This has to do with God's response to the world. It is the least understood aspect of divine compassion. George Matheson wrote:

> O Love that will not let me go,
> I rest my weary soul in thee:
> I give thee back the life I owe,
> that in thine ocean depths its flow
> may richer, fuller be.

1. God is all compassion, pure unbounded love

As I think of this I go back in memory to my childish faith, in which I was taught that God is omnipotent, that God is king, that God is judge. God can do anything, I was taught. I can no longer believe in a God like that.

Now I see God as always acting in the world as compassionate and persuasive love, infinitely patient and never acting by coercion. Let me illustrate this by contrasting the meanings of divine design and divine purpose.

The creative possibilities of God are not in the form of a blueprint for the future. Therefore it is misleading to speak of 'divine design'. The term 'design' implies a preconceived pattern. 'Divine purpose' is better because it does not have the same connotation. Nothing is completely determined; the future is open-ended. One reason for this is that God is not the sole cause of everything that happens. God exercises causality always in relation to beings with their own measure of self-determination—from protons to people and all the creative entities in between. The world lives by its incarnation of God in itself, not by external intervention.

What then do we mean by divine providence? I once thought it meant a divine plan by which everything was predetermined, as in an efficient machine. My job was to find out where I fitted into that plan. I now see things differently. For me, divine providence now means that there is a creative and saving possibility in every situation that cannot be destroyed by any event. So the Psalmist speaks of God:

> Whither shall I go from thy Spirit? Or whither shall I flee from thy presence? If I ascend to heaven, thou art there! If I make my bed in Sheol, thou art there! If I take the wings of the morning and dwell in the uttermost parts of the sea, even there thy hand shall lead me, and thy right hand shall hold me (Psalm 139:7-10).

God's creative influence can meet me in any situation, however dire, as a new creative possibility to transform my present circumstances. God is persuasive love that is never coercive. I spoke on one occasion to a bevy of Anglican bishops about evolution and creation. I presented the case for creative evolution as a response to the persuasive lure of God. One bishop asked, 'Why can't we have it both ways—God as persuasive love *and* God acting coercively by intervening from time to time?" My problem with the latter is twofold. First, I find no evidence for God's intervention in the world. I add that most problems about God are problems related to our understanding of the world. Second, the view of a manipulating, coercive God makes God malevolent. If God could have stopped the Jewish holocaust and didn't, then God is wicked. An earthly parent who stands by and watches while his or her child is killed by a madman is also guilty.

When Jesus overturned the tables of the usurers in the temple, he coerced a few tables but he didn't coerce anybody. His was not an act of coercion but of confrontation. That is the nature of divine activity.

Let me say as sharply as I can that God's use of persuasion is not based on voluntary self-limitation. God cannot choose from time to time to interfere coercively here and there at will. God does not put up special umbrellas to protect the faithful against this or that disaster, nor does God authorise any particular disaster. Some have said to me that this view limits God if he does not have complete control. But is God limited if he cannot work any nonsense in the world when he wants to, such as to create a stone so heavy that he could not carry it? It is also absurd to suppose that to carry out his work God cannot do so within the order of nature, as we have to, but has to destroy his creation to do his work.

Is God then powerless? The paradox is that in the end the only power that matters is that of persuasive love. It is the form of power that empathises with others and empowers them.

2. Our response to God's persuasive compassionate love

God acts by being felt by his creatures. In every event we are addressed by God (Martin Buber). God confronts what is actual in the world with what is possible for it. God elicits a response from creatures. A note on a tuning fork can elicit a response from a piano because the piano is fitted with a string tuned to the same note. So it is with God and the entities of creation. God acts in human life by being felt by us as persuasive love that is transforming. This is incarnation. Since the councils of the third century, traditional Christianity has restricted the word 'incarnation' to the presence of God in Jesus. Yet the Bible speaks of God as incarnate in all creation, for example, the references to the God of 'all things' in the first chapter of Colossians. All things subsist in God and are subjects of God's persuasive love. This is repeated six times in five verses.

The only adequate human response to God's compassionate love is to respond 'with all our heart and mind and strength' or, to use Paul Tillich's phrase, with 'infinite passion'. Because Jesus knew God to be compassionate and forgiving, he consorted with those who most needed compassion and forgiveness. The proposition of the group called 'Reworking Australia' concerning Australia's one million unemployed was: 'It is crucial to shift from some of the people having all of the work to all of the people having some of the work.' Jesus' message to Simon Peter was, 'If you love me, feed my sheep'. The message was simple. When you give food to the hungry, water to the thirsty, clothing to the naked, comfort to the distressed, companionship to the rejected and imprisoned, you are giving to Christ himself (see Mt 25:31-46).

But it is not only our fellow humans who need our compassion. The whole of creation is waiting for liberation from its bondage and decay. It is all there in Rom 8:18-25, which makes it clear that this liberation is directly linked to the emergence of God's new family, which is already experiencing 'the glorious freedom of the children of God'. This vision is a mandate for action in the environmental crisis by those who have already experienced 'the first fruits of the Spirit'. A redeemed community is the key to the redemption of creation. Why else would the writer picture creation as 'waiting in eager expectation for the sons of God to be revealed'? People are part of nature. If there is any true redemption at all, it must be a redemption of nature, including our nature. So it has always been. As soon as humans appeared on the world's stage, nature faced a new danger. I suggest that the 'fall' of humanity is not something that occurred at one time in the past; rather, it occurs every moment that our actual life falls short of the creative possibilities for that moment.

3. God's response to the world

God's response to the world is the least understood aspect of divine compassion. In the classical view, God is said to be loving yet without emotion, feeling or sensitivity to the feelings of others, including those of the whole creation. Aristotle said it first: God is mover of all things, unmoved by any. Aristotle's God is totally unaffected by what happens in the world. The same is true of the God of Saint Anselm, the God of Saint Thomas Aquinas and the God described in the first of the Thirty-nine articles in the Anglican Prayer Book: 'There is but one living and true God, everlasting, *without body, parts, or passions*; of infinite power, wisdom, and goodness; the Maker, and Preserver of all things both visible and invisible.' I can't believe in a God without passion.

Real love is reciprocal. Love that leaves the lover unaffected by the joys and sufferings of the one who is loved is not worthy of being called love.

Whatever we do makes a difference to God. God experiences the world's life in all its joys and its agonies. God must have experienced the holocaust, the excruciating suffering of the tormented. God must have felt the satisfaction of the tormenters and must have been tormented by them. God must have experienced the agony of D-Day at Normandy, with thousands perishing in a sea of blood. According to the Jewish scholar, Abraham Heschel, the 'pathos of God' is the central idea of prophetic theology in the Bible. We find God's pathos movingly expressed in Romans 8. God is not a playwright who observes the play from a distance. God is on stage with all the players, 'feeling every feeling in ways that words cannot express'. Not a sparrow falls to the ground without God knowing (and feeling) it.

In every event we are addressed by God's compassion. In every event we are to express God's compassion. In every event what we do makes a difference to God. In this vision of the divine who is not the supreme autocrat but the universal agent of persuasion, whose power is the worship he inspires and who feels all the feelings of the world, I find not only a new way of understanding the world, but also a new way of facing the tasks of today—the human crisis and the environmental crisis.

'A Grandeur Too Overwhelming to Express': Patrick White's Vision of God

Veronica Brady IBVM

'What I am interested in is the relationship between the blundering human being and God.'
—Patrick White (1912–1990)

Not every Christian would regard Patrick White as a religious writer. Interestingly, many secular readers do. Indeed, the religious strain in his work has led many critics to suspect him. To the 'realist' critics of the 1950s and 1960s, it was anathema. More recently, structuralist and post-structuralist critics have joined forces with Jungians like David Tacey to suggest either that White's religious interests were fraudulent or that they do not matter.

Throughout his career, however, White himself insisted on his interest in the question of God and maybe we have something to learn from him. In his autobiography *Flaws in the Glass* he wrote,

> What do I believe? I am accused of not making it explicit. How to be explicit about a grandeur too overwhelming to express, a daily wrestling match with an opponent whose limbs never become material, a struggle from which the sweat and blood are scattered on the pages of anything the serious writer writes?

Some might be troubled by the phrase, 'whose limbs never become material', since for Christians God was 'made flesh' in Jesus. But what White was talking about is the sheer otherness, the 'Godness', of God, who is 'unapproachably distant and unutterably strange' (Karl Barth), the permanent crisis confronting all human understanding.

For that reason White may have something important to say to those of us who tend to take the word 'God' for granted, something that may disturb but may therefore also be an occasion of grace. It is all too easy to construct God in our own image. White's vision reminds us that, as Karl Barth put it in his *Epistle to the Romans*, 'the activity of the [Christian] community is related to the Gospel only in so far as it is no more than a crater formed by the explosion of a shell and seeks to be no more than a void in which the Gospel reveals itself'.

White was critical of people who use the word 'God' as a cosmic security blanket. While many of us are content to use the word 'God' sentimentally, working off our feelings in words rather than deeds, White was not. 'God is everywhere they told me', he wrote in his autobiography. 'Is he in the bunya-bunya tree? Yes, everywhere. So much of my early life revolved round the bunya halfway up the drive at "Lulworth" I was almost convinced.'

Many of the most unpleasant characters in White's novels are people who call themselves 'good Christians', people like Mrs Jolley and Mrs Flack in *Riders in the Chariot*, the Bonners and their friends in *Voss* and Mr and Mrs Merivale in *A Fringe of Leaves*. In fact, all of them shrink from the 'call to go further', which is the call of faith. Their God is close to the caricature Karl Marx attacked as 'the general ground and consolation' of those who are prosperous and comfortable, the 'spiritualistic *point d'horreur*' of consumer society and, indeed, 'its moral sanction' and 'solemn complement'. They are really secularists because they do not acknowledge any level of reality beyond that of the observable world known to science. They put their trust in science and do not really acknowledge any meaning and purpose that transcends the merely human realm.

In White's work, however, discomfort rather than comfort is usually the mark of God's presence. This is true also of his life. According to his biographer, David Marr, White's definitive experience of God occurred in a moment one rainy day in the 1950s on his farm at Castle Hill. Carrying a tin of slops, he slipped and fell in the mud, covered with slops and cursing. But suddenly he realised how absurd this was; he was cursing someone in whom he said he did not believe. As Marr says, this was the moment of ecstasy in which he apprehended God in all existence around him. It was also the beginning of his faith and of his lifelong search for that presence of which he had fleetingly become aware. Not that his life was suddenly transfigured; he remained cantankerous, capricious and often unkind, and he still drank too much at times. But the centre of his life had changed. The shortest definition of faith is 'interruption'. White's life had been interrupted by 'a grandeur too overwhelming to express'.

All of the main characters in White's novels are engaged in a similar search. Voss, the arrogant man who comes to Australia in the 1860s determined to conquer the country, cross it from east to west and take possession of it by the power of his will, is perhaps the exception. But this exception proves the rule. God's power overturns ours, demands our submission. As Voss journeys further into the desert, he becomes aware of a force larger than himself manifested in the vastness of the desert. At the end, lying helpless and waiting for death, he comes to realise his place: 'I am not God. But man.' Just as importantly, he also glimpses the mystery of the God who shows himself as 'man with a spear in his side', the crucified one.

Since his first novel *Happy Valley*, published in 1939, all of White's books are concerned with the search for some similar point of realisation, of sheer intensity of existence—that point that defies any of our attempts at understanding or possession, which we call God. Scripture describes this point variously as the mysterious bush burning in the desert but never consumed, as the mountain trembling and wreathed in smoke, but also as the 'still, small voice' that called the prophet Elijah out of the desert. For Christians, of course, the supreme image is the Crucified One.

Patrick White had a strong sense of this mystery. His God is not domesticated. As Mrs Volkhov remarks in *The Vivisector*, we are all 'stroked by God'. God's understanding and purposes do not necessarily coincide with ours, and God's love can be terrible, as she realises one day walking along the golf links 'because something or everything had forced me out'. Nearby she sees a wasp nest. 'I got stung not by putting up my hand my hand was put. I was shocked white, it felt . . . It was like red hot needles entering at first very painful then I did not notice any more, only sea and sky as one, and me like a rinsed plate.'

Most of White's main characters live for the possibility of some such encounter. For some it comes at the point of death, as for Elizabeth Hunter in *The Eye of the Storm*. *The Tree of Man* concludes with Stan Parker's vision of himself, an old man seated at the heart of a series of circles in the garden he can no longer care for:

> It was perfectly obvious that the man was seated at the heart of it, and from this heart the trees radiated, with grave movements of life, and beyond them the

> sweep of the vegetable garden . . . All was circumference to the centre, and beyond that the worlds of other circles . . . The last circle but one was the cold and golden bowl of winter, enclosing all that was visible and material.

The final circle, of course, is God, the circle whose point is everywhere and circumference nowhere, the God Stan sees in all this large vision of splendour but also in a gob of spittle. He has found the secret that everything that lives is holy because God loves all things and works in all things, sustaining and empowering them.

Here, too, an explicit reference is made to a certain kind of Christian, the kind who thinks he or she knows all about, indeed, seems sometimes almost to own, God. A young evangelist presents himself before Stan, wanting to convert him, promising to 'show him books'. But Stan is overwhelmed by a sense of mystery. 'If you can understand, at your age, what I have been struggling with all my life, that is a miracle', he thinks as the young man stands before him so sure that he can 'give God' to another.

One is reminded of the contrast Dietrich Bonhoeffer made between 'cheap' and 'costly' grace. 'Cheap grace', he writes, 'means grace sold on the market like cheapjack's wares. The sacraments, the forgiveness of sin, and the consolations of religion are thrown away at cut prices.' But costly grace 'is the Gospel which must be sought again and again, the gift which must be asked for, the door at which [each one] must knock'. In these terms, Stan's position, which resembles that of White himself (a long search for the holy one, a readiness to wait on grace, living in hope and relying, as he put it in his autobiography, on 'moments which remain inklings rather than confirmation') seems closer to genuine faith. 'My work as a writer', White said, 'has always been what I understood as an offering in the absence of other gifts' to this unseen but living and loving God.

This mysterious presence calls White's characters beyond the mere moralising that sometimes does duty for faith. They may not always be respectable or even kind, but one thing they are sure of is that the universe is not closed and that their lives are open to moments of grace such as Mrs Volkhov's glimpse of the intensity, which in the same novel the artist Hurtle Duffield dies trying to paint, 'the otherwise unnameable I-N-D-I-G-O' (the colour of paradise). As those within the Protestant tradition will understand, this grace exceeds our human sinfulness, and Hurtle is a destructive human being. Similarly, Elizabeth Hunter, central character of *The Eye of the Storm,* is in many ways the epitome of the rich and emotionally ruthless woman. Yet all her life she longs to recover the vision of sheer being she glimpsed at the eye of a tropical storm and of herself as 'a being, or more likely a flaw at the centre of this jewel of light: the jewel itself, blinding and tremulous at the same time, existed, flaw and all, only by grace'. It is this grace that matters.

Characters like these are very different from and, I suggest, more properly religious than those like Mr Bonner in *Voss* for whom God is an adjunct of his self-esteem:

> Safe in life, safe in death, the merchant liked to feel. In consequence, he had often tried to calculate, for how much and from whom, salvation might be bought and, to ensure that his last entrance would be made through the last cedar door, had begun in secret to subscribe liberal sums to all denominations, including those of which he approved.

This is devastating. But the point White makes here is important. Belief of this kind disables us for life. Mr Bonner loved 'the fortune that rendered him safe, so he considered, from attack by life', and he associated God with that fortune as a further form of insurance. In fact, however, 'the shell-less oyster is not more vulnerable' than any human being. This is the point of *Voss* as a whole, dramatising the way in which Voss's pride in himself and his own powers is overwhelmed.

Pseudo-religious people like Mr Bonner, Mrs Jolley and Mrs Flack in *Riders in the Chariot,* Mrs Poulter in *The Solid Mandala* or Mr and Mrs Merivale in *A Fringe of Leaves* tend to ignore the question of evil and our power to say 'No' to God. Their God often seems to provide them with an exemption from evil. They are thus a long way from the overwhelming vision of Isaiah: 'I am the Lord, and there is no other. I form light and create darkness, I make weal and create woe. I am the Lord who does all these things' (Isa 45:6-7). They are also far away from the vision of the God who was crucified, himself 'made sin' for us, as Paul put it.

White's novels are preoccupied with this question of darkness, and it is this that disturbs many of his readers. But in his novels evil is called evil, not disguised as good. White had a vivid sense of the cruelties people perpetrate, often in the most civilised ways, of social injustices and divisions, and above all, of the painfulness of human history. For example, the memory of the holocaust is at the heart of *Riders in the Chariot*. Nor is it something distant. The Jew, Himmelfarb, dies after a mock crucifixion at the hands of his Australian workmates. *The Solid Mandala* tackles this question of evil even more explicitly. The father of the twins, Arthur and Waldo Brown, burns a copy of Dostoevsky's novel *The Brothers Karamazov* because he is terrified of the vision of God it proposes. As Arthur explains to his brother Waldo, 'It wasn't so much because of the blood, however awful, pouring out where the nails went in. He was afraid to worship some thing. Or body. Which is what I take this Dostoevsky is partly going on about.'

The God we are called to worship may be utterly Other. But God has also allowed himself to suffer the full onslaught of this obligation to worship and to be obedient to God's ways. In his own lesser way, Arthur also suffers this onslaught. A simpleton, a 'dill', by contrast with his intelligent and socially ambitious brother, Arthur is nevertheless gifted with the profound vision of simplicity. Waldo finds this increasingly unbearable because it challenges the pretentious emptiness of his life. He finally turns on Arthur in sheer hatred. Defending himself, Arthur kills Waldo accidentally and is taken away to be imprisoned in an asylum. But new life comes out of this death and this suffering. Mrs Poulter, until now a conventionally religious person, has a new insight into the meaning of God. The plaster image she has constructed for herself collapses 'in a thwack of canvas, a cloud of dust' as she contemplates the sufferings of the world. 'The flat faces of all those Chinese guerrillas or Indonesians . . . dragged out across the dreadful screen. All those Jews in ovens, that was long ago, but still burning, lying in heaps. Lone women bashed up in Mosman, Maroubra, Randwick . . . Little girls held to the ground.' This, she realises, is the suffering in which Arthur is involved. But the novel suggests his suffering echoes that of the Suffering Servant 'wounded for our iniquities and bruised for our sins'. This explains also why White had such a predilection for eccentrics, people somehow different from the rest of us and therefore much more likely to be vulnerable.

This will not be everyone's notion of Christianity. But it is biblical. White was intensely aware of the wisdom that is folly to human reason, the wisdom of the Cross. Like the philosopher, Simone Weil, whose thought influenced him, he believed that apart from rare moments of grace, glimpses of the sheer holiness of God, we know God as the suffering one who because of his love is involved in the pain of the world. This he also saw as the manifestation of God's sheer otherness, the antithesis of all that we regard as power and beauty, the abidingness that is the basis of all creation, which White figures forth in Hurtle Duffield's picture of God as like his parents' kitchen table '. . . which had borne with knives, and children's boots, and hot irons. Mightn't the whole have been finally contained from the beginning in this square-legged, scrubbed-down, honest-to-God, but lacerated table?'

The most extended exploration of this sense of what we may call the darkness of God is in *A Fringe of Leaves*. Here, significantly, the main character is a woman, Ellen Roxburgh. Women perhaps know more of this darkness, bodily as well as socially. Western culture is essentially patriarchal, and our cultural hero is Prometheus, who defied the gods and took possession of the light for himself. But women's bodily existence makes us more aware of our finitude and of our subjection to physical necessity, more aware of the need for the descent into the darkness of life if new life is to emerge.

A Cornish farmer's daughter, Ellen passes through a range of social experiences, marries a gentleman and comes to Australia with him only to be shipwrecked off the Queensland coast in the 1840s. After her husband is killed before her eyes by Aborigines, she becomes their captive and endures physical privations of all kinds until she manages to escape to 'civilisation'. But the key point of her story is a moment in which, desperate with hunger, she eats a piece of human flesh dropped from the dilli bag of one of her captors, themselves driven to extremity. This sounds disgusting. But as White presents it, this is a moment of communion in which she shares the bread of affliction with the rest of suffering humanity, completing her initiation when as a young woman she let herself down into the dark waters of a pool near her father's farm, a kind of baptism, a passing through the darkness of evil that nourished 'the darker needs of her hungry spirit'. She is 'moved' to do what she does in the forest and 'awed by the fact that she had been moved to do it'.

Simone Weil remarked that the point of life is to refuse our love to everything other than God. If God takes us to dark places, God is there in them and will bring us out again. Despite the horror implicit in the 'cannibal' scene, which needs to be read metaphorically rather than literally, it is a moment of joy and fulfilment. The voice here does not command but sings. Ellen is suddenly aware of 'the exquisite innocence of this forest morning, its quiet broken by a single flute-note endlessly repeated'.

This image of the bird, an image of transcendence, recurs after Ellen's return to the convict settlement at Moreton Bay in a shabby little church built by the only other survivor of the shipwreck. Over the altar is painted the legend GOD IS LOVE 'in the wretchedest lettering, in dribbling ochre'. God's grace often comes to us at the end of our human resources. So here, Ellen weeps for the betrayal of her earthly loves. 'All this by bright sunlight in the white chapel. Birds flew, first one, then a second, in at a window and out the opposite. There was little to obstruct, whether flight, thought, or vision.'

After this, she is ready to go on living. She returns to society to marry the kindly merchant Mr Jevons, whose working class origins, like hers, make him socially vulnerable and therefore aware of his human limits. Both of them, however, will continue to search beyond their limits.

White's vision of God may seem harsh, even elitist. But it is neither. Human beings do suffer, and White's sense of God is of one who suffers with us. This God, moreover, is much more available to simple people, to those who are poor in spirit and pure of heart, who are physically hungry or who hunger and thirst after justice, who are afflicted with suffering or are despised and excluded. Indeed, White's dislike of the rich and pretentious is prophetic in its intensity. Nor, finally, is his vision of God always painful. There is great joy in the moments of vision, moments that come often very simply, as, for example, when Amy Parker is looking at the dew glistening on the cabbages in her garden in *The Tree of Man,* or when Arthur Brown is making bread in *The Solid Mandala* or when Himmelfarb and Miss Hare are sitting under a flowering tree in *Riders in the Chariot*. God is never far from Patrick White's world, to be found not only in suffering but, as White wrote, 'less in what is said than in the silences. In patterns on water. A gust of wind. A flower opening.' His vision is always suspended between the seen and unseen. In the profoundly scriptural sense enunciated by the Jewish writer, Edmond Jabès, people called by God are always at home and always on the way:

What are you dreaming of?
—The Land.
—But you are on land.
—I am dreaming of the Land where I will be.
—But we are right in front of each other and we have
our feet on land.
—I know only the stones of the way which leads, as
it is said, to the Land.

White may for that reason always have had a suspicion of formal religion. Nevertheless, his exploration of the question of who God might be has much to say to those of us who are church people. He came back to Australia from England in 1948 in search, he said, of 'a state of silence, simplicity and humility which is the only proper state for the human being as the artist'. To the end of his career he kept searching 'with the drawing of this Love and the voice of this calling' (TS Eliot).

Part III

The Politics of Jesus and Christian Pacifism

Jesus—A Model of Radical Political Action

John Howard Yoder

It would be a mistake to assume that my title has a single self-evident meaning and that my task is simply to demonstrate how Jesus lives up to what 'radical political action' already means in the reader's mind. The word 'radical' has many definitions, some of them fanatical, some angry, some ideological. My task must rather be to describe who Jesus was and how he proceeded, and leave readers free to decide how to label it.

There was no separation between Jesus' thought or teaching and his action or 'career' as a political figure, as there was none between the 'religious' and the 'political' in his time. Yet my description may be more accessible if I tell the story twice, once from the perspective of ideas and once from that of public activity.

1. The good news of the kingdom coming

Everything about the early chapters of the gospel accounts conveys a sense of expectancy: the genealogies, the promises to Zechariah and Mary and Simeon, and the recognition by the shepherds and the magi. The very term 'gospel' signifies news. The first message of John the Baptist, of Jesus, and of the twelve Jesus sent out as messengers was, 'The kingdom is imminent'. Thus the first presupposition of 'radical political action' is the conviction that a real God is really intervening in human affairs to set things right. Jesus' actions were not mere human idealism; they were defined within a context of promises fulfilled and justice about to be implemented. This conviction undercuts the 'business-as-usual' assumptions with which most moral thought begins, on the presupposition (often called 'reason' or 'the nature of things') that profound change is not possible.

Jesus' Sermon on the Mount begins with this sense of newness. His phrase, 'Blessed are those who . . .', marks the contrast between the character of the imminent rule of God and what went before in clearly counter-cultural ways (see Mt 5:1-16). His declaration in Mt 5:20 that 'your righteousness must be greater than that of the scribes and Pharisees' spells out this newness in the form of six specific sample antitheses to the previously dominant ('you have heard it said . . .') moral assumptions about truth-telling, loving one's neighbour and sexuality (see Mt 5:21-48). In some cases the 'radicalising' that fulfils the law might be called 'internalising': what we are called to renounce is not only killing or committing adultery, but thinking that way. In other cases the 'radicality' is outward: loving the neighbour becomes loving indiscriminately, including the enemy; not swearing falsely expands to mean not needing the oath at all to validate what one says.

In both cases it is a misunderstanding to consider these 'radicalising' redefinitions as 'legalistic' or 'morally rigorous' in a traditional sense. They are part of the good news of the new world that is on the way in the power of the God who forgives and restores. They are not idealistic about human potential so much as they are realistic about divine power and about the substance of the divine intent.

The phrase, 'the substance of the divine intent', is a code label for a wealth of detail about concrete behaviour with regard to truth-telling, sexuality, work and wealth, social organisation and property. It is a mistake, however, to think that Jesus' primary originality was that he 'changed the rules'. Rather, as we saw, what he said was that he was filling them full, spelling out all their implications. That means that a full view of 'radical social action' should envision an agenda as broad as the entire Torah.

If taken alone, part of Jesus' Sermon on the Mount could be understood as 'tightening the rules', but what is more basic, more 'radical', is the grounding of these new possibilities in the coming of the kingdom. Nonetheless, it is possible that in education or in illuminating hard choices, some of Jesus' 'But I say to you . . .' sayings are crucial. 'Do not resist the evil person' became for Tolstoy 'the key to the gospel' because of all it implied. In our world, 'Love your enemy' or 'Blessed are the poor' may be the clearest way to articulate the radical nature of Jesus' message.

Action speaks. Jesus' image of the city on the hill or the lamp in the room makes of all behaviour a kind of speech. If the world is to learn of the kingdom coming, it will be by observing the law-fulfilling, truth-telling, enemy-loving lives of his disciples (Mt 5:14-16). Not only does such behaviour say that the kingdom is at hand; it also describes God. Jesus says that by loving their enemies his disciples will be 'like their heavenly father' (Mt 5:43-48; Lk 6:32-36). This is said of no other ethical issue.

2. The nonviolent liberator

The songs that open the Gospel according to Luke portray well the expectancy of Palestinian Jews. They expected a liberator who would exalt the lowly and bring down the mighty. The angel instructed Jesus' mother that her child should be named Yeshua, meaning 'the Lord liberates'. That had been the name of Moses' successor, leader of the original Israelite settlement in Canaan. John the Baptist's preaching in Mt 3:1-12 and Lk 3:1-17 described the coming change in terms of the 'repentance' required of those awaiting it: they would share with the needy. Those of John's listeners who were driven to ask, 'What should we do?', were precisely the representatives of Roman oppression, tax-gatherers and soldiers.

Jesus did not turn out to be the kind of violent liberator some were expecting; yet neither did he tell his hearers that he was not interested in their oppression. He used the political language of their expectation, speaking of God's kingdom and of righteousness. He offended Herod and the Sadducees who controlled local politics. He attracted large crowds who, when they heard him, wanted to make him King, and he formed a disciplined corps of disciples committed to his cause. He was executed on the grounds (false in detail, but credible in principle) that he claimed to be 'king of the Jews'. None of this would have happened if his concern had been to separate the religious from the political and deal only with the former.

Jesus faced authentically what the historian must call the 'Zealot temptation', although historians dispute how soon and how widely the actual term 'Zealot' was used. Violent revolution, intended to drive the Romans away and to re-establish a righteous commonwealth, was frequently undertaken by rebel groups and may well have been the initial expectation of most of Jesus' hearers, even of many of his close disciples. To reject that concrete political option, as Jesus very pointedly and self-consciously did, both for himself and for his disciples, made sense because of his world-view described above. He thereby made concrete the relevance of that world-view.

Yet Jesus' rejection of zealot violence was only important because it was in principle an attractive recourse. Jesus did see himself as a liberator.[1] He formed a people to be the bearers of the new principles of God's rule. He did not use the violence of the state or of war because that would have been a contradiction in terms, yet he and the community he left behind did incarnate the political newness of enemy-love, sharing bread and exalting the lowly.

With this account before us, it may be worthwhile to return to definitions. What is called 'political' may be almost anything. Candidates for prominent public office often say they are not being 'political' when what they mean is only that some particular action or statement is not motivated *only* by calculations of partisan electoral advantage. For others, the 'political' concerns only and specifically the state.

The Greek term *polis* means simply 'society'. The *political* in its root meaning, then, is whatever has to do with power, decisions, rank. The corporation is not less 'political' than the state; civil disobedience is not less 'political' than unquestioning loyalty; minority testimony is not less 'political' than imperial dominion. Thus, 'radical political action' does not automatically mean some way to press for specific state policies, although in some cases (Gerard Winstanley, William Penn, Gandhi, the German church struggle, Martin Luther King, Jr) that will be called for—and will also be called forth—by the good news of the kingdom.

3. The radical rabbi and nonviolent Zealot is our master

No theme is more widely present in the NT than that Jesus reveals what God wants of the believer. During his Palestinian ministry, Jesus warned his listeners not to join his movement without counting the cost: they would, like him, have a cross to bear, including social conflict and even death (Lk 14:25-33; cf Jn 15:18-27). If his fate was the cost of his incarnating a righteousness that the power structures of the world could not tolerate, then his followers should expect to be part of the same process.

---

1. My brief interpretation of Jesus' ministry in this light in chapter 1 of *The Politics of Jesus: Vicit Agnus Noster* (Grand Rapids, MI: Eerdmans, 1972; 2nd ed, 1994) continues to be reinforced by the work of scholars, some of which has been provoked by SGF Brandon's overstated thesis that Jesus was in fact a violent Zealot.

Different apostolic authors modulate in different ways the notion of sharing in Christ's life.[2] Some write of dying with Christ and rising with him, or of renouncing 'equality with God' as he did and sharing in his being given the title of 'Lord'. Some say that the Christian's posture in positions of subordination should be like his; others say that Christians in situations of power should become servants. In all of these ways, 'following Jesus' is not a rigid mimicry but a participation in the quality that characterised his political being. What is to be replicated in the believer's life is the spiritual and social posture of Jesus. It should not be caricatured by the naive 'imitation' language with which later Christians have forsaken marriage, or have gone barefoot, or have begged for a living or have made an issue of earning their living by manual labour (although any one of these specific paths may in some cases be dictated by the gospel and be politically significant).

4. The creative fidelity of the next generation

The standard account of the experience of the early Christians would have us believe that the radicality of Jesus was lost in a generation. We are told that by the time the gospels were written and perhaps even earlier, or by the time Paul had taken the Palestinian message into the Hellenistic world, the radicality of Jesus had to have been lost. What Jesus proclaimed could not be reduced to the dimensions of a real historical movement.

The postulate of necessary betrayal in the next generation of Christians is philosophically predetermined. It comes neither from the texts of the NT nor from the first-century reality. Scholars and preachers have read it into the texts by virtue of their prior philosophical prejudices. Yet to respond to this viewpoint we must review the same data independently.

For some, the early Christian acceptance of the structures of the family and the economy, which several apostolic texts write of in the language of 'reciprocal subordination', seems like a betrayal of Jesus' radicality because it did not abolish at one blow the institutions of family or slavery. But on closer scrutiny it becomes evident that such 'subordination' was the only authentic way for the tiny Christian movement to undermine oppressive structures. By the same token, the

2. The immense variety of modes of participation/discipleship is surveyed in chapter 7 of *The Politics of Jesus*.

acceptance of the presence of the Roman state (see, for example, Rom 13:1-4; 1 Tim 2:2; 1 Pet 2:13) represented not social conservatism but an extension into the Roman Empire of the subversive strategy of survival in dissent with which Jews since Jeremiah had maintained their moral integrity during centuries of imperial oppression. That God 'orders' the realm of 'the authorities' does not mean that their authority is unquestioned, but that it is limited and that the criteria that justify their role also condition it.

The most personal way in which the apostle Paul made sense of the power structures in the world, and of the church's testimony to them, was the ancient cosmology of 'principalities and powers'. In that set of concepts, which are more solid than 'metaphor' or 'myth' without being as prosaic as what we call social science, Paul contends that the power structures of our world are not devils but creatures, intended for the well-being of humankind yet 'fallen' and thereby oppressive. Jesus Christ disobeys the powers, disarms them and saves us from their enslavement by dying at their hands. He thereby 'tames' them and makes them useable in the service of human dignity. Twenty centuries later, this is what we would call 'radical social consciousness', that is, an analysis in terms of the cosmology of the times that defines how the minuscule community of disciples participates already in Christ's victory by its refusal to honour the fallen powers' idolatrous claims.

One other oft-maligned dimension of the early church's apostolic witness is the genre of apocalypse. When taken naively, or when abused by modern fundamentalism, visions of coming catastrophe can be used to depoliticise Christian witness. Yet the point of apocalyptic literature in the first century was to safeguard the young churches' confidence in God's ultimate victory against being abandoned on the ground of their present suffering. In such a world, apocalyptic literature is historically more realistic than other standard ways of reading history, for example, honorific inscriptions or laudatory chronicles.

5. The story, once begun, goes on

This being the nature of Jesus' message and his achievement, the story can by definition not stop there. If Jesus' primary intent and accomplishment had been to create a specific ecclesiastical institution, or to command a specific set of ritual practices, or to impart a precise body of insights about the nature of things, his job could have been done and no more history would have been needed. But if what Jesus 'came' to do was to light a fire on earth, to initiate an authentically historical process of reconciliation and community-formation, then the only way for that to proceed would have to be under the conditions of historicity, including the effects of ignorance, confusion, finitude and fallibility. The ambivalence brought into the Christian movement as a result of numerical growth, cross-cultural communication and incorporating non-Judaic religiosity could not be avoided; the occasion necessarily arose for dilution of the vision as well as its enrichment, for apostasy as well as faithful creativity.

Although the original message of Jesus was compromised in other ways, in the course of the processes that created 'Christendom', the most fundamental apostasy, which enabled and ratified the other kinds of betrayal, was the reversal of Jesus' attitude toward kingship in favour of the 'Constantinian' glorification of imperial autocracy and wealth. Thus the subversive memory of Jesus could not but respond in the finite, fallible, historical movements of radical discipleship that we call 'radical reformation': monasticism, St Francis, the Waldensians and Czech brethren, Anabaptism and Quakerism, Dorothy Day and Helder Camara, Clarence Jordan and Athol Gill.

These movements of radical discipleship regularly challenged the domination of violence, wealth, social hierarchy and empty ritual. Each such summons to the retrieval of discipleship confirms the centrality of Jesus in our history. Without the ongoing processes of distraction and reform we would not know today's form of Jesus Christ's call. We would not be asking the right questions that in every century renew the awareness that his summons retains the same radical substance and mediates the same empowerment.

Reading Yoder Down Under

Stanley Hauerwas

I have often written on the work of John Howard Yoder.[1] Indeed, I have not only written about Yoder but I hope that everything I write reflects what I have learned from him. That said, however, I feel that everything yet remains to be said because his work has opened up such fresh vistas that it will take some time even to begin to explore the implications of what he has written.

It should be said that Yoder did not want us to talk about Yoder. To write about Yoder as if he were yet another intellectual or academic theologian would be to misunderstand who he was and what he has done. After all, Anabaptists have always been reticent about honouring people. So to write about Yoder in order to honour him could not help but appear contradictory.

Yoder did not want our attention to be directed toward him but toward that to which his work directed our attention—God and the church's worship of God. We honour Yoder, then, by thinking and writing about what he cared about. I want to do that by suggesting how the situation of the church in Australia may present both a challenge to those of us who care about what Yoder cared about and a fresh appreciation of his work.

By proceeding this way I aim to put into practice lessons that Yoder taught me. For Yoder was tireless (indeed, almost tiresome) in insisting that theologians must attend to the context in which they find themselves. His essays were never written in the abstract. He always tried to clarify the question being asked, then answered that question as well as he could in line with the presuppositions of the one asking the

1. See, for example, 'The Nonresistant Church: The Theological Ethics of John Howard Yoder', in my *Vision and Virtue* (Notre Dame, IN: Fides, 1974; University of Notre Dame Press, 1981), 197-221; 'When the Politics of Jesus Makes a Difference', *Christian Century* 110/28 (October 13, 1993), 982-87. See also Stanley Hauerwas, Chris K Huebner, Harry J Huebner and Mark Thiessen Nation (eds), *The Wisdom of the Cross: Essays in Honor of John Howard Yoder* (Grand Rapids, MI: Eerdmans, 1999).

question. This was not a 'strategy' but rather an indication of his understanding of the character of Christian witness. There is no witness in the abstract, just as there is no theology in the abstract; rather, theology must be done as a conversation, a practice for building up particular Christian communities.

This accounts for the unsystematic character of Yoder's thought. He did not try to develop a theological system; rather, he did theology 'on the go', so to speak. In that sense his work reminds me more of the patristic writings than of the kind of systematic theology developed over the past two centuries. Like the church fathers, his work is biblical and occasional, seeking as he did to illuminate our challenges by past faithful witnesses. All this means that how Yoder is read and how he helps us to read the Bible in America may be different than in Australia.

Yoder and I have each been to Australia, but we never compared our impressions of this wonderful country. I have fallen in love with Australia partly because I love Australians. I think Australians are a lot like Texans because they have almost nothing to live up to! They simply accept that there is work to do and get on with it. Americans often consider that they are practical people with little use for theory. To my mind, such self-characterisation is misleading, but it does seem to be characteristic of Australians.

One of the first things that strikes an American about Australia is that it is a wonderfully secular society. The civil religion that pervades American life is simply not present in Australia, which is, after all, an outpost of the Enlightenment. In so far as Australia can be said to have a public philosopher, that person is Jeremy Bentham rather than John Locke.

Accordingly, Australians feel no need to explain why they are or are not 'religious'. The kind of generalised religiosity that characterises American habits and makes even 'secular Americans' feel the need to explain why they do not go to church seems not to exist in Australia. Australia genuinely seems to be a society in which the habits of Christendom have never been embedded so that the habits one finds in England, for example, do not exist in Australia, even as cultural lags.

Of course, this makes the condition of Christianity in Australia a struggle. Both for good and ill, Christianity in America continues to presuppose that people are generally disposed to think they ought to be 'religious'. We even think our public ethos, both socially and governmentally, should at least gesture toward such generalised religiosity. There seems to be no such presupposition in Australia, so Australians can elect political leaders who make no pretension to being religious in even the most generalised manner.

Such a situation would seem to be favourable to the kind of ecclesial practice entailed in Yoder's account of Christianity. In so far as the coercive character of the habits of Christendom is missing, the church can be a genuinely called and disciplined community. As Yoder reminded us in *The Original Revolution*, Jesus created a society that had never before existed. First, it was a voluntary society, and one could not be born into it. One could become a member only by repenting and pledging allegiance to its king. There could be no second-generation members. Second, it was a society that was mixed racially, religiously, economically, as well as containing a mix of quite different theological perspectives. And third, it was a society that had been given a new way to deal with offenders—by forgiving them. It was a society that had been given a new way to deal with violence—by suf-fering. It was a society that had been given a new way to deal with problems of leadership—by drawing upon the gifts of every member, even the most humble.[2]

This understanding of the church should be commensurate with the secularity of Australia. Such a view of the church would not generate, as it does in America, the charge of being 'sectarian', that is, of justifying Christian withdrawal from social responsibility. Such accusations often draw upon the presumption that the primary political reality for Christians in America is not the church but the nation. No Australian would presume that Australia is a nation with the soul of a church. Perhaps that is why I like Australia so much, as well as why I think Yoder is better understood in Australia than in America.

Yet I am left with some concern about Yoder's (as well as my own) favourable reception in Australia. My concern is that a 'voluntary church' in a society like Australia should not feel 'voluntary' to those who constitute it. I confess that the same challenge confronts the American church to the extent that both Australia and America are paradigmatic late capitalist societies. How do we sustain a called and disciplined body of people in social orders in which we think discipline is legitimate only to the extent that it is voluntary? In other

2. John Howard Yoder, *The Original Revolution: Essays on Christian Pacifism* (Scottdale, PA: Herald Press, 1977), 28-29.

words, I think the challenge for Yoder's and my own understanding of the church is to indicate the 'involuntary' character of Christian convictions in societies like Australia that tempt us to understand all our commitments as matters of choice.

After all, by its very nature discipline presumes a formation of the self and the community into habits that I could not have chosen freely before I had become so habituated. To be a well-formed disciple of Jesus requires that I be initiated into the way of life I have not chosen. Without such habituation I lack the resources to resist societies like Australia that form me to believe that any choice made when I did not know what I was doing must be coercive. The challenge before the churches in Australia is to become disciplined communities that are able to resist the secularism surrounding them that is legitimated in the name of freedom. I believe that challenge has been present in Australia from the beginning. To the extent that America is losing its endemic religiosity, it is a challenge we are only beginning to appreciate in America.

Yoder provided us with resources to meet this challenge by the way he exemplified the gospel in his work. One of the great strengths of Yoder's work is his confidence in Christian discourse and its disciplinary character. He never sought to demythologise or 'translate' the gospel, confident as he was in the language working among a people who have learned to speak it. What he never let us forget, however, is the challenges that are always present in learning to speak well as Christians. For, Yoder rightly reminded us, such speaking requires that we be embedded in the habits we have learned as part of a people who worship God by being made into the Body of Christ. Such 'making' becomes possible by being embedded in practices of that body that help us to discover that we were God's good creatures even before we knew it.

That is why Yoder did not feel the need to be polemical, at least not as polemical as my work tends to be, because he did not need to emphasise the differences, coming as he did from a position of difference. As a result, he could look for ways in which Christians can co-operate with non-Christians without fear that such co-operation might lull Christians into accommodationist strategies. If Christians have been confidently habituated into the practice of speaking of God non-violently, then we can approach the world with a joy that may even attract those who have not been made what we have been made.

Michael Cartwright has noted that one way to describe the difference between Yoder and myself is that Yoder thought of the church as being 'for the nations' whereas I tend to think of the church as being 'against the nations'.[3] Such a characterisation is certainly fair in so far as I have come from mainstream Protestant Christianity in America and find it necessary to confront what I perceive to be the accommodation of that tradition to the religiosity of America. Yoder felt no such compunction and he is certainly right to remind us that the church exists to serve the nations. It will be interesting to see the implications of that standpoint in societies like Australia where Christianity is not embedded in habits that make it feel 'natural'. As Christians in Australia struggle with that problem, there is no better resource for meeting that challenge than the work of John Howard Yoder.

---

3. See Michael G Cartwright, 'Radical Reform, Radical Catholicity: John Howard Yoder's Vision of the Faithful Church', in Michael G Cartwright (ed), *The Royal Priesthood: Essays Ecclesiological and Ecumenical* by John Howard Yoder (Grand Rapids, MI: Eerdmans, 1994), 1-49.

Toward an Australian Post-Constantinian Public Theology

Ian Barns

A feature of current public policy debates in Australia is the emergence of moral and spiritual issues that go beyond the usual concerns of economic development, distributive justice and due process. Debates over economic restructuring, native title, euthanasia, gay rights, environmental conservation, multiculturalism and the regulation of information and biomedical technologies have raised profound questions. What kind of people are we? What are the moral sources of human community and justice? What common vision should shape our public life and institutions? For example, by recognising Aboriginal ownership of Australian land prior to European 'conquest' (rather than 'settlement'), the High Court's native title decision in 1992 brought into question the legitimacy of Australia as a 'moral community'. Debates about the republic and multiculturalism have raised the question of what it means to be 'Australian' in a rapidly changing political, economic and cultural environment. Conflicts over environmental issues are not only about preserving endangered species and habitats, but more deeply about shared visions of 'nature' and our place within it. Even the economic restructuring that has dominated public policy making in Australia during the past decade has generated wide-ranging discussion about the moral purposes of Australian public culture and institutions. Debates about gender relationships and sexuality raise questions about publicly agreed definitions of sexual identity.

The re-emergence of such questions presents Christians with new opportunities to give public expression to our spiritual and theological convictions. Such opportunities have been scarce in the predominantly utilitarian culture of postwar Australia. Yet the 'deeper agenda' also poses a major challenge because in this erstwhile 'Christian' country, Christianity is perceived to have long occupied a privileged position from which it has oppressed non-Christian minorities and coercively imposed its views in areas such as sexual morality. Is it possible for Christians to commend the message of Jesus Christ as a public vision without implying a return to a position of cultural dominance?

Unfortunately, most Christian participation in public debates continues to assume an establishment or 'Constantinian' relationship between Christianity and Australian society. Australian Catholics and liberal Protestants present Christianity as an inclusive expression of the religious dimension of wider society, whereas fundamentalists and evangelical conservatives hanker after a more 'confessional' Christian society and press for legislative enforcement of a more exclusivist Christian vision that will shape social behaviour and 'values', if not faith. Despite their differences, all these groups believe that Christianity should provide the moral basis and conscience of the dominant social order.

My purpose is to draw on John Howard Yoder's writings to sketch a 'post-Constantinian' public theology relevant to Australian public policy debates. Why Yoder? Many dismiss him as a 'sectarian' theologian, interpreting his ecclesially centred theology as advocating a withdrawal from public life, thus providing little guidance for the moral ordering of a just and sustainable society.[1] On the contrary, Yoder's theology is neither sectarian nor socially irrelevant; indeed, by framing the public world in terms of the good news of the rule of Christ, rather than some supposedly more inclusive notion of natural law, 'order of creation' or civil religion, it represents an authentically Christian public theology that is neither sectarian nor accommodationist. After outlining the main elements of Yoder's public theology to demonstrate its coherence and applicability to contemporary public life, I consider how his 'evangelical' public vision might shape ways in which Australian Christians approach the challenges and opportunities raised by the public controversies mentioned above.

1. Yoder's theological framing of public life

1.1 The gospel as a public vision

Yoder claims that the gospel can and should provide a framework for Christian participation in public affairs. His gospel-centred social vision is a corrective to the distorting effects of what he describes as the

---

1. See James Gustafson, 'The Sectarian Temptation: Reflections on Theology, the Church and the University', *Catholic Theology Society of America Proceedings* 40 (1985): 83-94.

'Constantinian compromise' between the church and wider society.[2] According to Yoder, what underlies this Constantinian relationship is the assumption that moral order is derived from sources more general and inclusive than the gospel, such as natural law or creation, and that the church's task is to provide a sustaining civic religion. Within this framework, whilst the gospel is relevant to matters of personal discipleship and church life, it contributes little to broader questions of public life. Yoder rejects this claim, arguing that it is not because of alleged idealism, impracticality or other-worldliness that the gospel is deemed to have little or no relevance to the public sphere,[3] but because of the church's desire to justify state power in exchange for its support.[4] He also observes that despite the formal end of the Constantinian order, the basic Constantinian relationship between church and state or society persists, albeit in an attenuated form, even as the processes of secularisation have steadily weakened Christian influence in state and society.

However, Yoder does not wish to return to 'pre-Constantinian innocence'. Instead, he aims to recover the paradigmatic meaning of the practices of the NT churches in ways that address current challenges and deal with the ambiguous legacy of a 'Christianised' past. We need, he claims, a 'mid-course correction' in which the errors of Constantinianism can be overcome and the public integrity and relevance of the gospel recovered.

1.2 The rule of Christ and the war of the Lamb

The core of Yoder's public theology is the vision of the 'rule of Christ' over all things 'in heaven and on earth'. It is the rule of Christ, not a more general concept of natural law, creation or universal moral principles, that provides the primary category for interpreting the world, its history and its politics. Whilst this rule is known through the rev-

---

2. John H Yoder, 'The Constantinian Sources of Western Social Ethics', in John H Yoder, *The Priestly Kingdom: Social Ethics as Gospel* (Notre Dame, IN: University of Notre Dame Press, 1984), 135-47.
3. See John H Yoder, *The Politics of Jesus*, rev ed (Grand Rapids, MI: Eerdmans, 1994), 4-10, where he lists various reasons why it has been generally assumed in Christian social ethics that the teaching of Jesus is of little relevance to public life.
4. See John H Yoder, 'Civil Religion in America', in *The Priestly Kingdom*, 172-95.

elatory events of salvation history, it has an ontological as well as an historical dimension: 'what became human in Jesus was already present throughout creation enlightening everyone'.[5]

The rule of Christ is the outcome of the 'war of the Lamb', a metaphor that expresses the apocalyptic view of history entailed by the gospel story, in which all human affairs are reinterpreted in terms of Christ's victory over the principalities and powers.[6] This apocalyptic vision shapes Yoder's understanding of political authority. He rejects Reformed accounts of the state and other dominant social institutions as part of the 'order of creation', thereby granting them a 'creational' mandate to rule over us. Rather, Christians submit to the emperor or the modern democratic state because Christ has triumphed over them and made them subordinate to his rule.

The image of 'the lamb upon the throne' also signifies that the present and future rule of Christ is not like that of earthly rulers who lord it over their subjects. Jesus continues to be the same Lord who came as a servant and gave his life as a ransom for many. Moreover, the 'messianic ethic of Jesus' is not a utopian vision relevant only to the personal life of Christians. Rather, it is the mode of Christ's 'servant lordship' over the world, something not adequately recognised in the Niebuhrian tradition of 'political realism' that tacitly assumes the continuing autonomy of military, economic and cultural power.[7]

1.3 The church as the primary locus of public theology

In contrast to the public theology of mainstream theologians whose primary concern is to apply relevant Christian 'principles' to wider society, Yoder's public theology centres on the Christian *ecclesia* and its

---

5. See John H Yoder, *Body Politics: Five Practices of the Christian Community Before the Watching World* (Nashville, TN: Discipleship Resources, 1992), 69. Yoder does not develop this theme in terms of a trinitarian ontology and a theology of creation.
6. See John H Yoder, 'Ethics and Eschatology', *Ex Auditu* 6 (1990): 119-128. See also Michael G Cartwright, 'Radical Reform, Radical Catholicity: John Howard Yoder's Vision of the Faithful Church', in Michael G Cartwright (ed), *The Royal Priesthood: Essays Ecclesiological and Ecumenical* by John Howard Yoder (Grand Rapids, MI: Eerdmans, 1994), 7.
7. See Yoder's discussion of H Richard Niebuhr's 'Christ and Culture' typology in *The Politics of Jesus*, chap 1. See also Reinhard Hütter, 'The Church: Midwife of History or Witness of the Eschaton?' *Journal of Religious Ethics* 18/1 (Spring 1990): 27-54.

core practices. Whilst theologians such as Martin Marty and James Gustafson claim that a 'public church' must express itself in terms of the wider rationality of the public sphere, Yoder contends that the gospel worked out within the life of the church establishes the agenda and framework for public theology.[8]

Yoder's account of the Christian *ecclesia* begins with its fundamental otherness or difference, as the community constituted by the rule of Christ. It is a community that is not 'natural', but comes into being through the events of salvation history. It is also a distinctive polity. From *The Politics of Jesus* to *Body Politics,* Yoder has tried to overcome the depoliticisation of the church resulting from its Constantinian subversion and to recover the self-understanding of the church as a political community. Recovering the politics of Jesus, however, does not simply entail adopting the agenda and style of secular politics. Instead, it means taking seriously the 'upside-down' servant ethic of Jesus in the life of the Christian community and in its witness to the world.

Neither does the otherness of the church mean that it should turn away from 'the evil world' towards the alternative heavenly order. As the body of Christ, the church has a paradigmatic significance for the world, even as it stands against the world.[9] In its distinctive politics, it prefigures the eventual unity of the whole world within a perfected creation.[10] The church is a sign of the kingdom, an image to the wider world of its true destiny. The rule of Christ over all things is first displayed in the life, practices and ethos of Christian community. As Yoder puts it, 'The people of God is called to be today what the world is called to be ultimately.'[11] The alternative life-pattern of this com-

---

8. See John H Yoder, 'The Otherness of the Church', in Cartwright (ed), *The Royal Priesthood*, 53-64.

9. See John H Yoder, 'First Fruits: The Paradigmatic Public Role of God's People', in John H Yoder, *For the Nations: Essays Evangelical and Public* (Grand Rapids, MI: Eerdmans, 1997)), 23-29, for a discussion of Barth's essay, 'The Christian Community and the Civil Community', in which Yoder accepts Barth's notion that the church and wider society are 'connatural', that is, 'each is human, historical, social'. Cf Yoder, 'Why Ecclesiology Is Social Ethics: Gospel Ethics Versus the Wider Wisdom', in *The Royal Priesthood*, 103-126.

10. See Yoder, 'First Fruits', 27, where he writes, following Barth: 'the order of the faith community constitutes a public offer to the entire society'.

11. Yoder, *Body Politics*, ix.

munity will (or should) challenge and subvert the present social order. When the church is true to its calling, it anticipates the true ordering of society.

Yoder explores the church's paradigmatic role in *Body Politics*, where he examines five core 'political practices' of Christian community: communal moral judgement and forgiveness, baptism, breaking bread together, the expression of diversity of gifts within the life of the body and the practice of communal deliberation around the proclaimed word.[12] His concern is to show that these practices are not esoteric, so he describes them in such a way as to highlight their wider applicability.[13]

As a result, the otherness and primacy of the church implies not disengagement, but positive involvement in the issues, institutions and culture of wider society.[14] Moreover, this involvement is not simply for monological missionary proclamation; it entails ongoing participation that is genuinely dialogical in its respect for the otherness and freedom of the world before God. It is also reflexive because what it means to be the church is not pre-given, but is continually worked out within the context of ongoing involvement in the world.

1.4 Christian communicative engagement with the world

In various places Yoder gives careful and detailed attention to the conditions of dialogical communication between the Christian community and the wider world.[15] This relationship is approached in terms of the 'grammar' of gospel communication, the sharing of 'good news'.[16]

Yoder insists that we must maintain the particularistic language of the gospel rather than adopt seemingly more inclusive and universal-

---

12. These have been described in slightly different terms in John H Yoder, 'Sacrament as Social Process: Christ the Transformer of Culture', in *The Royal Priesthood*, 359-73.
13. Yoder, *Body Politics*, 77-78.
14. John H Yoder, 'On Not Being Ashamed of the Gospel: Particularity, Pluralism and Validation', *Faith and Philosophy* 9 (July 1992): 285-300.
15. There are interesting parallels between Yoder's focus on the conditions of communication and Jürgen Habermas's discourse ethics. Like Habermas, Yoder regards the context of communication as central to the self-identity of dialogical partners. For Yoder, however, genuine dialogical communication is made possible by the communication of the good news of the gospel.
16. See Yoder, 'On Not Being Ashamed of the Gospel', 290.

ist 'shared understandings' of the wider culture.[17] He disputes the universality of dominant languages as unacknowledged forms of particularity and tribalism. He also argues that the basic grammar of the gospel as 'good news' means that Christian communication does not express something already known, but shares real 'news'. Effective communication entails translation rather than dilution.[18]

Closely related is Yoder's insistence that however successful Christian communities may be in achieving acceptance and influence, they will always remain in a minority position within wider society. They remain 'children of the kingdom', occupying the 'servant location' of the rule of Christ.[19] One provocative implication that Yoder draws from this is that Christians ought not take responsibility for running society. It is a Constantinian habit to be concerned with the ethics of rule, reflecting the perspective of those who hold social power.[20]

This does not mean Yoder advocates a position of 'irresponsibility,' but rather a more theologically consistent, and politically realistic, understanding of the 'situated' position of Christians (and others) as social actors. He resists forms of inclusiveness that obliterate difference and obscure the inequalities of power relations. The 'view from below' is radically different from the view from the centre, with different questions, priorities and ways of dealing with social problems. Because the church's politics reflect not the efficacy of human power but the rule of Christ, the primary mode of Christian political agency is faithful witness, not exercising power.

Yoder has also considered the pragmatic use of the dominant language of the culture in which Christians live. For example, in '"But We Do See Jesus": The Particularity of Incarnation and the Universality of Truth', he argues that several diverse NT texts share a common strategic use of diverse pagan discourses to make the claim that Jesus is Lord.[21] A similar strategic expression and translation of biblical lan-

---

17. See Yoder, *The Priestly Kingdom*, 164, for his discussion of the semantic priority of the 'politics of God'.

18. See Yoder, 'On Not Being Ashamed of the Gospel', 291.

19. Yoder, *The Priestly Kingdom*, 162.

20. Yoder, 'Ethics and Eschatology', 121.

21. John H Yoder, '"But We Do See Jesus": The Particularity of Incarnation and the Universality of Truth', in *The Priestly Kingdom*, 46-62. See also his discussion of the prologue to John's Gospel.

guage occurs in *Body Politics,* where Yoder draws connections between specifically ecclesial practices and analogous practices in wider society.[22]

For Yoder, proclaiming 'good news' is not coercive but communicative, thereby creating a dialogical space that preserves, indeed, constitutes the freedom and dignity of the hearer; 'the other', whether enemy or stranger, is respected. Following the pattern of the self-limiting incarnation of the divine Word in John 1, gospel communication is vulnerable and self-limiting as it expresses its 'news' in the language of the host culture. As Yoder wrote,

> The reasons which count to move hearers to accept the 'news' as 'good' cannot already be provided by 'public and shared criteria' already present in every culture, for then no news would be needed, or possible. Nor can they be stipulated from outside the setting by the bearer of the message. The 'reasons which count' are present in the intra-subjective communication setting, by virtue of the fact that the news bearers have entered the scene, submitting to the language of the host culture, articulating and incarnating their values in the neighbors' terms. That vulnerability to the host community's criteria is the courage of witness.[23]

The process of gospel communication also involves a significant reflexive redescription of the message itself. In particular, expressing the gospel in the language of the dominant culture 'thickens' the meaning of the good news itself, making its 'universalistic' claims more explicit.[24]

1.5 The theological constitution of 'publicness'

This description of the dialogical conditions of gospel communication implies a distinctive account of 'publicness'. First, the claim that 'Christ is Lord' is intrinsically public. The gospel is not only about personal salvation, but also about the nature and destiny of 'all things'. It

22. Yoder, *Body Politics*, final chapter.

23. Yoder, 'On Not Being Ashamed of the Gospel', 292.

24. Here Yoder makes a point similar to John Milbank's account in *Theology and Social Theory: Beyond Secular Reason* (Oxford: Basil Blackwell, 1991) of the way metanarrative becomes incorporated into the primary narrative.

applies to everyone. Second, Yoder does not uncritically accept dominant secular notions of 'publicness', or what Stanley Hauerwas calls the 'self-policing' of Christian public practices.[25] For Yoder, the democratic sphere is not something 'given' in which Christians simply act as 'pressure groups'. Instead, 'publicness' is a practice of open dialogue (requiring deeper transcendent sources) that limits the exercise of elite power, making it accountable and giving voice to difference. It is the dialogical nature of gospel communication that creates an 'inter-subjective setting', a 'free space' within which the good news can be expressed, listened to, discussed and accepted or rejected, in short, a public sphere.

This is not only a theological claim. Referring to AD Lindsay's classic study of the democratic state, Yoder argues that a primary source of modern democracy was the Puritan and Quaker meetings:

> The origin of democracy in Puritan and Quaker meetings was not the product of a high view of human wisdom, nor were these people original at the point of their low view of human power. What was new was that particular commitment to the dignity of the adversary or the interlocutor which alone makes dialogue an obligation, and which can be rooted only in some transcendent realm.[26]

There are interesting parallels between Yoder's concept of publicness and notions of a thicker dialogical public sphere developed by some civic republicans and radical democratic writers.[27] These writers also view the public sphere as not simply a formal set of institutions, but a 'discursive space' constituted and sustained by communicative practices in which people present their claims in an open, accessible

---

25. Stanley Hauerwas, 'The Democratic Policing of Christianity', in his *Dispatches from the Front: Theological Engagements with the Secular* (Durham: Duke University Press, 1994), 91-106.
26. Yoder, *The Priestly Kingdom*, 168.
27. See, eg, B Barber, *Strong Democracy: Participatory Politics for a New Age* (Berkeley: University of California Press, 1984); C Mouffe (ed), *Dimensions of Radical Democracy: Pluralism, Citizenship, Community* (London: Verso, 1992); J Dryzek, *Discursive Democracy* (Cambridge: Cambridge University Press, 1990).

way so that such claims can be freely considered and interrogated. Yet by being wary of notions of inclusive moral community and common good, Yoder is perhaps closer to recent feminist and associational thought. Feminists such as Iris Marion Young[28] criticise a false liberal, or republican, universalism and argue that democracy is not characterised by a central 'established' discursive order, but by room for difference and contestation.[29] Young and others emphasise the need to contest the supposedly inclusive universalism of modern liberalism and to recover the 'situated' nature of one's position as a social actor. Similarly, associationalists such as Michael Walzer argue that there should be a shift away from the central, unitary perspective of the nation-state and that greater recognition should be given to the multiple perspectives of agents, groups and communities within civil society.[30]

1.6 The facilitative role of the state

The role of the state in a democratic society continues to be a central issue for both political theorists and public theologians. With the collapse of state socialism and communism, support for state ownership of public resources, provision of services and the regulation of social life has weakened. Even erstwhile Marxists such as Paul Hirst now regard the goals of socialism as not only unattainable but also misguided.[31] Contemporary statecraft is currently dominated by neoliberal notions in which the state has a neutral procedural role, thereby enabling the individual pursuit of different versions of the good life. This formal limitation of the state's role is reflected in the language of rights and in the present ascendancy of deregulatory or free-market approaches to public policy.

However, in a complex and interdependent industrial society, the state plays a central planning and regulatory role, something obscured, perhaps intentionally, by free-market rhetoric. Through its legislative, regulatory and budgetary activities, the state also provides an implicit, though not necessarily coherent, vision of the good life. The problem is

---

28. Iris Marion Young, 'Impartiality and the Civic Public: Some Implications of Feminist Critiques of Moral and Political Theory', in her *Justice and the Politics of Difference* (Princeton: Princeton University Press, 1990), 96-158.
29. Cf Yoder, 'On Not Being Ashamed of the Gospel', 291.
30. Michael Walzer, 'The Idea of Civil Society', *Dissent* (Spring 1991): 293-301.
31. See Paul Hirst, *Associative Democracy: New Forms of Economic and Social Governance* (Cambridge: Polity Press, 1994).

that the rhetoric of deregulation and the free market helps to consolidate state power, yet with reduced democratic accountability.

Many democrats believe that the legitimate role of the state in formulating and effecting collective moral purposes and in responding to 'common' problems must be recognised. Faced with a choice between a socialist state and a state increasingly co-opted by private interests, democratic theorists have turned their attention to renewing institutions of civil society: the network of free associations of families, communities, churches and the like.[32] By conceptualising the public sphere as broader than the state, the positive, though limited, role of the state in enabling the flourishing of civil society may be more clearly articulated.

Yoder's conception of the nature and role of the state has interesting parallels and differences with such views. As noted earlier, his political philosophy is shaped by an apocalyptic understanding of the rule of Christ over the powers. By framing political authority not in terms of an order of creation, but in terms of rebellious principalities and powers now subordinate to the rule of Christ, he develops a more critical and less submissive stance toward powers that be. There is much less expectation than is the case with 'established Christianity' that the just ordering of society will result from the activities of the powers themselves. For Yoder, good government is the result of democratic practices in wider society, including the leavening and limiting influence of the kingdom community that bears witness to the rule of Christ. In 'A Christian Case for Democracy', he limits the proper role of the state to one of facilitating democratic practices in wider civil society:

> We keep using the word 'democracy' as a code word for a better civil arrangement. Yet what is most at stake is not for the *demos* to be able to *rule* but rather for other entities, first of all faith communities, and then by implication other voluntary associations and

---

32. See Ian Marsh, *Beyond the Two Party System: Political Representation, Economic Competitiveness and Australian Politics* (Cambridge: Cambridge University Press, 1994). Cf S Ranson and J Stewart, 'Citizenship and Government: The Challenge for Management in the Public Domain', *Political Studies* 36 (1989): 5-24.

> household structures, to pursue their own ends without any more central management, by the *demos* or by anyone else, than the peace of the total community demands.[33]

Yoder does not thereby shift attention away from the state, either in terms of its public accountability or the positive role it might play in facilitating democratic life. In his discussion of the strategic use of 'beneficence' language employed by governing elites, he develops the basis for ongoing Christian contestation of elite power and community pressure on the state to act for the common good.[34]

2. Applying Yoder's post-Constantinian public theology in an Australian context

2.1 The 'thinness' of Australian public life

I turn now to consider how Yoder's post-Constantinian public theology might be applied in an Australian context. In recent years, concern has grown about the erosion of public debate and public institutions resulting from various long-term processes: the rhetoric and application of economic rationalism, the dominance of expertise, the imagistic discourse of the media and the pseudo-inclusive language of rights. Since the early 1980s, Australian public culture has been dominated by the discourses of economic 'restructuring' or 'competitiveness', liberal proceduralism (legal rights and due process) and cultural cosmopolitanism (inclusive tolerance of diversity, often criticised as 'political correctness'). Unfortunately, these discourses do not enable the differences and disagreements within Australian society to be adequately expressed and debated. Nor do they enable productive dialogue that could shape an agreed framework of common public values and purposes. Instead, they tend to produce increasing disagreements and conflict, as well as a less publicly accountable government and commercial sector.

The erosion of public life has prompted a search for ways to recover and renew public culture and institutions. There has been a revival of interest in notions of citizenship and civil society, and in applying to an Australian situation ideas from traditions of civic

33. Yoder, *The Priestly Kingdom*, 167.
34. Yoder, *The Priestly Kingdom*, 165.

republicanism, communitarianism, associationalism and social democracy.[35]

Christians have also been prominent in defending public institutions, particularly in relation to the effects of neo-liberal economic policies. For example, church leaders in Victoria have led the campaign against the reduction of government services, the sale of government assets and the promotion of a casino culture. They have campaigned against these measures not simply on the grounds of distributional inequity and the social misery they cause, but more deeply because they erode civic life.

As is the case with other defenders of the common good, however, Christians have failed to address what John Hinkson calls the deeper currents of 'economic rationality'.[36] Hinkson notes that a radical free-market individualism reflects, as well as produces, a culture of a technologically dynamic globalising capitalist economic system. It is not simply a currently fashionable economic doctrine. Politically active Christians have also failed adequately to address the underlying philosophical crisis of meaning in late modern societies reflected in the inability of enlightenment humanism to provide a coherent basis for self-hood, community and politics. Theologians such as Colin Gunton and John Milbank have argued that this crisis has deeper theological roots. As a result, the church's vital task is to deal with its own 'Constantinian complicity', to recover the trinitarian vision of God implicit in the gospel and to work out the implications of this vision for creation and society. The challenge for Christians is not simply to restore notions of common good, but to critique the discourses and practices of liberal secular reason and to demonstrate the alternative vision of the kingdom of God.

---

35. Recent examples include Eva Cox's 1995 Boyer Lectures and the work of the so-called Civic Experts Group. See Eva Cox, *A Truly Civil Society* (Sydney: ABC, 1995); S MacIntyre et al, *Whereas the People . . . Civic and Citizenship Education: Report of the Civic Experts Group* (Canberra: AGPS, 1994).

36. John Hinkson, 'Misreading the Deeper Current: The Limits of Economic Rationality', *Arena* 98 (1992): 112-32.

2.2 Recovering core practices of Christian community

Yoder reminds us that the church is central to a Christian vision of public life. Unfortunately, a church that embodies the 'body politics' outlined by Yoder is the exception rather than the rule in Australia. It is the exceptional church that practises the politics of Jesus as Yoder describes it. At a denominational level, church life tends to be framed by the neo-Constantinian politics of central church bureaucracies, whilst at a congregational level, Christian living is interpreted in largely individualistic and privatistic ways. Most Christians still regard politics as external to their faith. The core liturgical practices of corporate worship, baptism and communion have lost their paradigmatic political meanings. They are seen either sacramentally, in terms of a purely transcendent religious sphere; institutionally, in terms of practices authorised by denominational bureaucracies; or individualistically, in terms of personal spiritual needs. As a result, these practices do not enable Christian communities to revision society.

Recovering the politics of the kingdom does not imply that churches must be politicised and become directly involved in moral, social justice or environmental causes. Rather, the challenge is to embody the politics of Jesus in ways that display the paradigmatic meanings of the gospel for such issues. Even though many public issues are outside the direct experience of most Christians, the disciplinary and regulatory practices of Christian community can and should provide resources for reframing the various conflicts over land rights, euthanasia, sexuality and environmental conservation. This gospel authenticity of congregational life and denominational organisation, rather than public statements by church leaders, gives credibility to Christian involvement in public issues.

Of course, the task of renewing the politics of the kingdom cannot be accomplished overnight. It will involve overcoming the habits of Christendom, particularly the tacit division between the spiritual and secular realms. Most importantly, it will need congregational leaders who take seriously the identity of the church as an alternative polity and who are willing and able to equip lay people to work out the implications of their faith for everyday life.

2.3 Recovering a minority status

Yoder's view that we should not seek to preserve an 'established' position (either formally or informally) in society, but that we ought to take seriously our minority status as 'children of the kingdom'[37] is not shared by most Australian Christians. In most mainstream denominations (Anglican, Roman Catholic and Uniting) a Constantinian mind-set prevails. Notwithstanding the processes of secularisation, it is assumed that Christianity still occupies a de facto established position, representing the core values of Australian society. As is evident in moments of public tragedy or celebration, it is the Christian church that provides the spiritual expression of collective grief or joy. It is also expected that civil authority will continue to give tacit recognition to Christian institutions. Anglican and Catholic Bishops continue to occupy influential positions in Australian society. The major churches still own significant amounts of real estate, which provides the material and financial resources needed to maintain parish ministries and major programs in education and welfare provision.

Mainstream churches will not willingly surrender their political and cultural influence. Most Australian Christians would regard Yoder's advocacy of a minority position as an unwise and unnecessary surrender of the influence Christianity still has in public life. Surely it would mean losing a respected voice in public debate, not to mention material resources for ministry and mission. Yet closeness to power and large assets do not guarantee genuine spiritual influence. Historically, the most powerful sources of spiritual renewal have come from the margins. Indeed, in contemporary politics there is greater recognition that creative, democratising action is more likely to come from decentralised community action than from the centre of power.

This does not mean that individual Christians and Christian welfare and social justice agencies should not be actively involved in a wide range of situations, making use of the material, political and cultural resources of wider society to respond to the collective challenges of public life. However, such activities should reflect the vision and virtue of a kingdom community, not the Constantinian commitments of existing church bureaucracies.

37. Yoder, *The Priestly Kingdom*, 158.

2.4 The analogical extension of Christian practices

Yoder has drawn attention to ways in which institutional practices in American life, including processes of deliberative democracy and notions of economic equality, are legacies of the analogical application of a Christian social vision. Many of Australia's core values, practices and institutions also have their sources in Christian tradition. We live in a time when these practices are not only being cut off from their Christian sources, but are also being eroded by an increasingly nihilistic, individualistic and competitive restructuring of social life. We are also witnessing increasing levels of inequality, communal violence and hopelessness.

In this context, it is important for Christians to join others in seeking to maintain and defend practices of civility, compassion and care for the stranger. However, it is also vital to contest their changing meanings and to draw attention to their Christian sources. To claim that such core values have Christian sources will provoke strong disagreement from humanists, atheists and other religionists who defend such values on other grounds. Many Christians find it easier to join in common cause on the basis of shared values and to remain silent about metaphysical disagreements. Yet to do so at a time when the deeper sources of such values and meanings is becoming more problematic is disastrous. Despite such disagreements, we need to give a clearer public account of the gospel sources of notions of freedom, dignity of persons, equality, compassion and so on.

2.5 A dialogical 'gospel publicness'

Current debates about reconceptualising and renewing the public sphere provide opportunities for Australian Christians to articulate notions of gospel publicness. Even so, despite greater openness to substantive and spiritual issues, it is still a daunting task to promote a gospel vision in a public context. Australian public life continues to be utilitarian and pragmatic, and is thus not interested in questions of the deeper meaning of life. There is also a pervasive suspicion about, even antipathy toward, Christianity in many quarters. In a climate of cosmopolitan pluralism, it is not acceptable to assert the claims of Christian truth. Instead of remaining silent or being aggressively evangelistic, we need to develop the kind of practices of dialogical engagement suggested by Yoder.

The place to develop the skills and virtue of gospel dialogue is at home. Unfortunately, few churches in Australia have developed a dialogical culture. At a congregational level, church meetings are characterised by the monological dominance of clergy and the passive participation of parishioners. Of course, Australian Christians meet in small groups for fellowship and prayer. Yet this does not encourage the kind of public deliberation that Yoder discusses in terms of the 'rule of Paul'. At a denominational level, things are not much better, notwithstanding the annual gatherings of church synods and assemblies.

There is thus an urgent need in Australian church life for the creation of genuine spaces of publicness in which, within the framework of a gospel vision, ongoing communal conversation and argument is fostered. Most Australian Christians, I suspect, are captive to a liberal individualism that lacks a sense of how participative deliberation is essential for building up the body and for personal growth. Gospel dialogue needs to be recognised as a central ecclesial practice that enables Christians to listen to others, to express their own perspectives, to come to a common mind and thus to constitute a civic space. In the longer term, it will be through the flourishing of a gospel based deliberative democracy within the Christian community that Christians will contribute to the preservation of a wider public culture.

2.6 *Unmasking the powers*

The seemingly endemic corruption of government, business and law enforcement agencies is another important aspect of the erosion of Australian public life. In recent years there have been several Royal Commissions into official corruption: the Fitzgerald Royal Commission into police corruption in Queensland, the WA Inc Royal Commission and the Woods Royal Commission into police corruption in New South Wales. These inquiries revealed a dismaying level of venality and cynicism amongst public officials. In addition to blatant corruption, governments, businesses and other powerful public bodies act in ways that go against what were once accepted standards of public behaviour. At the level of policy, governments have initiated spending cuts that have adversely affected poor and disadvantaged groups and promoted 'industries' such as casinos, which foster corruption as well as increasing personal misery.

Making governments and other powerful organisations accountable for the abuse of power is a vital challenge in Australian public life. Those who seek to do so (ombudsmen, whistle blowers and the like) often find life difficult. Public administration and private sector management takes place in a complex environment; in the absence of 'watchdogs', there is always the danger that vital information and debate can be effectively suppressed. It is all too easy to be complacent about the resilience of democratic institutions and processes.

So long as Christians think about public life within a Constantinian mind-set, we will be inclined to regard government and other powerful institutions as part of the 'natural' or God-ordained order of things and thus fail to contribute to a culture of dissent by demanding openness and democratic accountability. By and large, Australian Christians hold a reformed or secular view of the liberal democratic state as a basically good institution. Corruption is interpreted as a lapse rather than the expression of hubris, sin and pride, which is the sin of collective power. In the context of endemic corruption and abuse of power, Yoder's understanding of government in terms of those 'rebellious powers' that have been brought under the authority of the rule of Christ provides a better perspective. On one hand, it recognises that all collective power tends toward idolatry, hence injustice and oppression; on the other hand, a vision of the powers as subordinate to the rule of Christ provides a basis for qualified, provisional submission to their limited authority.

The rhetoric of 'principalities and powers' should not lead to demonising the state; rather, it should encourage critical watchfulness of the rhetoric used by states, corporations and bureaucracies to mask idolatry, injustice and oppression. It should make us aware of the banality and smoothness of evil within the normalising processes of corporate, political and bureaucratic power. It should also remind us that resistance against such power requires the deeper spiritual resources of the suffering servant and the kingdom community.

2.7 *The facilitative state*

In Australia, the question of what we should expect of the state in relation to the shaping of public life is a matter of active debate. In the last decade there has been a strong move away from the notion of an active, developmental state. Public policy in relation to economic life has been dominated by economic liberalism. In areas of personal morality, there is opposition to the state enacting legislation to support a particular moral code. In a liberal proceduralist vision, it is assumed that the state remains neutral with respect to visions of the good life, ensuring instead the maintenance of equality and negative freedoms. Yet the rhetoric of the neutral state masks the role that the state inevitably plays in shaping some substantive vision. In reality, we expect the state to be more than a neutral umpire. What is really at issue is whether the substantive purposes of the state should be subject to public debate or should be 'privatised'.

Christians disagree about the proper role of the state. On one hand, conservative Christians endorse greater economic freedom but want the state to support (through education and legislation) Christian moral standards. On the other hand, liberal Christians want the state to intervene more in relation to economic life, but to protect the freedom of individuals in areas of personal morality. Whilst these differences are not as strong as in the United States, they are reflected in debates over abortion, homosexuality and welfare institutions.

In our contemporary context, it is unlikely that the church could reverse legislation on matters relating to homosexuality and the like. However, the deeper question is whether this ought to be our goal. If we had the influence to mobilise electoral support for legislation denying public recognition to a range of social practices, would this be desirable? To what extent should we seek to bring about conformity to a Christian social and political vision within public life? Should we seek to bring about acceptance of a Christian value system or worldview through control of key institutions and legislation?

In Yoder's perspective, the central regulatory purpose of the state is to facilitate the exercise of human freedom, though not the secular liberal sense of the term. The exercise of true freedom requires a normative vision: a moral order involving a rich culture of respect for persons, equality, the allocation of resources to enable those who are poor to have access to education and so on. To this extent it is a broadly liberal vision. At the same time, however, it contests current liberal accounts of the conditions of freedom: both that of those who espouse a purely 'negative freedom' approach and, more importantly, that of those based on a secular humanist morality. It thus makes the central question to be asked concerning the facilitative role that the state plays in relation to civil society, particularly in legislation, welfare and social policy, educational policy and so on: What are those conditions in which persons—and communities—may exercise the kinds of freedom that enable them to consider the truth claims of the gospel?

3. Conclusion

My purpose has been to show that Yoder's account of the politics of Jesus and of the Christian community provides a framework for an authentic and realistic public theology in Australia. His gospel-centred vision is neither sectarian nor utopian. In the context of a public culture in which deeper questions are being debated, yet in which the established moral, political and cultural order is in growing disarray, Yoder's theology provides a way of recovering a Christian vision of public life that is faithful to the confession that Christ is Lord, yet is not coercive. In particular, his analysis of the processes of dialogical gospel communication provides a basis for peaceful participation in what are often acrimonious public debates. His focus on the analogical application of core Christian practices within the wider world, whilst emphasising their specifically Christian sources, is particularly applicable to Christian involvement in social issues of justice, political deliberation and environmental concern. Above all, Yoder reminds us that the proper centre of public theology should be the life of the church, called to be a polity whose core practices bear witness to the coming of the eschatological kingdom when every knee shall bow and every tongue confess that Jesus is Lord.

Pacifism—*Not* Passivism

Philip Matthews

For many people in Australia, the label 'peace activist' continues to be a pejorative term used to describe 'left-wing radicals' with nothing better to do than to protest at any venue that will attract media attention. At the same time, Christian pacifists are understood as religious fanatics *unable* to protect themselves from harm and *unwilling* to respond to injustice forced upon others. This popular image is given added weight by media outlets that portray political 'peace' activists as violent revolutionaries and religious pacifists as passive bystanders. However, neither of these images comes close to describing the true nature of political peace protesters or religious pacifists. This article, whilst taking the opportunity to challenge the view Australians have of peace activism in general, primarily seeks to elucidate the diversity amongst Christian pacifists, with particular emphasis on the Mennonite tradition within the Peace Church heritage.

1. Political peace activism

In their historical review of *The Australian Peace Movement,* Malcolm Saunders and Ralph Summy suggest that the peace movement '. . . has been composed *exclusively* of neither blind fanatics nor extremely unselfish and highly rational individuals. Rather it has been and still is a collection of individuals and groups evincing an amalgam of principled struggle, creative expression, psychological catharsis, and political opportunism. Out of this blend has come some of Australia's most extraordinary figures'.[1]

The case against political peace activism is often prefaced by some banal remark such as, 'How can they claim to be peace activists when they involve themselves in violent demonstrations?' Two basic assumptions need to be debunked here: first, the historic misrepresentation that political peace activists are violent and, second, the im-

1. Malcolm Saunders and Ralph Summy, *The Australian Peace Movement: A Short History* (Canberra: ANU Peace Research Centre, 1986), 8.

plication that a 'real' peace activist could not be violent. Whilst the word 'violent' is a classic overstatement when used to describe the activities of the peace movement in Australia, it is a useful reminder that protesting against the violence of war can and should involve us in confrontation. The media myth of the peace protester as a young, unemployed communist with a penchant for violent confrontation tells us more about the forces that control the media than about the anti-war movement in Australia. It is focused entirely on the media-created image of anti-war demonstrations during the Vietnam War and ignores the diversity that existed (and still exists) in the Australian peace movement.

The second assumption, that a person who protests against war must be 'peaceful' (or passive) to be authentic, is simply naive. To be an anti-war protester enlists one in the struggle against the legitimised violence that surreptitiously infects social and governmental institutions worldwide. The peace movement in Australia was primarily an anti-war movement, not a 'peace' movement. To align oneself with the anti-war movement implies neither passivism (being passive) nor pacifism in the principled sense. Thus there is not the slightest reason why anti-war protesters should be passive and good reason to suggest that they should not be so. The assumption by media representatives, and thus those influenced by them, that political peace activists should be 'peaceful' and that religious pacifists could not be otherwise stems from a semantic confusion between *pacifism* and *passivism*. The following summary of the diversity within the Christian pacifist tradition shows that whilst some within the Peace Church tradition might fit the tag 'passivists', this is not the majority expression of present-day Christian pacifism—a pacifism exemplified by the activism of a peace*maker* rather than the passivism of a peace*keeper*.

2. Christian pacifism

Virtually all major religions have forms of pacifism and militarism as part of the spectrum of their religious expression. However, the commitment to pacifism as a principled expression of faith remains a minor focus in most, if not all, religions. Within the Christian tradition, the almost universal commitment to pacifism and nonviolence lasted for nearly three centuries before experiencing a dramatic decline in favour of militarism. Nevertheless, pacifism as an expression of Christian faith never died. The early sixteenth century saw a reemergence of Christian pacifism as a way of life during what became known as the Radical Reformation. Subsequently the Mennonites, Brethren in Christ and Society of Friends (Quakers) developed into what became known as the Historic Peace Churches.

After seventeen centuries of tacit approval by mainstream churches for the militarist response to conflict, it is not surprising that pacifism (as a principled expression of faith commitment) continues to be misunderstood by the majority of Christians. However, the decision to reject pacifism in favour of militarism was based primarily on pragmatic grounds rather than a rejection of the pacifist position per se. Even amongst Christians who endeavoured to develop a reasoned theological and/or philosophical justification for war (Augustine, Luther, Calvin, Reinhold Niebuhr, Paul Ramsey), one is left with the impression that pragmatic political and social considerations took precedence over the 'messianic' expression of pacifism most clearly espoused in the NT. Perhaps it is this pragmatic pretence that explains the anger and irrational violence directed at pacifists and others who refuse to be seduced by just-war reasoning. In the words of one of the more prophetic voices in Western Australia, 'I was shocked by the anger a discussion on pacifism could generate when I first spoke to a meeting of Baptist ministers almost twenty years ago.'[2] Whilst much of the *angst* concerning pacifism has dissipated, at least in Australia, the misunderstanding continues. Many within the Peace Church tradition added to the confusion by exemplifying a stance that resembled passivism rather than pacifism. For many non-pacifists, the traditional nonresistant stance was viewed admirably (even if condescendingly) as a lifestyle choice, but as a response to conflict it was considered impractical and thus was often presented apologetically by Christian pacifists. In recent times, however, representatives of the Peace Churches have stated their prophetic response more assertively:

> While the Brethren, Friends, and Mennonite fellowships are inclined to accept the designation 'peace church' . . . they do not see their pacifism as a sort of vocational gift or historical accident for which they should be admired, tolerated, reviled, or excused, as

---

2. Glen Brooks, a long-term activist and prophetic voice, paved the way for the modern-day re-emphasis of the Anabaptist heritage within Baptist churches in WA. He made this comment in the early 1990s.

> the case may be, but rather as a serious and faithful expression of the intention of Jesus.[3]

3. Varieties of religious pacifism amongst Mennonites

The following is an overview of how one part of the Peace Church tradition, the Mennonites, has grappled with what it means to be a Peace Church. Although care has been taken to interpret the scene objectively, using resources from within the Mennonite community, the internal nuances that have driven the debate amongst Mennonites could be misinterpreted by one who belongs to a sympathetic but non-Peace Church heritage.[4] John R Burkholder has provided an excellent introduction to the varied expressions of contemporary Mennonite peace theology.[5]

3.1 Historic Nonresistance stresses literal obedience to the teaching of Jesus in Matthew 5: resist not evil, turn the other cheek, love your enemies (Guy F Hershberger, Harold S Bender, John C Wenger).

3.2 'Apolitical' Nonresistance is an offshoot of the 'Historic Nonresistance' stance but with a stringent two-kingdom view of the Christian's place in the world; it seems to suggest that 'what's wrong for us (killing) may be right for them' (Sanford Shetler, J Ward Shank, James Hess, J Otis Yoder).

3.3 Radical Pacifism affiliates the rigorous nonviolent ethic of Jesus with aggressive social and political action (Ron Sider).

3.4 The Pacifism of the Messianic Community depends on confession of Jesus Christ as Lord and sees nonviolent obedience as enabled through resurrection power and lived out in a distinct counter-cultural community made up of those committed to the way of the cross (John Howard Yoder).

---

3. John K Stoner, 'Introduction' to Ronald Sider, *Christ and Violence* (Scottdale, PA: Herald Press, 1979).
4. The history of Baptists cannot be traced directly to the sixteenth-century Radical Reformation, but there has been a protracted debate about the extent of Anabaptist influence on early Baptist thought and practice.
5. JR Burkholder, 'Can We Make Sense of Mennonite Peace Theology?' in JR Burkholder and BN Gingerich (eds), *Mennonite Peace Theology: A Panorama of Types* (Akron, PA: Mennonite Central Committee Peace Office, 1991).

3.5 Political Pacifism is similar to 'Radical Pacifism' but is more optimistic about the possibility of effective nonviolent change in the world system; it also devotes more attention to secular analogues (Duane Friesen).

3.6 Post-Political Pacifism is a sophisticated return to a modified two-kingdom ethic, recognising the moral necessity for occasional state violence but supporting nonviolence (even radical nonviolent action) as the Christian ethic (Ted Koontz).

3.7 Social Responsibility is a response to the Niebuhrian critique that argues for a socially engaged stance that would not be troubled by ethical compromise, but holds to personal nonresistance (J Lawrence Burkholder).

3.8 Liberation Pacifism begins by standing in solidarity with the poor and oppressed; it emphasises justice (perhaps even more than peace) and is reluctant to establish absolute nonviolence as the norm (Arnold Snyder, Mark Neufeld, Perry Yoder).

3.9 Nonviolent Statesmanship views unconditional neighbour-love as the primary principle, but may call for political action that is contrary to personal conviction (Gordon Kaufman).

3.10 Canadian Pacifism has much in common with 'Political Pacifism' and 'Social Responsibility' and sees the modern democratic state as a positive arena for Christian participation.

4. From nonresistance to nonviolence

The text of Mt 5:39, 'Do not resist one who is evil', provided the foundation for the traditional evangelical Mennonite expression of 'Biblical Nonresistance'. Guy F Hershberger's *War, Peace, and Nonresistance* was the landmark work for Mennonites of North America.[6] In three editions (1944, 1953, 1969), he mapped out the standard North American expression of Mennonite nonresistance (although Canadian Mennonites have not been as strict in their interpretation of the Peace Church heritage). Tom Yoder Neufeld suggests that whilst the traditional Mennonite stance of nonresistance '. . . can accommodate a range of responses to complex social and political obligations, it is characterized more by *what is not done* than by what is done: as a follower of Jesus it is inappropriate to retaliate in the face of suffering

6. Guy F Hershberger, *War, Peace, and Nonresistance* (Scottdale, PA: Herald Press, 1981).

or oppression, whether at the hands of an individual, a group, or a system'.[7]

The term 'nonresistance' has provoked much thought and debate in the Mennonite community. After World War II many Mennonites, influenced by the 'Christian Realism' of the Niebuhr brothers, developed a form of pacifism referred to rather unflatteringly as 'just war' pacifism.[8] The Niebuhrs, who maintained that the only true pacifist position was nonresistance in its absolute form, proved to be strange bedfellows for conservative Mennonites. According to John R Burkholder, 'The Niebuhrs reinforced the common (conservative) Mennonite assumption that one must choose between the poles of purity or relevance. Reinhold Niebuhr vigorously set forth just two ethically consistent positions: either apolitical, pure pacifism or "responsibility"—which for him meant coercion, violence, and war.'[9]

'Christian Realism', made popular by Reinhold Niebuhr, was not a rejection of pacifism but an awareness that whilst nonresistance was the 'ideal', it could not be maintained in the modern secularised world. In other words, the pacifist teaching of Jesus is impractical for today's world. Niebuhr prefaced his argument for a 'realist' position by acknowledging that Jesus was a pacifist. He also said,

> Nothing is more futile and pathetic than the effort of some Christian theologians who find it necessary to become involved in the relativities of politics . . . to justify themselves by seeking to prove that Christ was also involved in some of these relativities, that he used whips to drive the money-changers out of the Temple, or that he came 'not to bring peace but a sword'.[10]

---

7. Tom Yoder Neufeld, 'Varieties of Contemporary Mennonite Peace Witness', *Conrad Grebel Review* 10/3 (1992): 245, italics mine. Neufeld also says: 'At one end of the spectrum of peace positions Mennonites are virtually indistinguishable from the majority of Christians.'
8. Neufeld, 'Varieties of Contemporary Mennonite Peace Witness', 244.
9. John R Burkholder, 'Mennonite Peace Theology: Reconnaissance and Exploration', *Conrad Grebel Review* 10/3 (1992): 264.
10. See Larry Rasmussen (ed), *Reinhold Niebuhr: Theologian of Public Life* (London: Collins, 1989), 241.

The question for Niebuhr was not whether Jesus meant what he said, but whether he meant for us to obey such a simple command now. In his mind, we cannot import Jesus' first-century social understanding into twentieth-century industrialised society; therefore the choice is either apolitical pacifism or 'responsibility'.

Conservative Mennonites (whom Burkholder describes as suffering from an 'inferiority minority complex') grasped hold of Niebuhr's 'backhanded' compliment as a way of maintaining the status quo against a more progressive interpretation of Christian pacifism. ('Historic Nonresistance' declared that resistance or coercion is wrong and that civil disobedience goes against the command in Romans 13 to obey civil rulers.) This narrow interpretation of biblical pacifism came under sustained attack from within the Mennonite community (John Howard Yoder, Ron Sider, Tom Yoder Neufeld, John R Burkholder) because it seemed that for many Mennonites 'Historic Nonresistance' had become a *raison d'être* rather than an expression of a faith commitment.

At the centre, nonresistance is grounded in a 'dualistic' or 'two-kingdom' understanding of the world. Using the 'two-kingdom' language of Martin Luther, the 'public' and 'private' spheres of life became the rationale for traditional Mennonites to maintain their peace witness whilst giving de facto support to civil authorities involved in military conflict. Neufeld summarises the variation within nonresistance by using the distinctive terms 'happy dualism' and 'sad dualism'.[11] For Neufeld, 'happy dualists' are those who reject the use of force but support the participation of others, including Christians, in the exercise of 'legitimate' force; they believe that God has created the state and endowed it with responsibility to exercise force and violence. 'Sad dualists', on the other hand, regret that there is little one can do other than to be faithful to the teachings of Jesus, whilst calling others to faith and faithfulness.

With the publication in 1972 of *The Politics of Jesus*, John Howard Yoder gave new impetus to the understanding that Jesus was a political figure and thus rejected the traditional dualism of conservative Mennonites.[12] Influenced by Karl Barth's rejection of dualism, Yoder

11. Neufeld, 'Varieties of Contemporary Mennonite Peace Witness', 247ff.

12. John Howard Yoder, *The Politics of Jesus* (Grand Rapids, MI: Eerdmans, 1972; 2nd ed, 1994).

challenged traditional Mennonite dualistic 'two-kingdom' approaches to social interaction. He laid to rest the image of Jesus as passive and nonpolitical. Burkholder says, 'Yoder provides a sustained critique of the ethical dualisms and forced options which he claims the brothers Niebuhr imposed on the mid-twentieth-century discussion of pacifism and politics.'[13] Yoder was part of a new wave of Mennonite thinkers who challenged traditional nonresistance. After taking a historical-critical view of the peace witness of Jesus and the NT writers, they adopted a radical-activist pacifism and rejected traditional Christian dualism. Christian pacifism should involve confrontation with individuals, governments and social forces that impose their will, either by political totalitarianism, economic imperialism or the violence of war.

Along with this new radical pacifism, Mennonites acknowledged that this advocacy role must of necessity involve coercion and resistance. Significantly, critics of Yoder's approach (Reinhold Niebuhr, Guy Hershberger and Paul Ramsey) viewed any form of coercion as beyond the scope of 'true' pacifism. Niebuhr's response to those who argue that the ethic of Jesus involves not (passive) nonresistance but (pacifist) nonviolent resistance was blunt but ultimately shallow:

> They . . . declare that the ethic of Jesus is not an ethic of non-resistance, but one of non-violent resistance; that it allows one to resist evil provided the resistance does not involve the destruction of life or property. There is not the slightest support in Scripture for this doctrine of non-violence.[14]

The discrepancy between Niebuhr's passive Jesus and Yoder's political Jesus is significant. Recent trends in the study of the Jesus of history tend to support Yoder's view that Jesus was indeed, at the very least, a political figure.

With regard to old-style dualism, the recognition by Yoder and others that the lordship of Christ was universal created quite a controversy. This 'new theology' proclaims that *all* society should come under the one moral standard. It entails the conviction that Christians should call *all* of society, including the state, to account for its conduct in keeping with the will of God as made known through

---

13. Burkholder, 'Mennonite Peace Theology', 264.
14. Rasmussen (ed), *Reinhold Niebuhr*, 241.

Christ.[15] Although the criticism of this new approach became quite vocal (once its full implications were realised), it is now the majority position for Mennonites and others from the peace-church heritage. One can see from the ten types listed above that most reject absolute nonresistance in favour of nonviolent direct action.

5. 'Radical pacifism' or 'just war'

So long as the rationalisation for the 'just war' remains the dominant position of all major Christian bodies, most people will continue to accept the just-war philosophy, even though an increasing number have come to the conclusion that traditional criteria for a just war can no longer be applied to modern warfare—an ironic turnaround considering Niebuhr's rejection of pacifism. Although this is a step in the right direction, it still fails to address fundamental inconsistencies inherent in the just-war approach. Once we accept the possibility of war in some circumstances, we practically determine that war will occur. Governments will build up armaments for when a just-war situation arises. Philosophical utility will ultimately succumb to the technical and political imperative for war because whilst the debate about war and peace is carried on by theologians, philosophers and other people of conscience, the decision to go to war is made by politicians, a male-dominated elite that makes 'moral' decision-making subservient to 'power-political' decision-making.

6. Conclusion

The initial goal of this survey was to help Australian Christians understand the difference between 'pacifism' and 'passivism'. We have seen that rather than being passive bystanders, most Christian pacifists are now active participants in the struggle against injustice of all sorts. Rather than presenting an 'idealistic' but 'unrealistic' philosophy of nonresistance, they espouse a theoretical and practical *nonviolent* alternative to conflict resolution. Rather than recognising the state as the legitimate protector of an ultimately illegitimate passivist lifestyle, contemporary Christian peacemakers are much more assertive in the way they challenge the state. The present-day advocacy role of the Peace

---

15. See Richard C Detweiler, *Mennonite Statements on Peace, 1915–1966* (Scottdale, PA: Herald Press, 1968).

Churches has influenced mainline churches to re-examine their positions on war and peace and to separate themselves, in a political sense, from the decisions of the state.

CS Lewis and Christian Pacifism

David Neville

In May 1953, at a seminar in The Netherlands on 'Modern Theological Thought and Its Criticism of Nonresistance', John Howard Yoder presented a paper on 'Reinhold Niebuhr and Christian Pacifism'.[1] In it he responded to Niebuhr's arguments in 'Why the Christian Church Is Not Pacifist', first published in 1939, the year World War II began, and subsequently as part of *Christianity and Power Politics*.[2] Yoder chose to focus on Niebuhr's arguments and presuppositions both because of his popularity and influence in the English-speaking world and because Niebuhr was concerned with pacifism as a central problem of Christian ethics.

While CS Lewis does not share Reinhold Niebuhr's stature as a theologian, he is arguably as influential as Niebuhr, if not more so, because of his durable popularity as a Christian apologist.[3] In *C. S. Lewis and the Search for Rational Religion*, John Beversluis noted that even before his death Lewis was regarded as 'one of the most influential spokesmen for orthodox Christianity in the twentieth century'. Indeed, according to Beversluis, 'Even the most lavish estimates of his influence are likely to be too conservative.'[4]

1. John Howard Yoder, 'Reinhold Niebuhr and Christian Pacifism', *MQR* 29/2 (1955): 101-117.
2. Reinhold Niebuhr, *Christianity and Power Politics* (New York: Charles Scribner's Sons, 1940), 1-32.
3. Cf John A Sims, *Missionaries to the Skeptics: Christian Apologists for the Twentieth Century* (Macon, GA: Mercer University Press, 1995), in which Sims discusses the apologetics of Lewis, Niebuhr and EJ Carnell.
4. John Beversluis, *C. S. Lewis and the Search for Rational Religion* (Grand Rapids, MI: Eerdmans, 1985), x. The 1998 celebrations commemorating the centenary of Lewis's birth confirm the accuracy of Beversluis's remark. In 2000 *Christian History* profiled Lewis as one of the ten most influential Christians of the twentieth century. See Ted Olson, 'C. S. Lewis', *Christian History* XIX/1, Issue 65 (Winter 2000). In addition to numerous biographies, see Walter Hooper (ed), *C. S. Lewis: A Companion and Guide* (Harper San Francisco, 1996); Jeffrey D Schultz and John G West, Jr (eds), *The C. S. Lewis Readers' Encyclopedia*

In 1940, the year after Niebuhr first published 'Why the Christian Church Is Not Pacifist', Lewis addressed a pacifist society in a talk entitled 'Why I Am Not a Pacifist'. While Niebuhr's non-pacifist arguments continue to be influential through their dissemination by Christian intellectuals, Lewis's case against pacifism is potentially more influential because of his appeal to ordinary people.[5] Without attempting to imitate Yoder's critique of Niebuhr, this appraisal of Lewis's argument against pacifism is nonetheless indebted to Yoder's pacifist vision.

1. Context

Born in Belfast, Northern Ireland, in 1898, Lewis turned nineteen in the front-line trenches of France. Early in 1918 he caught 'trench fever', but after recovering he experienced the horror of trench warfare—mud, human corpses, enemy fire and barbed wire. In April 1918 he was injured by shrapnel from an exploding shell and sent home.[6] It was a relatively short stint as a soldier, but one can assume that Lewis's memories of World War I remained with him.

In 1929 Lewis reluctantly revoked his atheistic stance and accepted God's existence. Two years later he became a Christian. During the 1930s he wrote, in addition to essays and a work of fiction, *The Pilgrim's Regress: An Allegorical Apology for Christianity, Reason and Romanticism* (1933) and *The Allegory of Love: A Study in Medieval Tradition* (1936). In 1940, the year in which he argued against pacifism, he published *The Problem of Pain*. He had yet to broadcast his BBC radio talks (initially published between 1942 and 1944) or to write *The Screwtape Letters* (1942), *The Abolition of Man* (1943), *The Great Divorce* (1945), and *Miracles* (1947), not to mention his later books. In short, 'Why I Am Not a Pacifist' was written relatively early in Lewis's literary career.

Introducing the revised edition of *The Weight of Glory and Other Addresses*, in which 'Why I Am Not a Pacifist' was first published,

---

(Grand Rapids, MI: Zondervan, 1998); Colin Duriez, *The C. S. Lewis Encyclopedia: A Complete Guide to His Life, Thought, and Writings* (Wheaton, IL: Crossway Books, 2000).

5. Lewis's friend Tolkien once referred to him as 'Everyman's Theologian'. See Humphrey Carpenter, *Tolkien: A Biography* (New York: Ballantine Books, 1978), 168-69.

6. For Lewis's experience of war, see AN Wilson, *C. S. Lewis: A Biography* (London: Collins, 1990), 50-56.

Walter Hooper says of this address: 'We know that Lewis never made any attempt to publish it, and it appears in print here for the first time.'[7] One should not take for granted, therefore, that it presents his final thoughts on pacifism and war. Lewis could, and sometimes did, change his mind. In 1948, for example, the Catholic philosopher Elizabeth Anscombe refuted his argument against Naturalism in *Miracles,* which had been published the year before. When *Miracles* was reprinted in 1960, Lewis revised it to take account of her criticisms.[8] Although he may have reconsidered his position on pacifism, this is doubtful because his account of why he was not a pacifist is of a piece with later writings. For example, he dealt briefly with the question of war in his broadcast talks on *Christian Behaviour* and evidently had not changed his view by 1952 when his three series of talks were published together as *Mere Christianity.* There one reads: 'It is . . . perfectly right for a Christian judge to sentence a man to death or a Christian soldier to kill an enemy. I always have thought so, ever since I became a Christian, and long before the war, and I still think so now that we are at peace.' A few lines later he declares: 'The idea of the knight—the Christian in arms for the defence of a good cause—is one of the great Christian ideas. War is a dreadful thing, and I can respect an honest pacifist, though I think he is entirely mistaken.'[9]

2. Argument

Lewis begins his address by noting that how one decides whether it is wicked, morally indifferent, or obligatory to participate in war if commanded by one's country raises a more general question about how one decides what is good or evil. He then considers this more general question, beginning with the role of conscience in moral judgment. Focusing on one particular understanding of conscience, namely, one's judgment of what is right and wrong, he asserts that, like the process of reasoning, it involves three elements: facts to reason about, based on experience or authority; the perception of self-evident truth, what he

7. CS Lewis, *The Weight of Glory and Other Addresses*, revised and expanded edition, edited by Walter Hooper (New York: Macmillan, 1980), xxii. Page citations to 'Why I Am Not a Pacifist' appear in the text. I am concerned with the general thrust of Lewis's argument, not with each point he makes.

8. See Beversluis, *C. S. Lewis*, 58-83.

9. CS Lewis, *Mere Christianity* (New York: Macmillan, 1952), 106-107.

calls 'intuition'; and the process of argument in which intuitions are arranged so as to demonstrate the truth or falsehood of a proposition.

Lewis also points out that we must rely on the authority of others not only for many of the facts required for moral deliberation, but also for many of our moral convictions because we simply cannot work through the reasoning required to defend all that we hold to be right or good. The importance of authority for moral judgment is particularly important, he argues, because it acts as a check against moral reasoning being corrupted by 'passion', his word for self-interest. This is a valuable insight, but Lewis overlooks the equally important point that moral judgment must often discriminate between conflicting authorities. This is especially pertinent in connection with Christian pacifism, but even when discussing the issue of authority later in his address Lewis does not adequately emphasise the vital question of the Christian's ultimate authority.

For Lewis, then, judgment about what is right or wrong, good or evil, 'is a mixture of inarguable [*sic*] intuitions and highly arguable processes of reasoning or of submission to authority' (38). After dismissing the potential claim that all killing of human life is self-evidently wrong, Lewis provides a method for resolving moral questions:

> We have seen that every moral judgment involves facts, intuition, and reasoning, and, if we are wise enough to be humble, it will involve some regard for authority as well. Its strength depends on the strength of these four factors. Thus if I find that the facts on which I am working are clear and little disputed, that the basic intuition is unmistakably an intuition, that the reasoning which connects this intuition with the particular judgment is strong, and that I am in agreement or (at worst) not in disagreement with authority, then I can trust my moral judgment with reasonable confidence. And if, in addition, I find little reason to suppose that any passion has secretly swayed my mind, this confidence is confirmed (39).

This method he now applies to the question of war.

2.1 Facts. Everyone agrees that war is 'very disagreeable', according to Lewis, but pacifists also contend that wars always do more harm than good.[10] After showing that this *alleged* conviction is impossible to substantiate because it involves 'a comparison between the actual consequences of some actual event and a consequence which might have followed if that event had not occurred', he opines: 'It seems to me that history is full of useful wars as well as of useless wars. If all that can be brought against the frequent appearance of utility is mere speculation about what would have happened, I am not converted' (39-41). Christian pacifists may or may not consider that wars always do more harm than good, but for many this is not the only, nor even the primary, consideration against participating in war.

2.2 *Intuition.* Lewis is brief on this point:

> There is no question of discussion once we have found it; there is only the danger of mistaking for an intuition something which is really a conclusion and therefore needs argument. We want something which no good man has ever disputed; we are in search of a platitude. The relevant intuition seems to be that love is good and hatred bad, or that helping is good and harming bad (41).

This seems unobjectionable, but Christian pacifists are not so concerned to act in accordance with indisputable and generally accepted moral principles as to heed one who revealed what God is like (Jn 1:18) and whose life patterned a way to be followed (Mk 10:42-45). Christian faith implies distinctive moral commitments that are never simply or obviously compatible with what 'no good man has ever disputed'. By seeking to base his argument on a universal ethical principle such as beneficence or nonmaleficence, which is in any case problematic,[11]

---

10. Lewis failed to distinguish between different pacifist positions, let alone different types of Christian pacifism. Cf John Howard Yoder, *Nevertheless: The Varieties and Shortcomings of Religious Pacifism*, rev ed (Scottdale, PA: Herald Press, 1992).

11. On the impossibility of a universal or unqualified ethic, see Stanley Hauerwas, *The Peaceable Kingdom: A Primer in Christian Ethics* (Notre Dame, IN: University of Notre Dame Press, 1983). For a discussion of similarities and differences between Lewis and Hauerwas on morality and ethics, see Jeffrey

Lewis inevitably restricts the teaching and example of Jesus to a subordinate role in moral deliberation.

2.3 Reasoning. Having identified what he thinks to be the relevant moral principle, Lewis next considers 'whether reasoning leads us from this intuition to the Pacifist conclusion or not' (41). Here his argument becomes intricate. He notes first that every good action is limited in some respect: 'Hence from the outset the law of beneficence involves not doing some good to some men at some times.' Following this obvious observation one reads: 'Hence those rules which so far as I know have never been doubted, as that we should help one we have promised to help rather than another, or a benefactor rather than one who has no special claims on us, or a compatriot more than a stranger, or a kinsman rather than a mere compatriot' (41-42). Despite Lewis's assertion that these 'rules' have, to his knowledge, never been doubted, they are at odds with the teaching of Jesus, who enjoined his followers to emulate the 'perfection' of God's *indiscriminate* love (Mt 5:43-48; Lk 6:32-36).[12] Then this leap on Lewis's part: 'And this in fact most often means helping A at the expense of B, who drowns while you pull A on board. And sooner or later, it involves helping A by actually doing some degree of violence to B' (42). Apart from the tenuous analogy between war and self-defence or defence of another against an individual attacker,[13] this is sheer hyperbole. Lewis is correct, however, when he says that 'when B is up to mischief against A, you must either do nothing (which disobeys the intuition [of beneficence]) or you must help one against the other' (42). Granted that one should assist someone being harmed rather than the one doing harm, there are nevertheless courses of action compatible with pacifist convictions.

Stout, *Ethics after Babel: The Languages of Morals and Their Discontents* (Cambridge: James Clarke & Co, 1990), 13-32, esp 15-21.

12. See John Howard Yoder, *The Politics of Jesus*, 2nd ed (Grand Rapids, MI: Eerdmans, 1994), 116-17. Cf 'The Political Axioms of the Sermon on the Mount', in John Howard Yoder, *The Original Revolution: Essays on Christian Pacifism* (Scottdale, PA: Herald Press, 1977), 34-51.

13. See John H Yoder, *What Would You Do?*, expanded edition (Scottdale, PA: Herald Press, 1992), 11-42. In 'Peace Without Eschatology?' in Michael G Cartwright (ed), *The Royal Priesthood: Essays Ecclesiological and Ecumenical* by John Howard Yoder (Grand Rapids, MI: Eerdmans, 1994), 161-67, Yoder critiques the type of 'lesser evil' argument used by Lewis.

Assisting someone being harmed does not necessarily entail killing the person doing the harm.

Lewis concedes that it is preferable to do as little violence to B as possible, provided it restrains B and is equally good for A. But he does not accept that killing B would always be wrong. In addition, while accepting that individual criminals might be adequately dealt with without killing, he avers: 'It is certain that a whole nation cannot be prevented from taking what it wants except by war' (43). This is a tendentious judgment, even if it reflects most political thinking. The contemporaneous example of Norway's effective nonviolent resistance to Nazi aggression illustrates an alternative to war, as do later examples of nonviolent resistance to Soviet aggression in Hungary in 1956 (following the failure of violent rebellion!) and in Czechoslovakia in 1968.[14]

For Lewis, the view that war is a greater evil than others rests on a 'materialist ethic' that regards death and pain as the greatest evils. He disagrees and considers the suppression of a 'higher' religion or culture by a 'lower' religion or culture to be more evil than war. While conceding that war is a great evil, he does not regard it as the greatest evil. Hence his apology for war in some circumstances, although he never refers explicitly to criteria that would make war justifiable.[15] Perhaps just-war reasoning should not to be expected from one who confessed, 'Nor am I greatly moved by the fact that many of the individuals we strike down in war are innocent. That seems, in a way, to make war not worse but better. All men die, and most men miserably' (43). Assuming Lewis here refers to 'innocent' soldiers rather than noncombatants, which would contradict a key just-war criterion

---

14. See Duane K Friesen, *Christian Peacemaking and International Conflict: A Realist Pacifist Perspective* (Scottdale, PA: Herald Press, 1986), 25-26. For a select bibliography on nonviolent defence alternatives, see John Howard Yoder, *When War Is Unjust: Being Honest in Just-War Thinking*, rev ed (Maryknoll, NY: Orbis Books, 1996), 165-66.

15. Lewis was familiar with just-war reasoning. In 1939 he replied to an article by EL Mascall, 'The Christian and the Next War', citing Aquinas on 'rules for determining what wars are just'. See *Theology* 38 (1939): 53-58, 373-74. His remark that war is less evil than the suppression of a 'higher' by a 'lower' religion or culture is an implicit appeal to just cause. In 'Christ, the Hope of the World', in *The Royal Priesthood*, 213ff, Yoder disputes whether war can save a culture.

for the proper conduct of warfare,[16] this remarkable statement is difficult to reconcile with his moral principle that 'helping is good and harming bad'.

Lewis considers another potential, but naive, argument for pacifism that adds little to his discussion and concludes: 'I do not therefore find any very clear and cogent reason for inferring from the general principle of beneficence the conclusion that I must disobey if I am called on by lawful authority to be a soldier' (45).

2.4 *Authority.* As an example of 'special human authority', Lewis notes that his own society had decided against pacifism, not only in his own time but through the centuries. He accepts that the authority of England is not 'final' but considers it to be significant. He then turns to 'general human authority' and asserts: 'From the dawn of history down to the sinking of the *Terris Bay*, the world echoes with the praise of righteous war' (46). He supports this claim by referring to the classical literature of Greece and Rome, as well as to Zarathustra, the *Bhagavad Gita* and Montaigne, but concedes that Christian pacifists may hold 'that the human race is fallen and corrupt, so that even the consent of great and wise human teachers and great nations widely separated in time and place affords no clue whatsoever to the good' (47). As if to grant that Christians answer to a different authority, but without underscoring the importance of this distinctive appeal, he next considers 'divine authority'.

Only at this late point does Lewis consider the relevance of Christian faith for the question of pacifism. He states, almost dismissively, that 'when we turn to Christianity, we find Pacifism based almost exclusively on certain of the sayings of Our Lord Himself' (47). On other issues such as forgiveness and sexual morality, Lewis accepted Jesus' teaching as binding. Why not here? He is right that 'if those sayings [of Jesus] do not establish the Pacifist position, it is vain to try to base it on the general *securus judicat* of Christendom as a whole' (47). For most of its history the church has accepted the validity and value of war. He is on shakier ground, however, when he asserts, 'All bodies that claim to be Churches—that is, who claim apostolic succession and accept the Creeds—have constantly blessed what they regarded as righteous arms' (48). This is simply untrue, unless one understands apostolic succession in its most rigid, Roman, sense. Apart from ignoring the

16. See Yoder, *When War Is Unjust*, 147-61, esp 157-58.

historic peace churches, this remark flies in the face of history. For the first three centuries of its history, the church appears to have been predominantly pacifist.[17] The earliest Christian authority outside the NT to whom Lewis appeals is Augustine (354–430 CE).

Returning to the NT, Lewis remarks: 'Nor, I think, do we find a word about Pacifism in the apostolic writings, which are older than the Gospels and represent, if anything does, that original Christendom whereof the Gospels themselves are a product' (48). By isolating the gospel records in this way, first by reference to post-Constantinian church authorities and then by contrast with the remainder of the NT, Lewis relativises their importance. He then observes, 'The whole Christian case for Pacifism rests, therefore, on certain Dominical utterances, such as "Resist not evil: but whosoever shall smite thee on thy right cheek, turn to him the other also"' (48). Ironically, this Christian apologist built a thick and high barricade against pacifism before considering the teaching of Jesus. Perhaps he was not addressing Christians, so did not think it appropriate to begin with the teaching of Jesus. Perhaps his conviction that in interpersonal relations 'Christ did not come to preach any brand new morality',[18] made him reluctant to make the teaching of Jesus normative. But whatever explains his mode of argumentation, it is seriously deficient from the standpoint of an ethic that accepts the normativeness of the life and teaching of Jesus.

Now that Lewis finally considers the relevant teaching of Jesus, how does he understand it? He first points out that one who takes the saying on nonretaliation at face value must also take other difficult sayings at face value. So far, so good, although each saying of Jesus needs to be considered in context and alongside others bearing on the same theme. He then offers three interpretations of the saying on

17. See Roland H Bainton, *Christian Attitudes Toward War and Peace: A Historical Survey and Critical Re-evaluation* (Nashville, TN: Abingdon Press, 1960), 66-84; Jean-Michel Hornus, *It Is Not Lawful For Me To Fight: Early Christian Attitudes Toward War, Violence, and the State*, rev ed, trans. Alan Kreider and Oliver Coburn (Scottdale, PA: Herald Press, 1980); Lisa Sowle Cahill, *Love Your Enemies: Discipleship, Pacifism, and Just War Theory* (Minneapolis, MN: Augsburg Fortress, 1994), 39-54. Cf David G Hunter, 'A Decade of Research on Early Christians and Military Service', *Religious Studies Review* 18/2 (April 1992): 87-94.

18. Lewis, *Mere Christianity*, 78.

nonresistance in Mt 5:39, which is the only saying of Jesus he considers: the pacifist interpretation that it 'imposes a duty of nonresistance on all men in all circumstances'; the 'minimising interpretation' that sees it as oriental hyperbole for saying that we should 'put up with a lot and be placable', a view he rejects; and his own view that 'the text means exactly what it says, but with an understood reservation in favour of those obviously exceptional cases which every hearer would naturally assume to be exceptional without being told' (49). How Lewis knows what Jesus' hearers 'would naturally assume to be exceptional' is not disclosed, but for him the saying applies only at the individual level, prohibiting personal retaliation against another individual. However, if motivated by reasons other than 'egoistic retaliation', such as protecting a third party or one's country, he finds retaliation acceptable, even obligatory. 'Indeed', Lewis continues, 'as the audience were [*sic*] private people in a disarmed nation, it seems unlikely that they would have ever supposed Our Lord to be referring to war . . . The frictions of daily life among villagers were more likely to be in their minds' (50).

What Lewis meant by the ambiguous phrase, 'private people in a disarmed nation', is unclear, but even so his position is contentious. He affirms that 'any saying is to be taken in the sense it would naturally have borne in the time and place of utterance' (50), but given the sociopolitical situation of those who heard Jesus one can hardly assume that they were only concerned with the frictions of village life. The 'Zealot option' was not far-fetched.[19] Galileans who encountered Jesus would be at least as likely to consider the implications of his teaching for those occasions when bullied by a Roman soldier as for how to deal with a village ruffian.

Lewis's view that Jesus' teaching applied to village life rather than to the question of insurrection or war against foreign or national enemies has been restated by Richard Horsley: '. . . there is no indication in the Gospels that loving one's enemies had any reference to the Romans or that turning the other cheek pertained to nonresistance to

---

19. The 'Zealot option' was real for Jesus even if there were no Zealots proper before the Jewish revolt of 66–70 CE. See Yoder, *The Politics of Jesus*, 56-58. See also William Klassen, 'Jesus and the Zealot Option', in Stanley Hauerwas, Chris K Huebner, Harry J Huebner and Mark Thiessen Nation (eds), *The Wisdom of the Cross: Essays in Honor of John Howard Yoder* (Grand Rapids, MI: Eerdmans, 1999), 131-49.

foreign political domination'.[20] While appreciative of Horsley's reconstruction of the social context of first-century Palestine, Walter Wink observes that 'on Horsley's reading, two of the most distinctive aspects of Jesus' ministry—loving and forgiving enemies and fellowshipping with outcasts—bite the dust'.[21] Even if Jesus' sayings on nonretaliation and love of enemies did initially refer to local community relations, Christians soon applied these sayings to situations in which they were forced to respond to the demands of foreign and national enemies, for example, when coerced to carry the packs of Roman soldiers, a practice alluded to in Mt 5:41.

A further point for Lewis is that a non-pacifist interpretation of Jesus' teaching 'harmonises' better with other NT texts such as Rom 13:4 and 1 Pet 2:14, which approve the use of the sword by magistrates. He also asserts that if we accept a pacifist interpretation of Jesus' saying on nonretaliation, we must conclude that all those close to Jesus in time, place and language misunderstood him and that it was only many centuries later that the true intent of his words was discovered. Again, this ignores the pacifist witness of at least some early church leaders.

Before concluding his talk Lewis reflects on whether his argument is influenced by self-interest. In fact, he is not quite honest because he does not so much examine his own motives as compare what soldiers and pacifists must face. According to Lewis, 'All that we fear from all the kinds of adversity, severally, is collected together in the life of a soldier on active service', whereas 'it is certainly a fact that Pacifism threatens you with almost nothing' (52). His comments about what a soldier must confront may reflect his wartime experience, but while what he says about pacifism may have been true on his side of the English Channel in 1940, it is certainly *not* a fact that the threat to pacifists is always and everywhere minimal. What might Lewis have said three years later to Franz Jägerstätter, the Austrian who because of his Christian faith refused to serve in Germany's war machine and was therefore beheaded as an 'enemy of the state'?

---

20. Richard A Horsley, *Jesus and the Spiral of Violence* (Minneapolis, MN: Augsburg Fortress, 1993), 150.

21. See the exchange between Horsley and Wink in Willard M Swartley (ed), *The Love of Enemy and Nonretaliation in the New Testament* (Louisville, KY: Westminster John Knox Press, 1992), 72-136.

Lewis concludes his address by saying:

> This, then, is why I am not a Pacifist. If I tried to become one, I should find a very doubtful factual basis, an obscure train of reasoning, a weight of authority both human and Divine against me, and strong grounds for suspecting that my wishes had directed my decision. As I have said, moral decisions do not admit of mathematical certainty. It may be, after all, that Pacifism is right. But it seems to me very long odds, longer odds than I would care to take with the voice of almost all humanity against me.

This final sentence typifies what I find to be most problematic about Lewis's address. He gives the impression that he made up his view on pacifism and war independently of his Christian faith or, at best, that what Jesus taught was only one among many considerations and not even the most important. It seems that for Lewis, some 'other light' than that of the life and teaching of Jesus provided alternative ethical guidance, thereby undermining the moral authority of Jesus. Although his case against pacifism was dissimilar to Niebuhr's in many respects, nevertheless he chose, like Niebuhr, '. . . to set up beside the Jesus of the canon and the creeds some other specific sources and contents of ethical obligation'.[22]

22. John Howard Yoder, 'Christ, the Light of the World', in *The Royal Priesthood*, 191. Cf p 184: 'the issue of war is a crucial and a most typical touchstone. Perhaps it is the most crucial test point for our age, the point where we are asked whether it is ultimately Jesus or some other authority whom we confess as "the light of the world".'

Contributors

Ian Barns is a Senior Lecturer in Ethics and Technology in the Institute for Sustainability and Technology Policy at Murdoch University. He is married with three adult children. He has a particular interest in the relationship between the gospel and contemporary techno-culture, including developments in the new genetics.

Charles Birch is emeritus professor of the University of Sydney, where he was Challis Professor of Biology from 1960 to 1983. From 1970 to 1985 he was Vice Moderator of the subunit of Church and Society of the World Council of Churches. In 1990 he was awarded the Templeton Prize for Progress in Religion. He has written extensively on the relation between science and religion and on the environmental crisis. He is the author of numerous books, including *Confronting the Future* (Penguin Books, 1976; rev ed, 1994), *On Purpose* (University of New South Wales Press, 1990), *Regaining Compassion for Humanity and Nature* (UNSW Press, 1993), *Feelings* (UNSW Press, 1995) and *Biology and the Riddle of Life* (UNSW Press, 2000).

Veronica Brady IBVM is a Roman Catholic religious sister, a member of the Loreto Order. She taught for many years in the English Department of the University of Western Australia where since her retirement she is now an honorary Senior Research Fellow. She has written widely on Australian literature, culture and belief, and her most recent book is a biography of Judith Wright, *South of My Days*.

Rowena Curtis is the Pastor of Collins Street Baptist Church in Melbourne. She and her husband Andrew commenced their urban ministry experience at the House of the Gentle Bunyip in 1980. After six years in the Bunyip community, she and her family moved to Sydney where she continued her theological studies and co-ordinated Scaffolding, a network of people and churches involved in urban ministry. In 1994 she took up the position of Pastor of Woolloomooloo Baptist Fellowship. She was ordained in 1999.

John Dunnill is an Anglican priest. He lives in Perth, Western Australia, where he is Senior Lecturer in New Testament Studies at Murdoch University. He is the author of *Covenant and Sacrifice in the Letter to the Hebrews* (Cambridge University Press, 1992). Currently he is working on issues in hermeneutics and the role of sacrifice in the Christian understanding of the body. John is married with three children.

Graeme Garrett is an Anglican priest and the Pat Wardle Senior Lecturer in Theology at St Mark's National Theological Centre in Canberra and the School of Theology, Charles Sturt University. He is the author of *God Matters: Conversations in Theology* (Liturgical Press, 1999).

Stanley Hauerwas is Gilbert T Rowe Professor of Theological Ethics at the Divinity School of Duke University. He is a member of the Society for Christian Ethics, the American Academy of Religion and the American Theological Society. He is the author of many books, including *A Community of Character* (University of Notre Dame Press, 1981), *The Peaceable Kingdom* (University of Notre Dame Press, 1983), *A Better Hope: Resources for a Church Confronting Capitalism, Democracy, and Postmodernity* (Brazos Press, 2000) and *With the Grain of the Universe: The Church's Witness and Natural Theology* (Brazos Press, 2001). In 2001 Duke University Press published *The Hauerwas Reader*, edited by John Berkman and Michael Cartwright. Stanley is married to Paula Gilbert.

William (Bill) Loader is Professor of New Testament and Head of the School of Social Inquiry at Murdoch University and Lecturer in the Perth Theological Hall of the Uniting Church in Australia. His recent books include *Jesus and the Fundamentalism of His Day* (Melbourne, 1998; Eerdmans, 2001) and *Jesus' Attitude Towards the Law* (Mohr Siebeck, 1997; Eerdmans, 2002). He has also written many articles, including ongoing electronic resources on his website (http://wwwstaff.murdoch.edu.au/~loader/). He is a Fellow of the Australian Academy of the Humanities and a member of Studiorum Novi Testamenti Societas. He has been teaching in Perth, Western Australia, since 1978.

Thorwald Lorenzen is on the pastoral team at Canberra Baptist Church. Before moving to Canberra, he was Professor of Systematic Theology and Ethics at the Baptist Theological Seminary in Rüschlikon, Switzerland. He is the author of *Resurrection and Discipleship: Interpretive Models, Biblical Reflections, Theological Consequences* (Orbis Books, 1995) and has chaired the Baptist World Alliance's Commission on Human Rights.

Chris Marshall is Reader in New Testament at the Tyndale Graduate School of Theology in Auckland, New Zealand. His two most recent books are *Beyond Retribution: A New Testament Vision for Justice, Crime and Punishment* (Eerdmans, 2001) and *Crowned with Glory and Honour: Human Rights in the Biblical Tradition* (Pandora Press with Herald Press, 2001).

Philip Matthews, co-editor of *Faith and Freedom*, was a Baptist pastor for fourteen years. Working in the Pilbara region of Western Australia provided him with the opportunity to engage with indigenous people and to explore some of the social difficulties arising from living in the Northwest. He now lectures in the Philosophy Department at the University of Notre Dame.

David Neville is Lecturer in New Testament at St Mark's National Theological Centre, Canberra, and the School of Theology, Charles Sturt University. He has written two books on the synoptic problem, and he edited *Prophecy and Passion: Essays in Honour of Athol Gill* (ATF, 2002).

Frank Nichol grew up in New Zealand, where he trained for the Presbyterian ministry from 1943 to 1949. He completed doctoral studies at St Andrews in Scotland and Princeton. He was a parish minister until he undertook further study at Heidelberg University, after which he was appointed Professor of Theology at Knox College, Dunedin, and later, Principal. He retired in 1986 and was honoured in 1990 with a Doctor of Divinity degree from the University of St Andrews.

Rick Strelan is an ordained minister of the Lutheran Church of Australia, having graduated in 1969 from Luther Seminary in Adelaide.

From 1970 to 1980 he worked as chaplain at the University of Papua New Guinea and Immanuel College in Adelaide. He is currently Senior Lecturer in the Department of Studies in Religion at the University of Queensland, teaching in the area of New Testament and Early Christianity. In addition to journal articles on various aspects of the Acts of the Apostles, he is working on a book entitled *Strange Acts,* which examines some culturally unusual episodes in Acts. Rick is also the author of *Crossing the Boundaries: Chi Rho Commentary on Mark* (Lutheran Publishing House, 1991).

John Howard Yoder (1927–1997) graduated from Goshen College in 1947. From 1949 to 1957 he served in Europe in the postwar relief work of the Mennonite Central Committee, and from 1959 to 1965 he administered the overseas program of the Mennonite Board of Missions. Between 1965 and 1984 Yoder taught at Goshen Biblical Seminary, after which he taught theology and ethics at the University of Notre Dame in Indiana. Yoder wrote *The Politics of Jesus* (Eerdmans, 1972; 2nd ed, 1994); *The Priestly Kingdom: Social Ethics as Gospel* (University of Notre Dame Press, 1984); *The Royal Priesthood: Essays Ecclesiological and Ecumenical* (Eerdmans, 1994); and *For the Nations: Essays Evangelical and Public* (Eerdmans, 1997). In 2002 his *Preface to Theology: Christology and Theological Method* was published posthumously by Brazos Press.

Author Index

Biblical References

Mark

Subject Index